Constructing Panic

Constructing Panic

The Discourse of Agoraphobia

Lisa Capps and Elinor Ochs

Harvard University Press
Cambridge, Massachusetts
London, England

Library of Congress Cataloging-in-Publication Data

Capps, Lisa.
   Constructing panic : the discourse of agoraphobia / Lisa Capps and
Elinor Ochs.
      p.   cm.
   Includes bibliographical references and index.
   ISBN 0–674–16548–9 (cloth)
   ISBN 0–674–16549–7 (pbk.)
   1. Agoraphobia—Case studies. 2. Personal construct theory.
3. Discourse analysis. 4. Discourse analysis, Narrative. 5. Panic
attacks. I. Ochs, Elinor. II. Title.
   RC552.A44C37   1995
616.85'225—dc20   95–22566

For Meg

Contents

Foreword

Jerome Bruner

This is a pioneering book. But to call it just that may be misleading. It is indeed a pioneer effort to explicate mental illness by a detailed and disciplined linguistic analysis of how it exists for the sufferer—in this instance, a sufferer from that increasingly familiar disorder called agoraphobia. But though the book launches into new territory, it scarcely does so with the rough-and-ready of old-style pioneering. For Lisa Capps and Elinor Ochs bring to their demanding task a wealth of subtle technical know-how—happily tempered by human insight. In this absorbing study, the two authors bring their partner skills of psychology and linguistics to the task of understanding what a sufferer means when she tells them about her severe agoraphobia. With the three of them, we travel not only into the experience of a mental disorder but also into the modern practice of linguistics, psychology, and, indeed, anthropology.

This is no word-counting exercise, nor is it the usual case history. It is a sensitive analysis of how a married mother of two in her mid-thirties uses language to construct her self-styled "abnormality," how she uses the rich devices of language to dig herself ever more deeply into a sense of helplessness, and how, through consummately crafted linguistic usage, she gives conventional shape and substance to the disabling anxieties that beset her "out of the blue" in unfamiliar places. The linguistic insights brought to this work are both powerful and subtle; but we expect nothing less from these authors. Even more impressive is how they

use their skills to explicate how a particular human being works her way
by words into the narratives that lock her into besetting difficulties—
and, at times, works her way out by the same means. It is an extraordi-
narily rich and moving study of the making of a "life narrative" and how
it shapes and is shaped by the life it recounts.

What endows this book with its moving, human quality deserves a
special word. Ordinary clinical studies are too often marred by the pre-
tensions to omniscience of the clinician who recounts the final story.
The "omniscient narrator," long shamed out of modern fiction by the
genius of writers since Flaubert and Joyce, is altogether too much in
evidence in psychology's clinical literature. Even Freud was dimmed by
it. In this tradition, the doctor knows how it goes, not the patient. But
not in the pages of this book. It is the sufferer who knows her reality,
knows it by suffering it. There is no hidden ontology to be found in
these pages: we know only the sufferer's world, the reality she brings
into being by her words and her stories. That is the book's focus. Lisa
Capps and Elinor Ochs scrutinize this process of life construction with
the care and perspective of, say, an architectural critic examining how
an architect has created a building. And much as the architectural critic
might ask what functions the building serves, given its particular design
in that particular setting, so the authors ask how and why and at what
costs a particular human being constructs the life she lives in her setting. Her medium, of course, is language and story, and the setting is
contemporary culture.

In the end this book is not about a "patient" but about a human being
who has got into deep trouble. Despite that, she holds the respect of the
authors. They never second-guess her or try to outsmart her. In consequence, the book has the rich particularity of well-wrought biography,
even to the description of a brightly painted, elaborately decorated
front door that marks the sharp boundary between the safe inside of the
sufferer's home and the perilous outside.

The authors offer no cures, no panaceas. It is a book not about therapy but about understanding trouble. Yet what it makes amply clear is
that the road back from "mental trouble," be it agoraphobia or any
other disorder of alienation from the world, requires a re-narrativizing,

reconstruing, another life construction. We do not know what it takes to undo the narratives whose construction comes to control a life—save for one big thing this book teaches us. The way back must obviously involve using language to reconstrue and, thereby, to construct a new narrative about our lives and our world. And as Toni Morrison so aptly said in accepting the Nobel Prize for Literature, lives and worlds are the work of words.

1

The Agony of Agoraphobia

The mind is its own place, and in itself can make a
heav'n of hell, a hell of heav'n.

—John Milton, 1667

"I'm afraid I can't really tell you how to get here from where you are.
It's been so long since I've been on the freeway."

Meg Logan has agoraphobia. She has not ventured outside a two-
mile radius of her house for the past six years. She is not alone. A recent
epidemiological study of psychiatric disorders in the United States sur-
veyed 15,490 individuals from five metropolitan areas—Baltimore,
Durham, Los Angeles, New Haven, and St. Louis—a sample over ten
times larger than in any previous investigation of agoraphobia. Over 4
percent of the individuals interviewed reported having suffered from
agoraphobia during the previous year.[1] This percentage is significantly
higher than those found in earlier investigations conducted in the
United States, England, Germany, and Switzerland, which reported
prevalence rates of agoraphobia ranging from .6 percent to 3.6 percent.
The higher percentage reported in the epidemiological study is attributable to the fact that participants were asked about symptoms over the
past year, rather than at the time of the interview, as was the case in the
other studies. Although agoraphobia is more common in urban than in
rural areas, its prevalence appears to be similar throughout industrial-
ized countries, across ethnic groups, and across age groups between
eighteen and sixty-four years.

The term 'agoraphobia' refers to a psychological syndrome as con-
ceptualized in American and European medical communities of practice. We use the term not to reify the label, nor to imply that agoraphobia is a universal reality,[2] but to explore an indigenous cultural
phenomenon, embedded in both a particular system of health beliefs
and conduct and, as we will demonstrate, a particular system of discourse practices. We describe Meg as agoraphobic because she consistently labels herself in this way. She even chooses descriptors that
match criteria found in the *Diagnostic and Statistical Manual of Mental
Disorders*, perhaps conveyed to her in the course of her psychiatric assessment and treatment.[3]

In American and European societies, the vast majority of individuals
diagnosed with agoraphobia are women. Indeed, the epidemiological
study conducted in the United States reported more than twice the
prevalence of agoraphobia among women as men. Though compelling,
this ratio is considerably lower than those reported in other investigations of agoraphobia, in which the relative percentages of females range
from 63 percent to 95 percent.[4] In the clinical literature, agoraphobia is
consistently referred to as a "woman's syndrome."

Discussion of the association between agoraphobia and women has
focused not only on prevalence rates, but on the similarity between
symptoms of agoraphobia and stereotypical female sex roles. From this
perspective, the socialization of stereotypic feminine behavior—helplessness, dependence, unassertiveness, accommodation—contributes to
the development and maintenance of the characteristics of agoraphobia.
The disproportionate percentage of women sufferers supports this
view, but it has also obtained some empirical corroboration. One study,
for example, found that agoraphobic men portray themselves as shy,
submissive, and not fitting into stereotypic male sex roles, and describe
entering relationships with dominant women who may have been more
likely to reinforce their unassertive behavior.[5]

Other studies, however, have not found evidence for the link between
agoraphobia and dependent, unassertive personality styles, which suggests that there may not be one consistent "agoraphobic personality."
This question remains open.

Sufferers of agoraphobia express fear of being in a place or situation where it may be difficult to escape or to obtain help should they experience a panic attack or develop other potentially incapacitating or extremely embarrassing symptoms. The term 'agoraphobia' means "fear of open spaces," but is more appropriately described as a fear of being anyplace where one might feel alone and vulnerable to fear and panic. Avoidance in response to this fear is a central feature of agoraphobia. Agoraphobic persons often describe feeling trapped by an ever-present threat of panic and their belief that they cannot risk leaving safe havens such as home.

As Lisa exited the freeway to meet Meg, the next participant in her study of agoraphobia, she mulled over Meg's disclosure that she could not provide Lisa with directions to her home. Lisa had met Meg while recruiting subjects for a study on the psychological adjustment of school-aged children of agoraphobic parents. Meg and her eleven-year-old daughter Beth had agreed to participate. Lisa made her way down the access road and turned onto the street where the Logan family lives. Their home lies in the center of a residential area spanning eight square blocks, bordered by the access road and three large busy streets. The freeway, though less than a mile away, is not visible. Tall shrubs buffer the residences from the sight and sound of traffic, creating a space in which children play safely.

Lisa pulled her car up alongside the curb and was immediately struck by the exterior of the Logan home. On the façade nearest the street and furthest from the entryway, the paint was peeling and worn away in patches, exposing older coats of color. The front door offered a strikingly different public statement. Satin red and ornately embellished with carved wood flowers and a shiny brass knob and knocker, it displayed painstaking attention to detail and high regard for appearance. It seemed to herald entry into an interior distinct from the outside world. The architectural contrast stood as a metaphor for a hallmark feature of agoraphobia: the attempt to exert control over a highly circumscribed space, to create a safe haven within a chaotic, often unwelcoming universe.

Meg, a slender thirty-four-year-old with hazel eyes and light brown hair, waved through the kitchen window, while her six-year-old son Sean and two barking dachshunds bounded to the front door. Meg unlocked it and let Lisa in. Two needlepoint plaques adorned the entryway: "Home is where the heart is." "The home of a friend is never far away." These sentiments cast the home as a safe haven. Yet paradoxically, while at home Meg spends much of her time ruminating over past experiences of panic and imagining similar experiences in other hypothetical situations. Home is not a safe haven, after all. It does not protect her from being engulfed by reconstructions of past events that channel rising tides of panic into the present. Home is a place where distressing emotions from past times and places creep up on, invade, and overwhelm Meg's experience. As John Milton writes in *Paradise Lost*, "The mind is its own place, and in itself can make a heav'n of hell, a hell of heav'n." Home is a paradise lost in that it cannot provide refuge from the mind and the scenarios it (re)creates.

What might account for this Miltonian lost paradise? There is strong research support for the role of genetics in the development of anxiety disorders in general and agoraphobia in particular. Research conducted in the United States and in Europe has documented higher rates of panic disorder and agoraphobia among first-degree relatives of individuals with the disorders than in the population at large.[6] Studies comparing identical twins (who begin life as a single egg, thereby having identical genes guiding their growth and development) and fraternal twins (who develop from two eggs, and are no more closely related to each other genetically than siblings from the same family) are used in genetic research. Because identical and fraternal twins share similar uterine environments and are reared at the same time in a family's history, comparing identical and fraternal twins affords a unique consideration of genetic contributions to development. Such studies have shown that concordance rates for anxiety disorders are far greater among identical twins than among fraternal twins. That is, if one of two identical twins has an anxiety disorder, the other is far more likely to suffer from anxiety than is the case among fraternal twins.[7] However, although these results suggest that there is a genetic component, the concordance rates for anxiety among identical twins are very low in comparison with those for medical disorders that are known to be transmitted genetically. Further, none of the identical twins studied shared precisely the same anxiety disorder, which suggests that a spectrum, rather than a particular disorder, is transmitted.

Efforts to understand the experience of anxiety and its perpetuation in families must take genetics into account. But anxiety is not solely attributable to genetic factors. Furthermore, identifying a genetic component does not delineate the scope or nature of what is passed on or the way that genetic and environmental processes interact. It is possible, for example, that anxious parents and their children share biological or psycho-physiological traits such as "chronic overarousal" that render them vulnerable to anxiety and panic.[8] Yet most models of anxiety suggest that additional factors are involved, factors that trigger the onset of anxiety and mediate its expression.

A number of factors may precipitate the onset of agoraphobia, including stressful life events, particularly those involving loss or separation from loved ones.[9] Some investigators, emphasizing the role of cognitive processes in determining the meaning and impact of such events, have suggested that cognitive styles contribute to the onset and maintenance of anxiety. Several cognitive styles have been attributed to individuals suffering from anxiety, including catastrophic misinterpretations of physiological stimuli, selective attention to negative events, hypersensitivity to social-evaluative information, and learned helplessness.[10] These cognitive styles are thought to mediate predisposed individuals' experiences in the world in ways that promote and maintain anxiety, particularly among persons with biological or psychophysiological predispositions toward anxiety. But establishing associations between various cognitive styles and particular anxiety disorders does not account for the development of such styles in the first place.

Clinical researchers have identified familial and interpersonal environments that may contribute to the development and perpetuation of the psychological and behavioral patterns that make up agoraphobia. There has been considerable speculation about the socialization experiences of children of agoraphobic parents, although our understanding of the processes involved is largely undetermined. One view holds that agoraphobic parents model caution and fearfulness, and that children develop anxiety by "internalizing" this stance.[11] Finding higher degrees of anxiety among children whose parents displayed more extensive avoidance behavior, another account suggests that children of agoraphobic parents who avoid a large number of situations "pick up" the tendency to respond to fear through avoidance.[12] Highlighting the role of perceived control, yet another conceptualization suggests that interacting with an agoraphobic parent undermines the child's sense of control, which, coupled with exposure to avoidance behavior, leads to learned helplessness and the eventual onset of anxiety.[13]

Psychoanalytic models of the development and perpetuation of agoraphobia emphasize the role of separation anxiety. These conceptualizations highlight a dynamic referred to as the "inversion of parent-child relationships,"[14] in which a parent with agoraphobia turns to her child to meet her own needs for closeness and alleviate her fears of being alone. The child then assures the parent that he or she will not become autonomous and leave. Not having established autonomy, the child is predisposed to repeat the same pattern with his or her own children. This model is supported by studies finding higher rates of separation anxiety in the children of agoraphobic parents,[15] and by agoraphobic adults' accounts of their parents as having overprotective caregiving styles.[16]

In addition to childhood socialization experiences, interpersonal interactions in adulthood may also precipitate the development and maintenance of agoraphobia; socialization occurs throughout life.[17] A running controversy in the literature on agoraphobia concerns the relevance and role of interpersonal conflict. On the basis of case histories, it has been proposed that women who are in unsatisfying intimate relationships, but feel unable to leave owing to fears of separation and independence, develop agoraphobia to "resolve" the predicament. Agoraphobia, rendering them "sick," provides justification for remaining in the undesired relationship. This hypothesis is supported by studies of agoraphobic women in which the majority reported marital conflict at symptom onset, whereas this was not the case among women suffering from other anxiety disorders.[18] It has also been suggested that the partners of individuals with agoraphobia manifest elevated levels of psychopathology.[19]

Alternatively, other investigators have asserted that this view of agoraphobia is derived from generalizations that have not been substantiated by reliable methods. On the basis of responses from agoraphobic persons and their spouses to standardized questionnaire measures of marital adjustment and diagnostic checklists, researchers such as W. A. Arrindell and P. M. G. Emmelkamp report that agoraphobic persons and their spouses do not show elevated degrees of marital distress.[20] Quoting A. Symonds, Arrindell and Emmelkamp claim that agoraphobia centers on "the patient's psychological make-up rather than the marriage or the husband, since the problem lies not in the marriage or the husband but with the patient herself."[21]

Ongoing debate about the socialization experiences that contribute to the development of agoraphobia and its perpetuation in families attests to the need for continued research. Further, at this point we can only speculate about the dynamics that might underlie empirically validated associations, such as that between adult agoraphobia and childhood separation anxiety. It seems critical to focus research on the socialization that occurs in the families of persons with agoraphobia. This was the rationale behind the initial study of children of agoraphobic parents in which Meg and Beth participated.

Meg and Beth each completed a battery of highly structured interviews as well as multiple-choice and true-false questionnaires—standard instruments used in making diagnoses and establishing clinically significant levels of fear and anxiety.[22] These instruments were designed to elicit information that is relevant to the diagnoses of various problematic behaviors and beliefs. Such methods are based on the notion that individuals may not be aware of the existence or nature of their problems, but will blindly reveal crucial information to the diagnostician or researcher through their responses to various questions. The instruments used in this endeavor do not solicit individuals' accounts of their difficulties or their self-understandings.

At the end of the study, Meg expressed frustration with the enterprise. While paying deference to the scientific method, she felt that interviews and questionnaires did not capture her experience. Beth echoed these feelings in a two-page note attached to her packet of completed questionnaires, in which she wrote, "I need to explain my answers in order for them to make sense."

Meg's and Beth's concerns opened the door to a novel way of understanding the agony of agoraphobia. Sensing that more attention needs to be paid to how agoraphobic persons talk about themselves and their experiences of panic, Lisa joined forces with Elinor, an anthropologist and linguist who had been working for a number of years on family narrative activity. Together we have delved further into agoraphobia by inviting Meg to recount her experiences of panic in order to closely analyze how sufferers of panic narrate such experiences. Our orientation has consistently been that the stories people tell construct who they are and how they view the world. How do sufferers of agoraphobia portray themselves in their narratives of personal experience? How do they portray panic? Lisa asked Meg if they could meet again, so that she could hear her stories in her own words.

"William is at work, and Beth is at school, so it's just Sean and I," Meg explained, and offered Lisa a glass of iced tea. They looked to each other for cues, neither sure how to proceed. As they sat down on the sofa, Lisa began taping their interaction. "I don't have a structured set of questions to ask. I want to hear about your experiences with panic and agoraphobia or anything else you'd like to tell me."

Sean came in, chasing a noisy battery-operated race car. Meg told him to go outside. She then lowered her voice and confessed that she fears being alone and depends upon Sean for companionship. She said she dreads the day that he will not be there to keep her company, and worries about how her dependence might affect her children.

For several hours Meg spoke of her panic experience with Lisa, an attentive listener. Meg recalled anxious episodes from childhood, through early adulthood, and up to the recent past.

Over the next two and a half years, Lisa returned to the Logans' home again and again. Although her conversations with Meg centered on Meg's experiences of anxiety, they revealed a great deal about Meg's life. Despite the confining nature of agoraphobia, Meg manages to work four days a week as a secretary at the local church just over a mile from home, where she and her family are also active members. Meg is very involved in the lives of the parishioners, and she refers to her office as "information headquarters." Although she was reluctant to begin working, fearing that the additional pressures would exacerbate her anxiety, Meg enjoys her job. She is grateful to William for encouraging her to take the position and for supporting her along the way. William frequently calls to check on her, and he comes to the church for lunch when she is feeling particularly uneasy.

On her day off, Meg sees a supportive psychotherapist. One of the main criteria in her selection of a therapist was location: she needed to see someone who practiced within her safety zone—the area within which she feels comfortable. When Lisa met Meg, she had been working with this therapist for two years. Although she is now able to drive herself to the office, this has not always been the case. At first the sessions were so anxiety provoking that she needed William to drive her and wait for her just outside her therapist's office. At this time Sean was an infant and Beth had just started school, so the whole family piled into the station wagon to make these trips. In this way, Meg's therapy became a family affair.

When she feels up to it, Meg volunteers in the neighborhood preschool that Sean attends. During Lisa's visits Meg received many telephone calls from her friends, and occasionally neighbors dropped in to say hello. Meg values her relationships with her friends and neighbors and works hard to maintain them, although this can be difficult when her symptoms are most severe.

During some visits to the Logans' home, Lisa talked not only with Meg but with Meg and her daughter Beth together about memorable events in their lives. On other occasions she observed and videotaped interactions involving the entire family, at dinnertime, on weekends, and after school.

Our interest in conversations between Meg and Beth and in family interactions stemmed from our desire to examine the socialization of emotions and beliefs. The research of Elinor and her colleagues on language socialization suggests that crucial dimensions of family and community culture are socialized through children's participation in everyday, completely ordinary conversational interactions.[23] Children come to adopt certain world views and ways of acting in the world not only by being told how to think, how to act, and what things mean; more pervasively they become socialized indirectly by simply attending to how persons around them are representing and constructing their world through language.

Lisa's earlier study of children of agoraphobic parents confirmed previous research suggesting that such children were more fearful and anxious than children of parents not suffering from anxiety.[24] Diagnostic profiles generated on the basis of children's and parents' responses to structured interview questions suggest that many (68 percent) of these children suffer from psychological disorders, particularly anxiety and depression, and that a small number had elimination disorders (bedwetting). The most common diagnosis was Separation Anxiety Disorder, found in 56 percent of the children. Replicating earlier research, the high prevalence of separation anxiety in the children of agoraphobic parents is noteworthy given that the symptoms of this disorder are similar to those of agoraphobia: avoidance, coupled with both the active search for environmental elements that provide safety and attempts to ensure that caregivers or home can be easily and rapidly reached. The study also examined *mothers'* anxiety over separation from their children—a phenomenon generally perceived as relevant among parents of infants. Agoraphobic mothers in this study reported significantly more anxiety over separation from their children, and perceived separation to be less beneficial to children, than did comparison mothers.

Children of agoraphobic parents perceive themselves as having less control over risks and dangers in the world, particularly those related to health, environment, and life-style. As a group, all of the children of agoraphobic parents also appear to lack the illusion of invulnerability (the so-called optimistic bias of "well-adjusted" mainstream American children and adults). A significantly greater percentage also reported worrying about death. In addition, children's perceived degree of control appears related to mothers' experienced anxiety over separation from their children: children of mothers who experience greater degrees of separation anxiety perceive themselves as having less control than children of mothers with less separation-related anxiety. Interestingly, children's perceived control did not vary as a function of parents' beliefs about the benefits of separation for the child. This may imply that children are more influenced by their parents' *experience* of anxiety in particular situations than by their parents' attitudes and beliefs about how children will be affected.

These correlations are provocative and disturbing and have implications for how anxiety is perpetuated across generations. The results do not delineate *how* children become socialized into these emotions and perceptions. Given the importance of narrative as a universal medium of socialization,[25] we examine the stories told by an agoraphobic mother for their socializing messages about fears, control, dependence, irrationality and/or other symptoms of this most debilitating disorder. Although we cannot crawl into the minds of children to mine their reactions to what they see and hear around them, we can and do examine how events are represented to them through the medium of storytelling. We also examine children as they listen and sometimes contribute to stories of anxious moments as they are recounted by an agoraphobic parent. Finally, we look at how an agoraphobic parent portrays children as protagonists within the tale world of panic experience.

Narrative activity is a path to penetrating the configuration of anxiety. We travel this path to understand how panic pervades Meg's life and the lives of those she loves. The settings and characters of Meg's stories vary, but their themes and rhetoric endure, giving rise to the master storyline that Meg lives by. This master storyline dominates Meg's existence, eclipsing her vision of alternative perspectives that lurk in the background of her stories. Listen to Meg's words for the dominant version of her suffering, but probe beneath the surface to apprehend a subjugated version, one that articulates an alternative, conflicting world view. This subjugated world view is not recognized in the official discourse of *The Diagnostic and Statistical Manual of Mental Disorders*. Nor is it fully recognized by the storyteller herself. Rather the subjugated world view of panic and self lies buried in background details of Meg's stories.

One would think that subjugated world views would gain prominence in the course of psychotherapeutic dialogue. And sometimes this is the case. More often, however, therapeutic interactions reinforce the official version. Why is this so? In part therapists are guided by the official narrative they have been apprenticed to detect and treat, the narrative codified as *The Diagnostic and Statistical Manual of Mental Disorders*. Perhaps more important, the subjugated world view is hard to detect. Identifying this world view requires piecing together disconnected elements of the story. In particular it involves retrieving elements of the story setting and connecting them to subsequent emotions and actions. But especially when recounting distressing events, storytellers often rush through and minimize elements of the setting in an effort to communicate the dramatic climax of some harrowing experience. In the absence of a taped recording of the story, the setting, which is the key to illuminating subjugated knowledges, eludes therapist and client alike.

In this day and age, we have access to technologies that allow us to electronically chart autobiographies in the making. We can decipher how storytellers structure their experiences to place a master story perspective in the foreground and to relegate an alternative point of view to the background. Audio and video documentation enables us to track the intertwining of such perspectives across stories that make up a life. Stories have an architecture that begs to be dismantled and mined for meaning. Because speakers the world over use narrative structure to make sense out of their experiences, it behooves us to look closely at how stories are built to penetrate the sense-making process. We believe that a look at how narrators routinely recruit linguistic forms to tell their stories—a look not only at words but at their grammatical and discursive shape—is an important step in illuminating how people, especially those suffering from psychological disorders, maintain and struggle to transform their lives.

2

In Her Own Words

We die. That may be the meaning of life. But we do
language. That may be the measure of our lives.

—Toni Morrison, 1994

Language is the greatest human resource for representing and structuring events in our lives. And no language practice has more impact in this direction than storytelling. Storytelling, one of the earliest forms of communication engaged in by young children, is universal to all human cultures and a powerful means of socializing values and world views to children and other intimates. In telling stories, interlocutors make sense out of their experiences. They use words, grammar, and narrative structure to weave a tale in which events are linked temporally, causally, and emotionally and protagonists are depicted with a particular evaluative hue.

We now begin to penetrate stories of daily lived experiences to illuminate how stories are shaped by their tellers and, at the same time, how stories shape the way tellers see and experience themselves in their worlds. Leslie Marmon Silko writes in *Ceremony*, "I will tell you something about stories, they aren't just entertainment. Don't be fooled. They are all we have, you see. They are who we are, and all we have to fight off illness and death."[1] This statement anticipates Toni Morrison's comments upon receiving the Nobel Prize for literature, that our doing language may be the measure of our lives. Morrison adds, "Narrative is radical, creating us at the very moment it is being created."[2] When we tell stories we not only reflect on the lives we are living, we also create and re-create our lives and ourselves.

Even after death, our words—our narratives—live on. In *Imagining Argentina*, Lawrence Thorton vividly portrays the perseverance of one woman's narrative in the minds of her survivors: "When it happened her words were heavy in the air, that, as the security men approached, her words were sounding in the minds of thousands of Argentines, and that those who ordered her abduction were frustrated in their knowledge that they could not also abduct her words, smash what she had said."[3] Words inhabit and shape present and future realms of existence.[4]

This quality of stories extends beyond those created by novelists to include everyday accounts of our personal experiences. Our quotidian stories create portraits of ourselves and others, which, through the process of telling, become portraits that we and our interlocutors remember and keep with us until they are modified through a new telling. Along life's span we *become* the stories we tell about our lives. Through narrative we struggle to bridge our past, present, future, and even imagined lives to formulate coherent identities. We travel along this narrative bridge in multidimensional time: we portray past, future, or imagined identities in present-time storytelling interactions with other people. Through this storytelling process, we reshape these identities in keeping with who we feel or hope ourselves and others to be at the moment. In this way, our present identities evolve out of complex temporally, linguistically, and interactionally organized communicative encounters.

Robert Jay Lifton touches upon this dynamic in *The Protean Self*, whose title refers to Proteus, the Greek sea god of many forms.[5] The essence of the protean self—a many-sided self in constant motion—lies in its fluidity. The protean self continuously undergoes shifts, rearrangements, and transformations. We continually restructure ourselves, feeding and maintaining evolving combinations in ways that ultimately permit a certain continuity: a form of life that is not in one-way, linear motion but, despite surprising jolts and changes of direction, composes a pattern.

The protean nature of the self stems from its permeability to inner and outer influences, which are never fully separable from one another. We are shaped by a complex interweaving of external events and inner experiences, which become indistinguishable. What 'actually happened' in some past event in our life is inextricably tied to the phenomenological meaning we ascribe—that is, to our experience of the event. And this meaning changes as we continually respond to the blending of external and internal forces that make up our ongoing experience—as we revise and reshape the story of our lives.

We experience events in association with an ongoing story about who we are, in which we struggle to achieve coherence and continuity rather than objective truth. Similarly, our memories do not consist of snapshots of our experiences;[6] rather, we store our experiences in memory in connection with a web of associations that is consistent with our narrative. Further, each time we store or recall an event, we invoke and reconstruct ("re-member") not an isolated occurrence but the entire web of associations: our story. This storytelling is central to the protean self's capacity to shift shape while sustaining its inner form.

Jerome Bruner, a pioneer in cognitive psychology and the study of narrative as the quintessential mode of human thought, proposes that "a life is not 'how it was' but how it is interpreted and reinterpreted, told and retold."[7] Despite claims to the contrary, no story constitutes the 'real story,' or the 'true story,' or even the final version. Events can be told in multiple ways. Even the same person may characterize a set of events and protagonists from many-sided, ever-evolving vantage points.[8] In many cases these differing accounts may be outcomes of differing interactional circumstances—different audiences, times, and emotional climates. In other cases, the same storyteller may construct different versions of the events in the course of a single recounting.

As a storyteller weaves events together, he or she creates a plot structure that links the actions, conditions, thoughts, and feelings of the protagonists. In particular, certain elements of a story are presented as temporally preceding and causing others. In one of her stories, for example, Meg presents a traffic jam as anticipating and causing the onset of a panic attack. The plot of a story is similar to a theory of events in that both reflect an author's attempt to provide an explanation of what happened. We tend to associate theories with the discourse of scientists, but all stories, whether historical, scientific, or personal, contain at least one theory about events.[9]

The plot structure of stories centers on a problematic event, which is temporally and causally linked to a circumstantial setting and which anticipates and causes psychological and behavioral responses. The plot structure of narratives of persons suffering from psychological disorders provides a window into how they understand their distress. The architecture of stories—how they are designed and built—reveals tellers' theories about the causes and consequences of emotions. We illustrate this perspective by focusing on Meg's experience of agoraphobia through an analysis of the plot structure of her narratives of panic. As we shall see, Meg's narratives present her theories about emotions, theories about herself, theories about other people in her life, theories about normality and abnormality, rationality and irrationality. Each of these theories is a thread in Meg's variegated weaving of her life narrative.

We mine Meg's stories for their theories of panic to gain insight into her experience of agoraphobia and perhaps that of other sufferers as well. Yet we also offer this analysis more generally, as a model for researchers and practitioners in an array of disciplines who are interested in understanding how people use language to craft portraits of themselves and others.

Just as different people generate multiple, conflicting interpretations of a single moment in time, one narrator may convey multiple, conflicting theories about a single event. Meg's narratives present two radically different theories of panic. One theory portrays panic as an irrational response to being in a particular location. This explanation of panic fuses emotions with physical space, such that the physical location becomes a reference point for panic. In her storytelling and in her mind, Meg cannot seem to separate her anxieties from the physical context in which they have arisen. Her attempts to avoid panic take the form of avoiding such locales.

Yet Meg's stories of panic present an alternative theory. In particular, in the settings of her stories, Meg provides details indicating that she has legitimate reasons for not engaging in a proposed activity. Rather than expressing those reservations, however, she accommodates to the proposal, participates in the activity, and panics. This alternative theory links panic and agoraphobia to a particular communicative dilemma, namely, an extreme reluctance or inability to express negative feelings when faced with an undesirable proposal.

Although we have identified these two conflicting theories in Meg's narratives, she herself does not. Instead, in describing her anxieties Meg dwells on the first theory, which links panic to place, and ignores the second. For example, in talking to Lisa one day, Meg remarked,

> It's to the point where I have a lot of anticipatory anxiety, and because of that I'm afraid to go out and *do* things. I told myself that I'm sure to *die*, or *panic* or *whatever* if I get on an airplane or a freeway.

At another time Meg added,

> I manage pretty well because I live within the bounds that I've established for myself. I know that if I don't (.3 pause)— if I stay off of elevators, freeways, and don't drive too far from home— that my— that I can keep my anxiety within manageable limits.

We suggest that one way to help Meg and others suffering from psychological distress is to listen to their stories, delve into their plot structure, and bring to conscious awareness the connections and theories they establish. Sigmund Freud and his colleague Josef Breuer discovered the therapeutic power of storytelling in treating the first patient of psychoanalysis, a woman they call Anna O. To their amazement, Anna was relieved of her hysterical symptoms after articulating memories and visions that haunted her psyche. Referring to this mysterious process as the "talking cure," Freud described how "completely her mind was relieved when, shaking with fear and horror, she had reproduced frightful images and given verbal utterance to them."[10]

Psychoanalysts since Freud and Breuer have examined the cascade of images, associations, and memories unleashed in narration to identify an underlying or latent story that powerfully influences their patients' ongoing experiences.[11] Some have teamed up with linguists to analyze particular forms of dialogue, such as question-answer formats, that characterize the therapeutic encounter.[12] William Labov and David Fanshel's *Therapeutic Discourse*, for example, analyzes the discourse patterns found in fifteen minutes of a psychotherapy session.[13] The linguistic shaping of sufferers' narratives has been generally glossed over, however, with the result that the therapeutic effect of telling one's life stories with another person remains largely a mystery. Psychoanalysts tend to look *through* narrative[14] rather than *at* narrative to identify underlying emotional dynamics and formative experiences. How a teller sculpts her tale—the grammatical form and the sequencing and intertwining of pieces of setting, enigmatic experiences, and outcomes—is not a focal point but rather a medium for exposing a deeper story.

We share the view that stories can offer a powerful medium for gaining insights not fully accessible to the narrator. Indeed we endorse the perspective, held by a number of philosophers and literary critics, that narrative creates stepping stones to self-understanding. To borrow the words of Vaclav Havel, narrative allows us to confront ourselves, "to return in full seriousness to the 'core of things,' to pose the primordial questions again and again, and from the beginning, constantly, to examine the direction [we are] going."[15] However, the medium itself has an architecture that begs to be dismantled and mined for meaning. Because speakers the world over use narrative structure to make sense out of their experiences, it behooves us to look closely at how stories are built in order to penetrate the sense-making process. Our analysis of Meg's narratives provides a model for doing so. We believe that a look at how narrators routinely recruit linguistic forms to tell their stories— a look not only at words but at their grammatical and discursive shape— is an important step in illuminating how people, especially those suffering from psychological disorders, maintain and struggle to transform their lives.

As the title of this book suggests, people play active, creative roles in maintaining and transforming the social, cognitive, and emotional order or, in the case of panic, disorder of their lives.[16] And narrative is the most effective resource known to humankind for doing so. *Constructing Panic* articulates how one sufferer of agoraphobia perpetuates a particular psychological orientation through narrative activity. As this sufferer narrates herself and her children as helpless protagonists in dangerous and uncontrollable worlds, other family members are engulfed and socialized into an anxiety-ridden world view.

We hope this book will enhance the efforts of sufferers, therapists, and others to alleviate distress. Like casting a pebble into a lake, as we penetrate the structuring of Meg's narratives, marking their grammatical and discursive contours, we become aware of ripples on the water. Each concentric circle expands the scope of our vision, opening vistas into agoraphobia, other forms of psychopathology, life stories, and collective histories in the making. And from each of these vantage points we move back and forth through the center.

From our perspective, the architecture of Meg's stories embodies her world views of panic, self, and others. When we carefully attend to how Meg "does language," she illuminates for us the worlds she inhabits and who she feels herself to be. Stories create the lives we live, and when we listen closely, they teach us about our lives.

Many people are troubled by the subjective nature of narrative, by the belief that narrative is *merely* a theory or a version of what 'really happened.' The inherent discrepancy between 'reality' and narrative accounts has long plagued psychologists and philosophers. Beginning with Freud, psychotherapists have expressed uneasiness over their inability to determine whether or not particular events in the lives of patients really happened.[17]

Psychoanalytic understanding involves tracing a phenomenon from the present to its origin in the past. In his case histories, which appear as narratives, Freud explains a given neurosis or psychosis by reconstructing a plot. His case histories lead to the revelation of a decisive event which, when placed in the sequence collaboratively constructed by the patient and therapist, is seen as the cause of the current situation. In his dramatic case of the Wolf Man,[18] for example, Freud's analysis of his patient's dreams and associations led him to conclude that at one and a half years of age, the child woke up to witness his parents copulating. Adopting the role of psychic archaeologist, Freud traces his way back into the patient's past and identifies this "primal scene" as the starting point of the series of events that lead to the present neuroses (in this case transformation of the memory into trauma). The crucial event is thus a product of an intellectual and emotional yearning to create a coherent life story.

Although Freud himself infers the occurrence of this event on the basis of the patient's discourse, in his initial notes on the case he argues vehemently that it truly took place.[19] In the end, Freud's formulation of the case both articulates and downplays the problem of knowing what really happened: "I should myself be glad to know whether the primal scene in my present patient's case was a fantasy or a real experience; but, taking other similar cases into account, I must admit that the answer to this question is not of very great importance."[20] Whether the decisive event is regarded as having happened or not, the establishment of a coherent and resonant story is the therapeutic end.

Although ascertaining what really happened is not critical for Freud, in today's world the resolution of legal and regulatory entanglements often hinges upon the determination of this very question. Particularly with respect to psychological issues such as alleged abuse and harassment, personal testimonies—narrative accounts of what happened—are often the sole basis for determining a verdict. Such cases typically involve drastically different accounts of what happened. Even expert witnesses produce radically diverse stories of events. In the 1992 trial of officers accused of beating the motorist Rodney King, for instance, a moment in a videotaped interaction between King and his apprehenders generated a proliferation of conflicting interpretations, even though all the witnesses and their audiences were viewing the same footage.[21] Each interpretation provided a different narrative of what happened.

Practitioners and scholars of the law recognize that the effectiveness of a witness's story rests not only on its internal logic and external corroboration but also on the rhetorical prowess of the witness and the examining lawyer as storytellers. For example, a *New Yorker* piece on the widely publicized O.J. Simpson trial notes, "The Simpson case, with its toxic stew of sex, race, violence, and celebrity, will demand a prosecutor who can do more than present the witnesses in the right order. It will need someone who can tell a story."[22] Similarly, a profile of a forensic psychiatrist credits his success as an expert witness in part to his virtuoso storytelling performances:

> Gazing steadily into the faces of the jurors when he returned to the stand, Dr. Dietz began to tell a story that would have seemed rather innocuous if its likable, hardworking, mild-mannered protagonist had not within the space of one night slaughtered thirty-four-year-old Polly Seguin, seven-year-old Danny, and five-year-old Amy . . . With none of the psychiatric terminology that jurors find so intimidating, he spoke of [the defendant's] insecurity about his performance in his new job . . . Dr. Dietz . . . began to build a wall of damning fact, brick by brick, in concert with the prosecuting attorney. One week later the jury found the defendant guilty.[23]

On the basis of divergent versions of events, jury members construct a narrative that is plausible and coherent in their eyes, but the truth is beyond their reach. In this sense, rendering a verdict is analogous not to ascertaining the facts but to determining an official story.

From our perspective, far from being a problem, the subjective, multifaceted nature of narrative is critical to understanding how people perceive themselves and others in their worlds. We view stories not as flawed renditions of reality but as windows into individual and collective theories of reality. In our view, theories organize lives; they give meaning and coherence to ongoing experience. It is not what 'really' happened but rather experiencers' theories of what happened that provide continuity between past, present, future, and imagined lives.

People with agoraphobia spend much of their time ruminating over past experiences of panic and imagining similar experiences in other hypothetical situations. A central argument of this book is that agoraphobia is in part kept alive through these repeated psychological reconstructions of panic, and that one very important form of reconstruction is storytelling. Meg ruminates over panic episodes in ways that linguistically transport past distress into the here and now. We can track on a linguistic plane how Meg's narratives construct theories of a world in which emotions creep up on, invade, and sometimes overwhelm the present rather than being contained at a distance. In this sense, agoraphobia can be seen as an outcome of theories individuals develop as they act and interact with others in the world.

Psychiatric diagnoses in general, and agoraphobia in particular, are defined as disorders in rendering reality. In the sense that sufferers maintain a Weltanschauung[24] that is deemed irrational and debilitating, agoraphobia is centrally a phenomenological problem. That is, it is a problem in how one relates to and understands objects in the world, including oneself. Conceptualizations of mental health and illness rely on notions of Weltanschauung in that they presuppose a normal world view. Those diagnosed with mental illnesses are differentiated from normal, rational members of society, who are assumed to share commonsense understandings of themselves and the world.

People like Meg who are deemed abnormal by themselves and others tend to give authority to prevailing commonsense understandings. Meg frequently laments her struggles to deal with situations that are "not at all threatening to normal people" and her fear of doing things that are "not really frightening." In one story from her childhood, for example, Meg describes relying on her friend's judgment that anyone can dive into the deep end of a pool and does so, even though she knows she can't swim. Meg recounts feeling inferior because she had fears that her friend did not share: "And I *remember* . . . thinking I was going to drown, and being very *afraid*, and after that thinking of myself as um (.3 pause) *not* measuring up."

Meg's sense that there is a discrepancy between her world view and that of normal others makes her anxious. While most members of society—those who are deemed normal by themselves and others—believe that their thoughts, feelings, and actions are similar to those of people they know and respect, Meg and others like her do not share this belief. She senses that her view of the world is distorted and that others see the world that really exists. When Meg interacts with other people she has the feeling that their vision of themselves in the world is clear—uncontaminated by the imposition of idiosyncratic ideas.

Meg is like a philosopher in her reflexive thinking about self and the world and in her preoccupation with the distinction between reality and representation. She becomes mired in questions about how and why she has come to see the world in a particular way, and she struggles to regain a normal, commonsense perspective. Meg relentlessly reflects on her inability to gain access to an orientation to the world that others take for granted. Her ruminations illuminate the importance of an authoritative Weltanschauung in the construction and maintenance of both mental health and mental illness.

Despite its significance in differentiating mental health and illness, the ontological status of a commonsense world view, that is, its status as something real and universal, has only recently been questioned by diagnosticians in clinical settings.[25] Decades of psychological wisdom have equated mental health with contact with reality and mental illness with deficits in commonsense renderings of reality. Counter to this perspective, recent research indicates that being normal involves a good deal of illusory thinking.[26] These studies suggest that depressed individuals are more likely to process information in a relatively realistic fashion, whereas normal people appear to "view the world through rose-colored glasses."[27] Yet these studies continue to rely on the assumption that there is one reality that is apprehended by some (depressed persons) and distorted by the rest.

This assumption ignores centuries of philosophical discussion of the relationship between reality and a person's subjective awareness of objects in the world. It also overlooks insights from sociologists and anthropologists who posit that common sense is cultural in character, fashioned historically and interactionally. Common sense is neither universal nor objective. When the sociologist Harold Garfinkel refers to common sense as "What Anyone Like Us Necessarily Knows," he does not mean that it is rational and sensible across all communities of the world.[28] For Garfinkel, common sense is a set of local expectations, understandings, and practices that members of a community agree is practical and reasonable. Similarly, the anthropologist Clifford Geertz argues that common sense is a form of cultural logic, embedded in local concepts of what is sensible and judicious. Common sense is a kind of vernacular wisdom, grounded in local authoritative construals of "things as they are." In this vein, Geertz argues for treating common sense as "a relatively organized body of considered thought, rather than just what anyone clothed and in his right mind knows."[29]

Geertz's argument contains an invitation to contemplate, rather than take for granted, the nature of commonsense understanding. Like scholars in an array of academic disciplines, Meg engages in this process. Yet unlike members of the academy, Meg legitimizes rather than relativizes the prevailing world view of what counts as common sense. Further, Meg is not rewarded for her reflexivity; she is deemed, and deems herself, mentally ill. Reflexive thoughts about differences between her reality and the reality that normal people perceive permeate her narratives; they are inextricably woven into the story of her life. In talking with her family over dinner, for example, Meg begins to recount an incident from her day: "You know what happened today when I went to the bank? Not that anything *happened*, but . . ." Here Meg begins to separate her lived experience from 'what happened.' Meg goes on to describe her experience. She sees the bullet-proof window in the bank and it triggers recollections of an armed robbery that had occurred some months before and hypothetical speculations about menacing persons "who'd want to shoot over it and hurt the tellers." These perceptions and speculations are not supported by family members seated around her, who shift the focus away from Meg's associations to situations they agree really happened. In so doing, they may reinforce the dichotomy and discrepancy between what happened and what Meg experienced.

As Meg makes her way through the world, she senses that the realms she inhabits exist in her mind, that what happens to her didn't really happen. In contrast to philosophers who insist that reality is a product of subjective experience, Meg assumes that normal people live in worlds that really exist. Meg remarked to Lisa during a telephone conversation:

Sometimes I get to the end of the day and I feel exhausted by all of the "what if that had happened" and "what if this happens." And then I realize that I've been sitting on the sofa—that it's just me and my own thoughts driving me crazy.

We now join Meg on her sofa, and move inside her stories of panic. Meg's words create and illuminate the vortex of mental activity she inhabits; they reveal her desperate struggle to experience the reality that she attributes to normal people.

3

Telling Panic

History has the uncanny propensity to repeat itself, to
return at unexpected and unwanted moments . . .
Attempts to remedy this uncertainty are equally
caught in the dilemmas of temporality, tied to the
inhospitable context of the here-and-now at the same
time as imagining a there-and-then.
                                    —Anthony Vidler, 1992

Agoraphobia pervades Meg's existence. To understand Meg's struggle—*how* agoraphobia pervades her being—we had to go beyond standardized questionnaires that isolate specific factors and enter her daily
life. In so doing, we became immersed in the thoughts, feelings, and
stories expressed by Meg and other members of the Logan family. Joining Meg in her home offers a window of understanding into agoraphobia that is otherwise inaccessible, allowing us to enter the very places
where Meg's panic resides. Whether on her sofa, at the family dinner
table, or in her car, Meg's ruminations about past and imagined bouts
of anxiety maintain the presence of panic in her life. In these places and
in this way, agoraphobia is kept alive through narrative. Meg's repeated
reconstructions of past and imagined panic experiences within the
confines of her daily routines color and perpetuate her restricted existence. By delving into these narratives we can enter into her panic
where she lives it: in her own tellings, in her own words. And we can
witness the psychological universe that Meg inhabits taking shape
around her.

Over the course of two and a half years, Lisa observed and recorded Meg in various circumstances. On many occasions, Lisa and Meg talked together about Meg's concerns. During these interactions Lisa asked Meg about her experiences of panic. On other occasions Lisa talked with Meg and Beth about important moments they shared. Lisa returned to the Logan household many times to record the family members' interactions with one another, especially during dinner. At these times Lisa left a video camera on a tripod in the dining room to allow the family to eat in relative privacy.

These audio and video recordings capture a plethora of narratives whose structure and message content illuminate the dynamics of panic. The narratives constructed with other family members provide particularly rich insights into the socialization of emotion. In Chapter 9, we mine a corpus of fifty-three narratives with an eye toward understanding how Sean and Beth are portrayed as accomplices in Meg's panic episodes and as protagonists out of control. But first, in this and following chapters, we focus on Meg's world view of panic. This world view and its narrative embodiment underlie the socialization of anxiety.

Guided by our interest in how Meg's panic experiences are narratively perpetuated when she is at home, we examine eighteen narratives that center on panic experiences. Our analysis of these tellings illuminates the discursive and grammatical forms and the interactional demeanors that rekindle Meg's anxiety and maintain its presence in the life of the family. These stories may be about Meg herself or they may be about someone Meg knows. What is important is that Meg characterizes these figures as experiencing anxiety. The panic stories are predominantly told by Meg and vary in terms of the portrayed severity of panic, ranging from anxious feelings to full-blown panic attacks.

How to Read a Transcript

Transcripts are the backbone of the analysis of spoken language. Through transcription we are able to re-present the shape and content of unfolding stories. When we look at a transcript of a story, we can see

what was said, how it was said, and who said it. Transcripts allow us to
see the choreography of story construction. With a transcript in hand,
we can return to parts of a story that otherwise get overlooked. We can
see how tellers build up a point of view subtly but systematically. An
important part of this process is noticing specific grammatical constructions that a storyteller may routinely exploit to paint a portrait of herself
and others. Transcripts also illuminate the co-authorship of stories and
the ways that interpersonal relationships are built through storytelling
interactions.

Transcripts are never exact representations of the spoken word.[1]
Transcribers make decisions about what to transcribe and what to ig-
nore. Journalists, for example, often present persons' spoken words as a
running text, even though speakers may have backtracked and revised
their words. Journalists usually don't show where two people talked at
the same time, overlapping or interrupting one another. And readers
usually are not privy to the pauses that intersperse the production of a
single thought or linger between the turns of one speaker and the next.
It is easy to read dialogue that is transcribed in this way; however, we
believe, along with our colleagues who analyze spontaneous conversational discourse, that meaning arises as much from *how* something is
said as from the semantic content of what was said. We are interested in
how messages are delivered. False starts and pauses, for example, convey important information. They may signal a storyteller's tentative-
ness, distress, or self-doubt. In addition to false starts and pauses, discourse analysts mark intonation and voice quality, pitch height,
emphatic stress, and loudness, among other features of delivery upon
which meaning depends.

It is not easy to read a transcript filled with stops and starts and symbols. For this reason, we annotate only a few features of talk in the narrative passages incorporated in most chapters of the book. We *italicize*
utterances delivered with emphatic stress. We use dashes to note self-
corrections, false starts, hesitation, interruptions, and repetition, for example,

It's just afrai— just af— just *pure fear*

We represent pauses between utterances in parenthesis, and record their duration in tenths of a second, for example,

I (.4 pause) uh became aware of feeling (.4 pause) just *anxious.*

We represent concurrent talk by using brackets to indicate the point at which one speaker overlaps another:

Lisa: [Uh-huh
Meg: [stop obsessing about my rapidly beating *heart.*

Additional features of talk, including intonation, voice quality, pitch height and loudness, and inhalation and exhalation, are represented in certain portions of the text to facilitate discussion of grammar. In these cases, we delineate transcript conventions.[2]

In this chapter we introduce and reflect upon selected passages as Meg presents them. Later we present transcripts as running sequences, showing speaker change and overlaps. At times it is useful to pull a part the lines of a story to see how a sequence of communicative acts or ideas unfold in the course of telling a story, or to facilitate close analysis of grammatical forms. Although simply looking at a written transcript is a boon, the less compacted the transcript the better able we are to visualize the process of constructing a narrative and a life. When we are interested only in the semantic content of what is said, we present a compacted transcript, but when we want to focus on features of the language, we pull apart the utterances and lay them out line by line. Somewhat like E. E. Cummings or Gertrude Stein, we manipulate the transcript in different ways to lead the reader to new perspectives on language.

Meg's Panic Stories

Meg Narrates with Lisa

Most of the panic narratives are drawn from conversations between Lisa and Meg in which Lisa asks Meg to describe times in her childhood and adult life when she has experienced anxiety. These questions typically unleash a flood of narratives, one flowing to the next. Within moments, it is clear that Meg is relating tales to Lisa that she frequently reflects on herself. She prefaces stories by noting that the experience is fresh in her mind, for example, "Just the other day I was thinking about a time I went swimming with a friend . . ." In talking with Lisa, Meg tells her panic stories in chronological order and in order of intensity, climaxing with the experience she refers to as the "Big Mama" or the "Granddaddy of them all." Although she delivers the Big Mama story within its chronological sequence, this incident leaks into her telling of other panic stories, as into the telling of the story of other significant moments in her life.

Meg's encounter with anxiety begins in childhood when she panics after complying with her friend's suggestion that they jump into the deep end of a swimming pool, despite the fact that she cannot swim. In this narrative, which we call the "Water story," Meg states,

> And I remember just gulping water and *panicking*, and feeling like a chicken then because I didn't want to go in the deep end.

Meg also recounts a childhood experience on a train with her mother when she felt petrified of falling through a gap between the train cars ("Train story"). After relating these incidents, Meg raises the issue of rationality, suggesting that these episodes differ from panic episodes in her adult life:

> I don't know that this was irrational fear for a child . . . I don't know if you'd call that *anxiety*, you know? It's pretty *rational*, and I didn't *obsess* over it.

But this commentary contradicts the content of her ruminations and prefaces to her story such as "just the other day I was thinking," which indicate that she remains preoccupied by these events.

Meg's encounter with anxiety continues some twenty years later, on the night of her thirtieth birthday. On this occasion, she experiences what she now identifies as her first panic attack ("Thirtieth Birthday story"). Her story portrays panic as abrupt and elusive in the way it becomes known to her. The family has just returned from her birthday dinner. Meg is reading a book in the living room, when she becomes overwhelmed by inexplicable sensations and emotions. She describes being "outside of herself," severed from an awareness of herself and her environment as familiar and knowable. The story ends with a telephone call to her sister, a pre-medical college student, who labels the episode a "panic attack." Finding words for her experience brings Meg temporary relief, yet the threat of recurrence looms large:

> I don't know in a *way* that alleviated my *worry* because I— at least I was able to put a *name* to it . . . B— but it didn't— I still had the *anxiety*. And I— it was hard for me to get to sleep that night . . . But then I did—the next day—worry that it might come *again*.

Meg then loops back in time, differentiating this experience from fears she had as a child:

> See *that* was the first time I remember having (.8 pause) what I would term anxiety, just pure anxiety with no *cause*. I mean with the swimming I had this fear because I nearly *drowned* . . . And with the train there was a real fear that I might have fallen between the cars. (.3 pause) This was sort of fear for no reason.

Meg continues her telling with a story about taking a ski trip with her family and enduring terrifying fear that something might happen to her en route in a place where help was not available:

> You have to drive through some pretty remote *areas*, through the desert and stuff to *get* there. I remember just kind of *white* knuckling it in between sign posts of civilization . . . We'd see a sign that would say hospital, or you know *town*. And I would think oh there's help . . . If anything happened to me now we could get to help.

Meg remains riddled with anxiety when they reach their destination, and solicits help:

> Um the first night the anxiety *really* got to me. And I remember um (.3 pause) calling back (.3 pause) to California, and speaking with our

pastor's wife . . . But sh— I remember her b— trying to really comfort me with the Scripture and stuff. And I remember calling her and saying, "I just don't think I can *back* this. I'm feeling terrible. I'm *really* afraid."

Following these incidents, Meg's anxiety went into remission. It returned five years later, during the last month of her pregnancy with her second child, Sean, when she felt trapped and unappreciated: "I remember having some of it during my pregnancy with Sean, having moments where I was anxious thinking I am stuck." While almost nine months pregnant, Meg has a "stupid squabble" with her husband over what she has cooked for dinner ("Taco story"): she has made tostadas, but he complains that he had wanted tacos. Meg describes running off to the bedroom crying, feeling furious and helpless:

I'm so *damn mad* I could just— storm out of here in the *car*. But— I can't leave. I'm nine months preg— almost nine months pregnant. I can't— (.4 pause) If I *wanted* to leave I *couldn't*.

Meg relates her pregnancy to her struggle with panic in other ways. While pregnant with Sean she suffered repeated visual disturbances that caused her to worry about the health of the baby she was carrying ("Vision story"). Meg goes on to construct a story about pregnancy that blends past, present, and imagined realms of anxiety ("Pregnancy story"). That is, she contaminates the past experience of anxiety during pregnancy with her present, more intensified agoraphobic condition. She explains,

At the time I had anxieties but I hadn't become agoraphobic yet. I had, you know, like I said the *glimmerings* of what was to come, but it wasn't full blown yet.

Meg then generates an anxiety-ridden hypothetical story scenario in which she is pregnant:

When I think about pregnancy *now* I have a lot more anxieties. Pregnancy *itself* is kind of a form of confinement. You're in it for the *long haul* once you start. It's *irrevocable*. You can't— shouldn't take drugs. What if? What if you get high anxiety? You can't be popping Xanax, you know? . . . But what if I need some intervention? My gosh if I were pregnant I'd— you know? You can't—

Meg grafts this imagined scenario onto her past pregnancy with Sean, rendering herself unable to cope now with the situation she has handled in the past:

Plus the very thought of being deposited without my *car*. I remember when I had Sean I wasn't phobic yet . . . But *how* could I *endure* that? If I were to have to be hospitalized now I— I don't know how I could endure without my *car*, without feeling that I could get up and leave at will.

Notice how Meg narratively constructs her past pregnancy: rather than casting it as an accomplishment, she casts it as a pre-agoraphobic event. Rather than casting herself as competent at this point in her life, Meg casts herself as not yet but soon to be incompetent. This story illuminates how present anxieties and self-categorizing impinge upon and organize her memory of the past. In this manner autobiographies fuse past, present, future, and imagined experiences. In keeping with the words of Anthony Vidler, we see how Meg, in her struggle to overcome her anxieties, is "caught in dilemmas of temporality, tied to the inhospitable context of the here-and-now at the same time as imagining a there-and-then."

In talking with Lisa, Meg constantly foreshadows the worst panic attack of her life ("Big Mama story"). Lisa asks for details, but Meg prefers to continue her chronology: "Well there was the Big Mama one on the freeway, but I realize that even before that I had some that were sort of like precursors." Meg goes to describe these episodes, locating them within a rising tide of emotion that would culminate in the attack on the freeway. Meg's references to the Big Mama imbue each panic episode with a menacing sense of the inevitability of what is to come. In this manner not only single incidents but also whole sequences of incidents become organized in terms of current anxieties. Each story is shaped to fit Meg's overarching autobiography and Weltanschauung of panic.

Meg's anxieties intensify over the two years following Sean's birth.

She becomes overwhelmed with anxiety while visiting Niagara Falls ("Niagara Falls story"), panicking at their base when she realizes "there's no way out but through that *darn* elevator." After resurfacing from the depths of the Falls, Meg finds that she is afraid to take elevators at the hotel and at the airport; the prospect of entering an elevator triggers "the same kind of feelings I'd had in Niagara." Meg marks this episode as the beginning of her ongoing avoidance of elevators.

Meg's anxieties continue to crescendo, reaching a peak during the Christmas holiday season. She experiences a panic attack while driving a group of friends back to the church after a luncheon ("Piaf's Cafe story"). Meg describes being overwhelmed by inexplicable sensations and emotions:

> And we got halfway back to the *church* and then I started when I started having (.6 pause) those weird just ph— *pure physical* anxiety. I began to feel shaky inside, like a (.6 pause) like a— (.5 pause) like a *motor* was vibrating inside me. I just felt shaky inside, like you would if— if you were *really* afraid of something. I could almost feel like my teeth were going to chatter if I didn't get this (.3 pause) feeling of shakiness under control . . . And then I felt (.4 pause) uh like an urge to run or g— or (.4 pause) uh to *escape*. But I didn't know what it was I was supposed to be *escaping*.

Meg reports that although her body eventually quieted down, she remained haunted by the threat of panic:

> But the *memory* of that stuff stuck with me in the days ahead. And I wondered what is *happening* to me.

At this point in the telling Meg takes a deep breath and launches into the story of the most intense and momentous panic attack in her life: "And then the *Granddaddy* of them all was about a week and a half after that, when we got stuck in traffic on the freeway." In this story, which is the longest in the corpus, Meg describes traveling with William and the children to the Marriott Hotel to take William's cousin Harriet out to lunch. Meg reports that on the way to the Marriott she experienced "those same trembly (.3 pause) scary feelings that I had had driving back from that *luncheon* that day." Meg suffers in silence, managing to control her anxiety during lunch. William then proposes that they take Cousin Harriet to visit his father. On the freeway en route to William's father's house there is a traffic jam. It is at this point that Meg experiences "the *worst symptoms* I've ever had of *anxiety*." She portrays herself as "just *dying*" in the back seat of the car. She engages in futile attempts to alleviate her distress—reading a book, trying to distract herself—and eventually communicates her agony to William, imploring him to get off the freeway. After a ten-minute delay, the congestion clears and they soon arrive at William's father's house. Meg, however, remains agitated and preoccupied over the fact that they still have to return Harriet to the Marriott: "and the worst thing was we had to take her *back*." Meg desperately pleads with William to take surface streets rather than the freeway, imagining the recurrence of her panic:

> I begged William, "*Don't* get on the freeway when we take her back to the Marriott. Let's just take surface streets. *Please* . . ." I said I just can't. I *cannot* live through another episode like what I just *endured*. And if we get on that freeway, and we get *stalled* again in traffic (.4 pause) I— I— I just can't *bear*— I just can't *bear* that.

After some resistance, William complies with Meg's request, and they travel surface streets. Meg marks this as a turning point in her life:

> Yeah so then the whole pattern of avoidance began to set in, and I began to feel that I had to protect myself from any— (.4 pause) from any place where I might get *trapped*.

The Big Mama becomes the basis for Meg's fear of venturing far from home to visit friends and relatives. After receiving an invitation to a friend's graduation, Meg contemplates making the trip ("Graduation story"). As captured in her tone of voice, the very thought evokes high anxiety and a pressing need to avoid the situation:

> I'm thinking well that's out of my safety— safety zone. I can't go over there because— (.4 pause) There again it's another one of those *can'ts*. I *can't*. I can't go to Hamilton . . . It's out of my boundaries.

Yet despite the imperative quality of her avoidance, Meg feels guilty: "if I were a really good friend to her I should be able to overcome my anxiety and make the attempt because I care about her."

These emotions also arise during a subsequent telephone conversation with her mother ("Dutiful daughter story"). Meg stresses the underlying message of the call,

> She *implied* that if I really cared, if I were really a dutiful daughter, I would come home and see her and Dad before they die.

Meg goes on to express frustration over her mother's limited understanding of the severity of Meg's anxiety. Articulating the implications of her mother's words, Meg expresses her guilt over not being able to visit her parents. After voicing her frustration with her mother, she describes her own struggle to make sense of the agony of her agoraphobia. In posing her questions to herself, her voice crescendos and then trails off to a whisper:

> I just can go on and on and on analyzing it. *Why* me? Why am *I* afflicted with this? You know? Why me? Why *me? Why me* and not someone *else? Why?* (.3 pause) You know? Why me?

Meg and Beth Narrate with Lisa

Additional panic narratives are drawn fr m Lisa's conversations with Meg and Beth, in which Meg and Beth relate vivid memories of experiences they have shared. In these conversations, Meg and Beth reconstruct anxious moments in their lives. One such experience took place when Beth was six years old, and she and Meg were shopping at a mall near their house ("Mall story"). The trouble begins when Beth soils her pants in a fabric store. Anxiety mounts as they hurry to the car to rush home, and peaks when they realize the car won't start. They eventually contact a tow truck and return to safety, but the memory of being stuck in the parking lot remains fresh in both of their minds.

Another such narrative centers on Beth's distressing interactions with a bully at school who harasses Beth during chorus (Sarah the Soprano). Beth's interactions with this bully give rise to a series of attempts to make sense of the injustices done her and a barrage of questions about the persecution of innocent persons. These questions unleash Meg's memories of her own childhood struggles as an innocent victim, which give way to a portrayal of herself as an innocent victim in the grip of panic.

Family Dinner Narratives

Still other panic narratives are drawn from recordings of family interactions at the dinner table. These storytellings offer penetrating insights into narrative practices that ignite Meg's anxiety and fan its flames in the direction of her children and husband. On three occasions, anxiety invades the dinner table through stories about pit bulls, notoriously fierce dogs. In the first of the three stories in the pit bull trilogy, Meg relates an unexpected encounter with two menacing pit bulls while paying a visit to her father in law ("Pit Bull story #1"). While casually conversing in the backyard, she is startled by the sight of the dogs: "I looked over the wall and this dog, it— it *came at* me." In animated detail Meg describes the dogs' "*wicked* expressions" and "snarling jaws," asserting that "if he ever got *loose* that'd be the end of us. He could scale this wall and kill us."

Anxiety escalates as Meg narratively dismantles the wall that protects people from the dogs' vicious attack: she refers to it as a fence, and then as a gate, thus gradually increasing its permeability, reconfiguring what was once a protective barrier into a designated means of access. Meg further develops her rendition of the gate as a way out for the dogs by reporting that they have partially destroyed it:

And then the *fence*— the um *gate* going into the— in and out of this man's backyard, uh— uh— it had about *five*— originally it had maybe about five wooden slats? And the *dog* had just knocked out— there were like two pieces of wood *left* where the dog had— I mean this dog's *powerful*. He just chewed them. I don't know *how* he got— whether he (.3 pause) just threw his *weight* against it or what.

Paralleling the way the dogs penetrate the gate and are unleashed upon the world, Meg's anxiety breaks through her narrative about the past into the present and, unconfined, pervades the dinner table.

Pit bulls return to the dinner table a few weeks later, when William reports having seen an advertisement for a puppy on his way home from work ("Pit Bull story #2"). William proposes that the family adopt this puppy—part pit bull, rottweiler, German shepherd—as a pet. This proposal rouses anxiety in Meg, who, clearly not amused, comments, "Who needs a *gun* with a dog like *that?*" Immediately thereafter, Meg relates an incident in which a neighbor's mother-in-law unwittingly locks herself in the backyard with a ferocious pit bull ("Pit Bull story #3"). This sequence begins somewhat light-heartedly, but, as in the telling of the previous pit bull stories, leaves Meg mired in anxiety about the possibility that such a bloodthirsty dog—not just the particular dog in the story, but "any pit bull actually"—might attack and kill someone.

Anxiety enters the family dinner domain in other forms as well. On one occasion Meg describes her unnerving encounter with an inquisitive neighbor, Charles. Charles fiddles with bullets while interrogating Meg about their plans to paint the front of the house ("Interrogation story"). Meg's anxiety mushrooms as he shifts the focus of discussion to guns and his shooting expeditions. On another occasion Meg recounts a trip to a bank in which the tellers work behind ceiling-high bullet-proof windows. Seeing the bullet-proof windows lets loose a cascade of associations, including recollection of a terrifying armed robbery that had occurred some months before, and hypothetical speculations about other menaces to society.

Narratives constructed at the dinner table illuminate the amplification and perpetuation of anxiety as specific events from the past are reconfigured in present and hypothetical realms. These storytelling interactions demonstrate how, in Vidler's words, "history has the uncanny propensity to repeat itself, to return at unexpected and unwanted moments," overwhelming present experience and ripe for renewal in the future.

Stories Present Problematic Events

Although these stories vary in content and in the circumstances of tell-ing, they share a common structure. Like exposing the interior scaffold-ing of a building, delineating narrative structure reveals the linguistic resources tellers habitually draw on to create and maintain emotions, actions, and identities. Each of Meg's panic narratives focuses on a *cen-tral, problematic experience*, sometimes referred to as an *inciting event*[3] or an *initiating event*.[4] Like stories of personal experience in general, each centers on at least one problematic event, which provokes one or a se-ries of psychological responses and behavioral attempts to resolve the problem and ensuing consequences. The problematic event arises in a temporal, spatial, and psychological framework known as the *story set-ting*.[5]

In this set of panic stories Meg and other members of the Logan fam-ily portray an array of problematic events. As we have seen, Meg jumps into the deep end of a swimming pool without adequate swimming in-struction:

I remember a friend of mine who was a *very accomplished* swimmer and a diver. And she took me swimming one time. (.4 pause) And she said, "Come *on*. Let's jump in *here*." And very trustingly I did. And it turned out to be the deep end of the pool.

Traveling with her family through isolated areas en route to a ski vaca-tion is also problematic:

I— I would be scared in between turn-offs because I would think, Here we are. You have to drive through some pretty remote *areas*, through the desert and stuff to *get* there.

Being stuck at the base of Niagara Falls is yet another problem:

You can take this— this elevator that goes down this *shaft* through the rock. We got on the elevator and went down and— we got down and— (.5 pause) and— and *inside* the rock is just like a— a maze of tunnels. And you— eventually you emerge to (.4 pause) a spot right behind where the actual (.4 pause) *water* is *falling*. And when I got down there I became *claustrophobic*.

Perhaps the biggest problem Meg faces takes place on the freeway, where she is trapped with her family and William's cousin Harriet:

So we got on the freeway to head up to um (.8 pause) t— to Westland. And *darn* it if there wasn't some kind of (.4 pause)*tie*-up. I don't know if there was an accident. You couldn't *see*, the cars were piled up for so far ahead of us. But for one reason or another, traffic came to a standstill. And there we *were*. (.8 pause) And all of a sudden I realized we weren't moving.

Yet another problematic event occurs in the familiar location of her father-in-law's yard. While casually conversing with her father-in-law, Meg encounters two ferocious pit bulls:

I was standing there talking to your *dad* by the back *wall*. And I just happened to remember these dogs. (.6 pause) I looked over the wall and this dog, it— it *came at* me.

Recasting Events as Problems

Tellers build events as problematic through their structuring of stories. Stories are structured in ways that establish temporal and causal connections between elements of the story, conveying tellers' theories about events. Storytellers construct events as problematic by locating them in sequences that cast them in a negative light. Tellers may do this in more than one way.

One way to build an event as a problem is to portray it as triggering one or a series of *subsequent* negative *psychological responses* or behavioral *attempts* to resolve or reverse the situation or undesirable consequences. These subsequent narrative components *recast* the event as a problem. By portraying protagonists as having negative responses to an event, tellers construct a particular world view of the problem. In Meg's set of panic narratives, she recasts events as problematic by linking them with a particular negative psychological response: panic.

For example, Meg's jumping into the deep end of the swimming pool is cast as a problematic event in light of the psychological response that follows:

> And I *remember* just gulping water, and thinking I was going to drown, and being very *afraid*, and after that thinking of myself as um (.3 pause) *not* measuring up when it came to swimming . . . And I felt *inferior* to my friend, and *embarrassed* that I'd nearly drowned.

Being at the base of Niagara Falls with only one elevator becomes a problem when Meg realizes that this is the case, panics, and communicates her imperative desire to leave:

> And I— I *realized* there's no way out but through that *darn* elevator. And I *remembered* clutching on to my *daughter* and saying, "Beth I'm— *Mama's really afraid.*" (.3 pause) And— and um (.4 pause) and um (.4 pause) I— er I— I mean *instantly* regretted that I had (.4 pause) *told* her that I was afraid. But I— I *did*. I clutched on to her. And I remember asking her to *pray* with me because I was *so unnerved*. (.8 pause) And I— I said, "I wanna go *up* now." And (.4 pause) I told William, "I've got to get out of here. I'm not— I'm not *feeling* good."

Similarly, traveling mountain roads and staying at the ski lodge with her family are problematic events because they are narratively linked to Meg's panic and her desperate attempts to find comfort through a telephone call to her pastor's wife:

> Um the first night the anxiety *really* got to me. And I remember um (.3 pause) calling back (.3 pause) to California, and speaking with our pastor's wife . . . But sh— I remember her b— trying to really comfort me with the Scripture and stuff. And I remember calling her and saying, "I just don't think I can *hack* this. I'm feeling terrible.

I'm *really* afraid." I was crying over the phone to her and she said some reassuring words.

In the same way, Meg's encounter with the pit bulls is problematic because of the ensuing anxiety that she experiences and relates at the dinner table:

And this dog it— it *came at* me. I mean thank *God* it was *attached* but— to the *chain*. But I went, *"Eeyow!"* And I jumped back off the tree stump. (.4 pause) And your dad said "For heaven *sakes!* Don't *run!* That's the worst thing you can do."

The triggering events and circumstances are not inherently problematic; they are *made* problematic in the context of Meg's subsequent panic and the consequences that ensue. In telling about her experiences, Meg constructs the meaning of events in her life. Events become problematic because she experiences them as such, not because of what 'really happened.' Meg's narrative accounts of her experiences embody theories of what happened, theories that create continuity between past, present, future, and imagined lives.

All stories convey one or more theories about the narrated events. These theories, or "challengeable explanations," are embedded in the architecture of the story—how it is designed and built. In constructing a story, tellers create causal connections among a series of events. These causal links organize elements of the story into a sequence that presents the teller's explanation of what happened. We have seen how Meg connects components of her panic stories within a causal sequence in which one event (for example, being stuck at the base of Niagara Falls) triggers a series of psychological responses that trigger further attempts to resolve the situation. This narrative sequencing constructs a chain of events that identifies the problem and, in so doing, offers an explanation of panic. An alternative sequencing of these story components would have spawned an alternative explanation of the narrated events. Hence theories embodied in narrative are challengeable. In this sense, stories are a medium not just for communicating facts and ideas but, perhaps even more important, for constructing and evaluating theories and interpretations.

The particular theory being constructed throughout Meg's narrative renderings of panic explains panic as an irrational response to being in a particular location. By fusing her panic response with the particular location in which it arises, Meg's portrayals recast being in certain physical locations as a problematic event—the circumstance that triggers the distressing emotions and consequences that ensue. Panic, while narratively tied to particular locations, is portrayed as inexplicable, or unaccountable. Meg depicts events as problematic for her, but not for others in her midst. This discrepancy contributes to her problem; it is the basis for her portrayal of herself as an irrational and abnormal protagonist, struggling to cope with circumstances that others deem ordinary.

Meg reinforces this theory through the connections she builds *among* stories of panic. In talking with Lisa about her panic experiences, Meg journeys chronologically from one account of anxious experience to the next, systematically excluding those that have a legitimate, reasonable cause:

I remember having some other fears. Um but I don't know that they were *irrational*. I mean if there was a *reason*, and I didn't *obsess* over it, I don't know if I would term that *anxiety*.

Precasting Events as Problems

As an alternative to casting events as problems on the basis of subsequent story components, a teller can cast an event as problematic through components of the story that *precede* the event. By delineating circumstances that make an event understandably troublesome for a protagonist, a teller can *precast* the event as a problem. In developing the story setting, the narrator provides crucial details about the psychological dispositions of protagonists by locating an event within particular social and physical circumstances. These circumstances are portrayed as anticipating or causing a problematic event.

When we reexamine the panic narratives, focusing our attention on the story settings, we see a recurrent communicative dilemma in which Meg has reservations about participating in a proposed activity, does not communicate these reservations, participates, and then panics. The emotional climate developed in the setting precasts the event as problematic. Meg sets the stage for the Water story, for example, by explaining that she had never been given adequate swimming instruction and cannot swim:

Meg: My mother never bothered to give us swimming lessons
       [until I was thirteen.
Lisa: [Aw
Meg: And so I had a fear of water
Lisa: Um-hm
Meg: I liked to *swim*, but I would never go in the deep end. And I was
       okay as long as I stayed *out* of that deep end.

This setting precasts jumping into the deep end as understandably problematic. The psychological and behavioral responses that follow—sensing she is drowning, feeling afraid and embarrassed—are linked not only to the event but to the setting.

At the beginning of the Niagara Falls story, Meg describes feeling reluctant to go down in the elevator with her family to the base of the Falls, but doing so nevertheless:

And I'd never *really* been afraid of elevators before, but I— I realized I didn't want to do it. (.3 pause) But I was afraid to ruin everybody's good time, so I put on my little *rain* jacket that they give you and we got on the elevator and went down.

Meg neither voices nor acts on her reluctance, joins her family in spite of her fears, and then panics.

Meg recounts a similar experience in the Ski Trip story, when she describes having reservations about going on the trip, but does not express her hesitations to other members of her family and goes anyway:

There was the time we went on our ski trip with my husband's parents. I remember being very reluctant to do that, having some reservations about making the trip.

These unexpressed reservations precast or anticipate problematic events. Being at the base of the Falls, on remote roads to the mountains, or at a ski lodge far from home are problematic events before Meg panics—because she does not want to be there.

Causal connections among the story settings that anticipate problematic events, responses, and consequences construct an alternative theory of panic. This second theory links panic to a set of extenuating circumstances that render participating in a proposed activity problematic. On the basis of this alternative theory that is embedded in the structure of her stories, we propose that Meg's panic is tied to a recurrent communicative impasse in which she, as protagonist, does not communicate reservations about taking part in upcoming events. Instead, she participates in the proposed activity and panics. Although we identify this theory in Meg's narrative, she does not. In a sense this second theory is the narrative's, not the narrator's, theory of panic.

The stories we tell about ourselves often convey understandings that are not readily accessible to us. We frequently go back to our writings and see things about ourselves that we were not fully cognizant of, or did not entirely comprehend. It is always the case that there is more to our stories than meets our eyes and ears. In talking with others we often learn about ourselves through the things they hear us say, things that we may not have heard at all or may not have understood in the same way. Our conversational partners cast our stories in a new light, illuminating our evolving sense of who we are.

We now delve into the theory of panic that links panic to a fear of particular places. This theory is most salient in Meg's accounts as well as in the clinical literature on panic and agoraphobia. We look first at how this theory is narratively built and, later, in Chapter 4, at the grammatical resources that are recruited in constructing this view of panic. From the poststructuralist perspective that people actively shape the social, cognitive, and emotional realms they inhabit, we can see how Meg uses grammar and discourse to establish and perpetuate her identity as an agoraphobic woman.

Building the Core Panic Episode

Meg builds a place-centered theory of panic during the dramatic climax of each panic story. This is the part of the story that is most vivid, elaborated, and captivating. After the story ends, the core panic episode remains most prominent, resonating in the minds of teller and listener alike.

Core panic episodes highlight a problematic event or circumstance, which triggers a panic response in the protagonist—including feeling overwhelmed, helpless and trapped—and a series of attempts to escape the problematic situation, often including a communicative act such as "get me out of here." These components form the dramatic core of the panic narratives, serving as the foundation for Meg's world view of anxiety.

THE PANIC EPISODE

1. A climactic *problematic initiating event* that triggers
2. A *psychological response*, including *panic*, and
3. A series of *attempts to escape* the problematic situation, often including a *communicative act* that makes this goal explicit.

The climactic panic episode dominates not only Meg's narratives but the clinical literature on anxiety as well. For example, the *Diagnostic and Statistical Manual of Mental Disorders* identifies panic as "discrete periods of intense fear or discomfort that are unexpected, i.e., did not occur on exposure to a situation that almost always causes anxiety, and are not attributable to organic factors."[6] Diagnosing panic and agoraphobia involves soliciting accounts centered on the triad of elements that form the dramatic core of Meg's panic narratives. Panic is diagnosed in individuals who report distress over their experience of fear and anxiety in situations that do not warrant such a response. Agoraphobia is diagnosed in individuals who experience both panic and the imperative desire to prevent its recurrence, which is expressed by avoiding situations in which panic has arisen. In this sense, Meg's accounts of her experiences and those enshrined in diagnostic profiles of agoraphobic persons reinforce each other.

By illuminating the narrative structuring of Meg's panic episodes, we gain insight into how she builds a turbulent emotional universe associated with a psychological syndrome. The medium of narrative brings to the fore unresolved, fragmented, and disconcerting aspects of one's relation to the world. We draw from Meg's telling of the Big Mama incident, the most intense and momentous panic attack in her life, to depict the basic narrative components that make up the dramatic core of her tales of panic: a problematic event; psychological responses, including panic; and attempts to escape the problematic situation, often involving a communicative attempt that articulates this goal. Although we focus on the Big Mama story for purposes of exposition, these three components characterize Meg's other panic narratives as well. We have included comparable, albeit slightly abbreviated analyses of additional narratives in the notes.[7]

The core elements of Meg's panic narratives vary in terms of their intensity. The Big Mama story merits its title by virtue of the extensive, dramatic development of these narrative components. Stories that relate experiences prior to the Big Mama attack are paler versions of this drama. As we shall see, narrative components may appear in any order in the narrative. They may appear more than once, and they may be intertwined in the very same utterance. A characteristic of informal narrative accounts, regardless of whether they concern panic, is that elements of the story are not necessarily related in chronological order. Aspects of the narrated events tumble out as they are recalled and symbolically reexperienced.

In the Big Mama story, the climactic panic episode occurs after Meg and her family have lunch with Cousin Harriet at the Marriott. They are on the freeway, en route to William's father's house, when they find themselves in a traffic jam. Meg describes this climactic problematic event:

And *darn* it if there wasn't some kind of (.4 pause) *tie*-up. I don't know if there was an accident. You couldn't *see*, the cars were piled up for so far ahead of us. But for one reason or another, traffic came to a standstill.

Although Meg's "*darn* it" foreshadows the problem as such, she goes on to articulate additional psychological responses that frame the event as a problem: namely, acute awareness that they are stuck, which is reinforced by her futile attempts to locate an exit.

But for one reason or another, traffic came to a standstill. And there we *were*. (.8 pause) And all of a sudden I realized we weren't moving. And I (.4 pause) looked out and saw there was no uh we weren't near an exit . . . There was a big high chain-link fence bordering the freeway at that point where we were.

These psychological responses recast the event as a problem by identifying it as triggering a negative response. In turn, they are rendered part of a sequence that provokes panic:

All of a *sudden* all of the *symptoms*, the *worst symptoms* I've ever had of *anxiety* just overtook me. And I felt like I was— if I didn't get out of that (.4 pause) *car* and out of that freeway, that I bet something *terrible* was going to happen to me.

These panicky sensations and emotions precipitate a series of behavioral attempts to escape the problematic situation, beginning with the communicative acts of pleading with William to exit the freeway, "William can we get *out* of here?" William provides his own reaction to Meg, stating that this is not a realistic possibility:

What do you *mean* can we get out of here? You know we're in *traffic*. We just have to *wait*.

Meg reiterates her plea twice:

Well can't you get on the shoulder?
Can't you just like get on the *shoulder* and drive *off*?

Again William deems this impossible: "Well *no*. There *isn't* any shoulder here."

This narrated interaction presents Meg's panic responses and her explicit desire to escape as unreasonable. William's responses to Meg's pleas suggest that her requests deviate from what would be expected of a normal person with a commonsense understanding of the situation at hand.

William then asks Meg, "Are you all right?" and Meg responds in a desperate whisper: "I'm not *doing* very good." William further queries, "W— Well what *is* it?" to which Meg haltingly replies, "Well— well you know I just—(.3 pause) I'm feeling *anxious*."

Cousin Harriet then echoes William's question to Meg: "What's wrong Honey?" But William voices Meg's response:

> *Well* she uh—Well she has claustro—*claustrophobia*. Well I think she's just a little claustrophobic.

Lowering her voice, Meg parenthetically remarks to Lisa, "For lack of a better word. He didn't know what to say."

Shifting to a tone marked by increasing urgency, Meg portrays the intensity of her experience to Lisa: "*Meanwhile* I'm just *dying*."

In the vortex of the panic episode, Meg makes various *attempts* to alleviate the situation by distracting herself:

> I'm I had this *book* that I had brought with me to read. And I was trying to preoccupy myself and *distract* myself by reading the *book*. But I was so anxious it was just *futile*. I remember I took out writing paper and a *pen*, and tried *writing*, just *writing* anything, just— just to distract myself . . . I tried— I remember clutching the *headrest* behind me, just thinking if I (.3 pause) do *anything* to just sort of burn off some of this nervous energy, maybe I could get *through* *this*. It was *agonizing*.

This portion of the Big Mama episode ends ten minutes later when the traffic clears and the Logans make their way their way to William's father's house. Meg reports that she was "agitated the rest of the day."

The structuring of this and other panic stories presents a particular world view of panic. The Big Mama typifies Meg's panic narratives in that it portrays panic as the outcome, albeit irrational, of being trapped in a particular physical space far from home. Whether the freeway or the base of Niagara Falls or on a plane, the *physical environment* is what Meg portrays as the source of distress.

After telling this portion of the Big Mama story, Meg appears wired, yet somewhat drained. She slowly departs from the narrative she is reliving, and returns to the room. Taking a sip of tea, she draws in her knees, tucking her legs beneath the folds of her skirt. She sighs, as if relieved to have reached the point in the story where panic subsides, yet conscious that it could return, unannounced, at any moment. Meg structures her narratives in a way that gives panic a force of its own, a force that consumes and overwhelms her experience, sweeping her up into its grip. We now go through the panic episode once again, this time viewing it not as a linear sequence but as a spiraling, self-perpetuating vortex of events, responses and consequences.

How Panic Spirals

An essential characteristic of Meg's panic narratives is that psychological and behavioral responses to problematic events are built as problems in themselves.[8] Mapping the structuring of these events, responses, and actions is crucial to understanding how panic is perpetuated through narrative. Meg frames her panicky feelings and actions—feelings and actions that arise in response to a particular problem—as further problems. These feelings and actions then incite further psychological and behavioral responses, which in turn are framed as problematic, generating a spiraling of interconnected problems and frustrated responses. In this way she portrays herself as a protagonist responding not only to one but to an accumulation of intertwined problematic circumstances—an entangled web of feelings of panic, failed attempts to terminate these feelings, as well as the troublesome situation that triggered the panic in the first place. Indeed the nesting and spiraling of intertwined problems may be a hallmark of panic experience itself.

Returning to the Big Mama story, we can see how Meg spins a spiraling web of problems. Meg starts out by casting being stuck on the freeway as the major problematic event. However, she goes on to narratively construct an interwoven set of problems spawned by that event. For example, Meg's immediate realization that the car wasn't moving and they weren't near an exit becomes a second problem—that is, she experiences a heightened awareness of being stuck on the freeway, which itself distresses her. This heightened awareness, coupled with the initial problem of the traffic jam, incites additional, intensified, panic responses—"the *worst symptoms* I've ever had of *anxiety*," constituting a third, nested problematic event. Meg's subsequent attempts to communicate her desire to escape to her husband, and her failure to achieve this goal, form a fourth problematic event. This problem is linked to the psychological responses that precipitate it, and results in yet a fifth series of problems—her futile attempts to distract herself. This vortex of frustrated attempts to resolve the problem lead to a respiraling of panicky feelings, captured in her emphatic assertion, "It was *agonizing*."

HOW PANIC SPIRALS

Problematic Event (being stuck on the freeway) provokes:
   Psychological Response (heightened awareness) that becomes:
   Problematic Event that provokes:
      Psychological Response (panic) that becomes:
      Problematic Event that provokes:
         Attempt to handle Problematic Event
         (communication) that becomes:
         Problematic Event that provokes:
            Attempt to handle Problematic Event
            (distraction)

Looking at this sequence in reverse—starting with her attempts to resolve the problem and working back through the problem sources—

we can see that Meg's attempts to alleviate the situation address not one but a tangled web of problems. Her (failed) attempt to alleviate her distress by distracting herself addresses not only the problem of being stuck on the freeway but her unsuccessful attempt to communicate with her husband, her panic response to heightened awareness of being stuck on the freeway, and this heightened awareness itself.

The nested, spiraling structure of panic episodes illuminates how Meg relives and perpetuates panic through narrative. Panicking involves becoming trapped in a web of rapidly interlocking distressing circumstances and emotions. Meg's emotions and actions not only fail to alleviate her distress but contribute to its escalation. The discursive structure of core panic episodes portrays panic as a response to being stuck in a place from which there is no way out. It creates this portrait by forging causal links between components of the story.

In this sense structuring a story is like painting a picture and explaining how its parts are interconnected. The teller creates a coherent plot, providing a framework for interpreting events, emotional dispositions, and actions, and understanding their meaning in the lives of the protagonists.

From this panoramic view of panic stories, we now narrow our scope, focusing on the way the teller grammatically constructs each component of the story. Like the painter's palette and brush, grammar provides a medium and a tool for creating the propositions, actions, and dispositions. We use the term 'grammar' broadly, to cover how the teller puts words together in sentences (syntax), how words themselves are structured (morphology), and the sound system (phonology) that speakers draw upon to make meaning. Grammar gives shape, color, texture, and intensity to elements that make up the picture as a whole. It allows us to penetrate the construction of panic, stroke by stroke.

4

A Grammar of Panic

That which is presumably closest is by no means that
which is at the smallest distance from us.

—Martin Heidegger, 1962

Language is a potent and sometimes frustrating instrument of human-kind. It is our primary medium for symbolizing how we construe reality: we experience an emotion and try to put that emotion into words. We think a thought and struggle to communicate it to ourselves and others. This is the representing function of language, the function of language that many feel distinguishes us as a complex species. This side of language infuriates speakers and writers, because words often seem static and pale in comparison with the intricate torrents that make up a lived or imagined experience. "That's not what I want to say!" we say, as we rail at the inadequacies of our code.

Language, however, is also a triumphant configurer of experienced reality. It influences how we think and feel about ourselves and others; about actions and conditions; about time, space, and causality; about illness and health; and about right and wrong. Although we are not prisoners of language, we are influenced by the vocabulary and grammar we speak. As children, we come to know the world largely through how those around us represent the world through language. Language draws children's attention to objects and relationships and properties. Speakers of different languages, in this sense, see the world somewhat differently, a principle referred to as 'linguistic relativity.' The anthropologist and linguist Edward Sapir captures this notion:

The relation between language and experience is often misunderstood. Language is not merely a more or less systematic inventory of the various items of experience which seem relevant to the individual, as is so often naively assumed, but is also a self-contained, creative symbolic organization, which not only refers to experience largely acquired without its help but actually defines experience for us by reason of its formal completeness and because of our unconscious projection of its implicit expectations into the field of experience.[1]

Sapir speaks of not only grammar but also "fashions of speaking" as influencing how we think and feel.[2] It is not simply that grammatical structures and lexicons of languages carve up the world in different ways, but also that we as speakers of these languages routinely draw upon particular structures and words to construct an idea or point of view. The ways in which we habitually use language shape our perception of events.[3]

This last point is most relevant to understanding the perpetuation of psychological dispositions such as agoraphobia. A hallmark of agoraphobia is the way in which sufferers sit at home mulling over anxious experiences, communicating to themselves or to themselves and others at once. This ongoing rumination organizes how sufferers see past, present, future, and imagined events in their lives. We cannot penetrate the mind of the ruminator to examine the form of silent self-communication, but we can look at the form of their linguistic expression in social interactions with others. Identifying the linguistic forms that speakers habitually use in building and maintaining portraits of themselves and others allows us to see identities, relationships, and world views in the making. In this sense, attending to grammatical form is central to understanding how people make meaning through language.[4]

That a sufferer would draw on grammatical forms that articulate defining characteristics of panic is in itself not surprising. Yet what do we know about the grammatical forms that construct this crucial portrait of the self? Next to nothing. Certain grammatical forms flood the narratives that sufferers of panic relate to their intimates and to clinicians. And these forms are fundamental to the diagnostic process in that diagnoses hinge upon particular modes of self-representation. When self-representations are maintained, diagnoses tend to endure; when self-representations change, diagnoses tend to change. Despite the essential role of grammar in constituting self-representations and the role of self-representations in experiencing life, grammatical realizations of dispositions have not been delineated.

In telling stories of anxious moments, Meg habitually draws upon a set of grammatical structures and lexical items to paint a portrait of herself as abnormal, helpless, and out of control. Over time Meg's past experiences and her linguistic shaping of them have become blurred. Her thoughts are identified with her words:

> I'm not a person who travels any more. And I can't—(.3 pause) And I um I you know I— I realized I've adopted this really negative way of thinking, and it's you know I tell myself what I— I define myself in terms of what I *can't* do anymore.

In this comment Meg describes her negative way of thinking, which she identifies as what she tells herself and how she defines herself. When Meg says, "I tell myself" and "I define myself," she speaks of enduring messages. From our perspective, these linguistic acts, as well as those that dominate Meg's interactions with others, structure her self-image.

What are the grammatical structures Meg routinely uses to etch a landscape of her emotions? Can we speak of a grammar of panic—a repertoire of forms that compose the agony of agoraphobia? Here we chart a grammar of panic. We traverse the intersection between panic and grammatical form without precedents to guide our way—there are no existing grammars of emotion or standard anxiety-language checklists to consult. While we use ecumenical language to describe features of talk central to anxiety disorders, we are not relaying a diluted version of what specialists in linguistics or psychology already know. Rather, we present a sophisticated analysis of grammar and suffering. We hope this grammar of panic will be useful to persons interested in the relationship between grammar and psychological dispositions as well as those interested in the nature of panic. Our exploration casts grammar in new light, and takes us into facets of panic that have been glossed over or not otherwise considered.

We begin by turning to the grammatical core of Meg's affliction in an effort to elucidate her lament, "That's what I torture myself with and that is what keeps me from living a normal life." To shed light on *what* is torturing and keeping Meg from living a normal life, we explore *how* these tortuous and debilitating thoughts are linguistically formulated. That is, we travel the grammatical topography of Meg's world view. Our passage shows us that how Meg puts her thoughts and feelings into words shapes her ongoing experience.

We have noted that Meg's stories build at least two theories of panic. As discussed in Chapter 3, the most elaborate and explicit theory coincides with clinical characterizations of agoraphobia. In this theory, panic is viewed as an irrational response to being in a particular location, for example, a freeway or an airplane. We now explore the grammatical resources that Meg relies upon to build this theory.

Grammar of Abnormality

Consistent with diagnostic accounts of panic, Meg uses grammatical forms to portray panic as coming on unaccountably and marked by a heightened self-preoccupation, fear of losing control, including going crazy or even dying, and a sense that there is no end in sight. In constructing this emotional journey, Meg relies on a consistent set of grammatical forms.

Reason Adverbs and Adverbials

Lexical adverbs and adverbial phrases are grammatical elements that express conditions such as where, when, how, why, or the extent or intensity of an action, event, state, emotion, belief, or other notion predicated in a sentence. When we look at the core episodes of panic in Meg's narratives, we find that she relies on a limited set of adverbial expressions to delineate her transition into a state of panic. Not surprisingly, in light of the clinical literature on agoraphobia, Meg routinely marks the onset of panic with adverbs and adverbial phrases that denote the unexpected and unaccountable. Indeed, the *Diagnostic and Statistical Manual of Mental Disorders* defines panic as coming on unexpectedly.[5] Among the adverbial expressions she most frequently uses are the lexical adverb "unaccountably" and the adverbial prepositional phrases "all of a sudden"[6] and "out of the blue."[7] Meg uses these grammatical resources to describe her senseless passage into panic in locations such as on the freeway:

> And all of a sudden I realized we weren't moving.
> And I (.4 pause) looked out and saw there was no uh we weren't near an exit.

after celebrating her thirtieth birthday:

> Um (.6 pause) I was just reading a book.
> We had gone out to dinner to celebrate my birthday.
> And um when we came home,
> and I was sitting on the living room sofa reading a book.
> And all of a sudden
> I (.4 pause) uh became aware of feeling (.4 pause) just *anxious* unaccountably.

on an airplane trip, after visiting Niagara Falls:

> All of a sudden
> I realized I wanted very much to be off the *plane.*
> (.5 pause) But we had to wait for our turn
> to get up to the— (.3 pause) the— the— *whatever.*

and in a score of other scenes:

> I mean I had all these *attacks*
>   that just seemed to come out of the blue.

> And I began to feel that I really couldn't trust my *body* anymore to
> *behave.*

These adverbial phrases are abnormalizing devices in that they mark a
transition from a normal to an abnormal condition. Indeed, such
phrases are not only used to construct an unexpected onslaught of
panic, but are resources for constructing any unusual or abnormal experience.[8] Meg recruits these forms to frame the onset of panicky feelings
as both sudden and inexplicable. In so doing, she portrays her panic
experiences as unlike the feelings and conduct of others who are with
her during these moments. In using these adverbials, Meg begins to
build a narrative portrait of her emotions and herself as both portentous
and beyond her control.

Mental Verbs

Within her reconstructed panic episodes, Meg progresses into a heightened sense of self-awareness. While this progression is consistent with
clinical accounts that describe panic as involving "anxious self-preoccupation"[9] Meg's stories breathe life into such terms. By examining how
she builds her narrative accounts, we see how the psychological terrain
she inhabits is created and maintained. In Meg's panic narratives, she
steps outside of immediate external situations into a dialogue with herself. These internal dialogues are grammatically reconstructed through
mental verbs, such as "think," "realize," and "become aware." Meg uses
mental verbs to frame her thoughts as messages, in this case unspoken
messages formulated as reflections addressed to herself. Meg usually
represents the communication as if it were a direct quote. In these cases
she captures the sense of exact quotation by preserving the tense of the
original message. She replays her sense of awakening anxiety as if it is
happening here and now, as her story unfolds. This is evident in her use
of the present and future tense to relive her heightened self-awareness
while traveling to a family ski resort. Speaking in a whisper, as if to
herself, Meg explains:

I would think, Okay.
This sign says next town you know 20 miles.
And I would think, I can make it for 20 miles.
I would kind of just say I can— I can make it.
I *will* make it.

Returning to her normal tone of voice, Meg continues:

And then I would— whew!
We'd get into a town and I would think, Okay there's a *hospital* and a
   doctor's office, and if anything should *happen* to me . . .

Similarly, Meg uses the future tense to dramatize her silent self-communication during the panic attack that mars her thirtieth birthday:

I remember thinking
I'll just go *do* something *normal*. D— you know?

She relates her thoughts methodically, as if delivering a list:

I'll go up*stairs*
and I'll brush my *teeth*,
and wash my *face*,
and get ready for *bed*.

In this passage Meg at first uses mental verbs ("I remember thinking")
to report her thoughts directly but then slides into a style of narration
that has the character of what literary critics and linguists call "free direct speech."[10] In free direct speech, the reporting verb is omitted and
only the reported speech is expressed. In the case of reporting thoughts,
the mental verb is often omitted and the thought laid bare. We are in
the experience, inside Meg's head, privy to her private thoughts.
   Alternatively, Meg sometimes takes more emotional and temporal
distance in telling about these moments of heightened self-awareness.
In these cases, Meg tends to couch her thoughts as having occurred in
the past. Further, she portrays her reporting of these thoughts as paraphrases rather than direct quotes of the original. For example, in de-

scribing her thinking while in the grip of panic on the airplane, Meg reports,

> I realized I wanted very much to be off the *plane.*

> I realized we weren't moving.

Mental verb constructions help to illuminate the grammatical face of consciousness. When Meg uses forms such as "I remember thinking, 'I'll just go *do* something *normal,*' " she is reporting not only *what* she is thinking and feeling but also *that* she is thinking and feeling. In this sense mental verbs bring into focus Meg's consciousness of engaging in the activities of thinking and feeling. In recounting these narratives, Meg gives the impression that the absorption with thinking and feeling that she associates with particular past events is not completed but, rather, continues through the moment of storytelling.

Meg also conveys the impression that she often dialogues with herself in this way. She uses mental verbs in the progressive tense ("I remember thinking"), which implies recurrence. She also prefaces mental verbs with auxiliaries such as "would," which imply habitual or enduring activity:

> I would think, Okay.
> I would think, I can make it for 20 miles. I can—

Lowering her voice to a whisper, she continues:

> I would kind of just say I can— I can make it. I *will* make it.

When Meg repeatedly uses mental verbs that depict recurrent or enduring involvement in thinking and feeling, she communicates over and over again to her interlocutors and herself that she is caught up not simply in specific worries but in the web of worrying itself.

Place Adverbs

Given that agoraphobia is identified with anxiety about movement away from safe places, it is not surprising that place adverbs play a salient role in the panic narratives of an agoraphobic person. In the present discussion we focus on the use of the place adverb "here," because it is widespread in Meg's panic narratives and because it is very rarely used by Meg in narratives *not* on the topic of panic experiences. We consider how Meg imbues "here" with emotion—creating an emotional space—and the implications of emotional spaces for the maintenance of agoraphobia.

One might think, as we did, that Meg would link "here," which denotes closeness to the speaker, with positive experiences in her life. We had expected "here" to be associated with the safety and comfort of home. In Meg's stories, however, "here" is decidedly associated with negative experiences. Meg routinely uses "here" to depict painful or uncomfortable situations she feels trapped in, desires to escape, or otherwise intensely dislikes. For example, in telling the story of the biggest panic attack of her life (the Big Mama story), Meg, in a desperate, pleading voice, recalls,

> And I remember telling William,
> "William can we get *out* of here?" . . .
> I *mean* I don't *think* I let on the *extent* of the— m— of the *agony* I was going through.
> But I d— I remember *urging* him saying, "Can you— *please* get off here?"

Similarly, Meg reports that in the throes of a panic attack at the base of Niagara Falls,

> I told William, "I've got to get out of here. I'm not— I'm not *feeling* good."

And as panicky feelings well inside her on the way to a ski vacation, Meg thinks,

> I— I would be scared in between turn-offs because I would think, Here we are.

In telling a story about being stuck in a predicament at the mall with her daughter, she reflects,

> So here I *am* with a little girl.

After Beth pipes in with the name of the mall,

> We were at Rosemont.

Meg goes on to lay out the negative circumstances:

> with poop running down her leg.

Finally, in a story centering on her frustration in response to her husband's culinary demands, Meg voices a desperate, pleading rendition of her troubling thoughts:

> And—and then I *realized*,
> Well what can I—?
> I felt real *helpless*.
> I thought, Here I *am*.
> I'm so *damn mad* I could just— *storm* out of here in the *car*.
> But— I can't *leave*.
> I'm nine months preg— almost nine months pregnant.
> I can't— (.4 pause)
> If I *wanted* to leave I *couldn't*.

These passages suggest that "here" is not where Meg wants to be. "Here" is where Meg is in agony or scared or furious or in difficulty.

In many ways, Meg's use of "here" parallels her use of the present and future tense. The constructions bring temporally remote events into a present-time vividness and spatially remote events into the immediate proximity of Meg and others as storytellers. These are among the grammatical resources used by good storytellers, who try to involve interlocutors in the story realm by dramatizing the story events as if they are taking place in the here and now.

The semiotician Karl Bühler discusses this practice as one of two strategies that narrators use in depicting a set of events. They may frame the events as taking place in distant time and space, using past tense and distant deictic forms such as "there." He characterizes this strategy as "Mohammed goes to the mountain." That is, the storyteller moves the story away from the immediate circumstances. Or, alternatively, storytellers may frame the same events as occurring in the here and now. That is, the mountain comes to Mohammed.[11]

Bühler's concern is with how speakers use language to shift the subjective orientation to a given situation, a linguistic and psychological process referred to as "displacement" in the English translation of Bühler's work.[12] Sophisticated narrators may use linguistic forms such as "here" to direct interlocutors to displace their usual orientation by imagining absent entities as present and/or distant events or circumstances as proximal. Building on Bühler's framework, we focus on the impact of the mountain coming to Mohammed on Mohammed—in this case, on Meg as narrator and protagonist.

Bühler's formulation suggests that narrators have an equal choice between two rhetorical strategies. Yet for Meg, and likely for other agoraphobic persons recalling their panic experiences, the two strategies may *not* be equally accessible. Rather, panic experiences may be so vivid and pressing that they force their way into current consciousness. We suggest that Meg uses "here" because she is engulfed and overwhelmed by the mountainous experiences of panic she is reconstructing. Indeed, Meg's ongoing concern is that she can't achieve any distance from this mountain. It keeps invading her thoughts and her life.

In this perspective, the mountain is ever-present, close by, much like the notion of existential spatiality explored by the philosopher Martin Heidegger.[13] For Heidegger, there is a difference between physical space and lived space. Lived space is the space that my interests, cares, and attention define. For something to be near to me, it is not necessary for it to be physically close, but, rather, it occupies my current thoughts and concern. "That which . . . is closest is by no means that which is at the smallest distance from us."[14] The existential condition of Being-in-the-world involves this experience of nearness, achieved through acts of "de-severance" in which farness vanishes, remoteness disappears, and entities and circumstances enter into a caring closeness to oneself.

Heidegger's notion of existential spatiality is crystallized in the construction "here I am" in Meg's stories. The three words that compose this phrase represent the three essential dimensions of lived space: "here" = nearness, "I" = subject, "am" = present being. When Meg, or anyone for that matter, states "here I am," she draws attention to her existence at a singular point in experienced time and space. When Meg utters these words, her distressed existential circumstance is the focal concern. Sometimes Meg intensifies this existential focus by placing emphatic stress on the verb "am" and drawing out the vowel sound (marked in transcription by a colon), as when she recalls, "I thought here I *a::m*."

In many ways, "Here I am" seems like an empty expression. When Meg says "Here I am," she is telling her interlocutors that she exists, but not where in particular she is located. "Here I am" is elucidated only when it is connected to the rest of the unfolding story.[15] Because interlocutors have to listen further to unpack "Here I am," this construction is also a powerful attention-getting device. Meg's use of "Here I am" illustrates how particular grammatical forms shape both her life and the lives of others, in the story and in the telling.

In Meg's narratives, what follows "Here I am" is a litany of phrases and clauses that depict aspects of her existential predicament. Consider how "Here I am" prefaces and projects a series of distressed circumstances (marked by {}):

Here I am:
    {with a little girl}
    {with poop running down her leg}

Here I am:
    {I'm so *damn mad*}
    {I could just— *storm* out of here in the *car*.}
    {But— I can't *leave*}
    {I'm nine months preg— almost nine months pregnant.}
    {I can't—(.4 pause)}
    {If I *wanted* to leave}
    {I *couldn't*.}

We suggest that Meg uses "Here I am" together with mental verbs to anticipate and draw attention to her distress. When Meg says "I remember thinking," we do not know what she is thinking. We anticipate the unpacking of the contents of her mental activity. The following passage outlines how mental verbs act like "Here I am" by prefacing and projecting a series of thoughts (marked by {}):

> I remember thinking
>   {I'll just go *do* something *normal.*}
>   D— you know?
>   {I'll go up*stairs*}
>   {and I'll brush my *teeth,*}
>   {and wash my *face,*}
>   {and get ready for *bed.*}

"Here I am" and mental verbs capture and maintain interlocutors' attention over an extended sequence of discourse. Meg may sustain her interlocutors' attention even further by using the two constructions in series:

> And— and then I *realized*
>   {Well what can I—?}
>   {I felt real *helpless.*}
> I thought
>   {Here I am.}
>   {I'm so *damn mad*}
>   {I could just— *storm* out of here in the *car.*}
>   {But— I can't *leave*}
>   {I'm nine months preg— almost nine months pregnant.}
>   {I can't—}
>   {If I *wanted* to leave}
>   {I *couldn't.*}

This strategy extends interlocutors' attention by unpacking the contents of a mental verb construction with "Here I am," which in turn needs to be unpacked to be understood. In this manner Meg, and perhaps other agoraphobic persons, can prolong the narrative reconstruction of panic experiences as a focal point of current consciousness—for

Meg herself or for the researcher, clinician, or family members involved in the storytelling.

Meg uses "Here I am" and mental verbs both to point to her predicament and to lay out more fully details of her existential condition. More generally, the adverb "here" and mental verbs give panic the property of endurance: panic experienced at some past time and physically distant place endures as a current focus of attention across extended stretches of narrative. Meg presents panic not as a completed episode but as an experience that continuously "gnaws into the future and swells as it advances."[16]

Grammar of Helplessness

So far we have seen how Meg uses grammar to portray herself as abnormal. She uses grammatical constructions that frame her panic experiences as irrational and as involving heightened consciousness of her existential predicament. Let us now turn to how Meg characterizes her role in this predicament.

In European and American world views of panic, a fundamental diagnostic feature is that sufferers feel helpless and out of control. As noted earlier, it is not surprising that a sufferer would draw on grammatical forms that articulate these characteristics. But how is helplessness grammatically realized? The answer to this question is neither transparent nor simple. The English language offers a vast array of grammatical possibilities for expressing loss of control that are far subtler and more potent than bald statements such as "I feel helpless." These forms assume varying degrees of control over actions and emotions. They are resources for the presentation of self-in-everyday-life[17] as in or out of control or sliding somewhere in between. The grammatical resources that Meg uses to tailor herself as helpless and out of control are widely used to construct an array of identities, especially victims of one circumstance or another.[18] A grammar of helplessness is central to the linguistic construction of many psychological dispositions, although this claim awaits delineation. Like the painter's palette and brush, the grammatical repertoire in a person's speech community provides means for portraying shades and textures of impotence and vulnerability. Grammatical forms can intensify these qualities or dilute them—can bring them to the foreground or relegate them to the background. Like painters, language users coordinate forms to compose a coherent emotional landscape of helplessness.

Meg paints a self-portrait of helplessness by consistently (1) referring to herself in semantic roles other than agent or actor, (2) using grammatical forms such as modal verbs that frame her action as arising out of necessity rather than as a voluntary act, (3) using grammatical forms that imply failure to achieve a goal, and (4) using grammatical forms that intensify her vulnerability and deintensify her ability to cope and control.

Nonagentive Roles

Perhaps the most obvious grammatical strategy that Meg uses to convey her helplessness is to cast herself in semantic roles other than that of agent or actor.[19] With the important exception of verbs of communication (to be discussed in Chapter 5), Meg generally does not portray herself as a person who purposefully initiates or causes actions.[20] Rather, in telling about panic episodes, she tends to use grammatical constructions that place her in the role of experiencer or affected object. The role of experiencer includes cognitive (one who thinks) as well as emotional (one who feels) experience. An affected object is one who is affected by an action. When Meg casts herself in these semantic roles, she renders herself as relatively impotent.

When Meg represents herself as an experiencer, she uses her tacit knowledge of grammar to modulate her prominence as a referent in the sentence. In so doing, she modulates her prominence and power in the world of her stories. Like an author describing a character in a novel, Meg colors herself as more or less in control of her thinking and feeling, although the predominant hue is passivity. For example, although thinking is potentially an act of empowerment, Meg habitually represents her thoughts as unwanted. Meg portrays herself as unable to control not only their content but also their onset and duration. Similarly, when Meg refers to herself as experiencing emotion, she frames her emotions as unwanted and unbridled. This pattern is illustrated when Meg tells Lisa about experiencing panicky emotions and thoughts after celebrating her thirtieth birthday:

Meg: And all of a sudden I (.4 pause) uh became aware of feeling (.4 pause) just *anxious* unaccountably. It was more a feeling of almost being outside myself and looking— (.3 pause) looking *on* as it were.
Lisa: Um-hm
Meg: And *realizing* that I was aware of every (.3 pause) thought and feeling that I had. And I couldn't seem to (.3 pause) *shake* this
Lisa: Um-hm
Meg: self-preoccupation. And that was *alarming* in *itself*.

In this passage, the experiencer, Meg, is a focal point. She is the grammatical *subject* of the utterances, for example, "I (.4 pause) uh became aware of feeling (.4 pause) just *anxious* unaccountably," and "I was aware of every (.3 pause) thought and feeling that I had." In other cases Meg puts panic in the prominent position of subject, and relegates herself to the relatively minor position of *direct or indirect object* in the sentence. In these positions, Meg casts herself as acted upon by the force of intense anxiety. In detailing the agony of panic during the freeway traffic jam, for example, Meg recounts,

All of a *sudden* all of the *symptoms*, the *worst symptoms* I've ever had *of anxiety* just *overtook* me.

Here Meg casts anxiety, indeed the worst Meg has ever experienced, as the subject of the sentence and as the agent that overtakes a helpless self ("me"). This grammatical pattern is frequent in Meg's reconstruction of panic. At the climax of the story about going on a ski trip, for example, Meg reconstructs the panic she experiences upon arriving at their destination:

> But I remember when we got to Utah,
> um the first night the anxiety *really* got to me.

At this moment in the story, Meg casts anxiety as a force that acts upon her. Meg deputizes her sensations as the creative subject[21] and becomes a passive destination for their catastrophic energy.

Meg uses grammar to further diminish her prominence and agency by omitting herself from utterances that are nonetheless about her. In these constructions, we infer Meg's role as experiencer on the basis of the surrounding narrative context. Meg makes herself invisible when she constructs clauses such as the following:

> And then a feeling of impending *doom,*
> just— that's the only way I can describe it.
> It's just afrai— just af— just *pure fear.*

> And it was *so* awful, the *feeling* of that fear was so awful and—

> So then the whole pattern of avoidance began to set in.[22]

Where is Meg in this reconstruction of the panic experience? In articulating her role as an experiencer of emotion, Meg nominalizes feelings as "a feeling of impending *doom,*" "the *feeling* of that fear," and "the whole pattern of avoidance" rather than saying "I felt impending *doom,*" "I was afraid," and "I began to avoid." Nominalization is a rhetorical strategy widely used by speakers of English to avoid mention of persons. It is emblematic of scientific and legal discourse, for example, where authors wish to deemphasize their part in some outcome.[23]

Diminished Agentive Roles

Meg's preference for putting herself in nonagentive roles in her narratives of panic does not mean that she never portrays herself as a volitional agent or actor in the world. Yet when she articulates her roles as agent or actor, she typically uses other grammatical features that severely weaken these roles.[24]

Verbs of Necessity

When Meg grammatically portrays herself in the role of agent or actor, she often casts herself as acting in the grip of forces larger than herself. She is agent or actor only because these external forces impel her to carry out some action. In other words, she is a *causal* but not a *willful* agent/actor. Meg constructs this state of affairs by continually using verb constructions such as "got to [verb]," "have to [verb]," and "can't [verb]." These forms, often called modal verbs, indicate that someone undertakes an action out of obligation or, as in Meg's stories, necessity, or that someone does not undertake an action because it is impossible.[25] Meg uses modal verbs that indicate that her actions must be performed out of necessity; they are compelled by the panic welling inside her. For example, feeling trapped at the base of Niagara Falls, Meg tells her husband,

> I've got to get out of here. I'm not— I'm not *feeling* good.

Meg does not narrate herself as wanting to go, as in "I told William I want to get out of here" but rather as having to go, "I've got to get out of here," citing illness ("not feeling good") as a warrant. Similarly, in the story about her husband's culinary demands, Meg cites being nearly nine months pregnant as a warrant for her inability to leave in protest:

> I'm so *damn mad* I could just *storm* out of here in the *car*. But— I can't *leave*. I'm nine months preg— almost nine months pregnant. I can't— (.4 pause) If I *wanted* to leave I *couldn't*.

Hypothetical Past Constructions

Meg also weakens her volitional control over actions and emotions by talking about them as taking place in a *hypothetical past world*. When Meg describes a past action or psychological state as hypothetical, as when she says "If I did . . ." or "If I wanted to . . .," she is not making the neutral claim[26] that some action or some volition could or could not have possibly occurred. Rather she implies that she did not carry out the action or did not have the intention. In the passage in which Meg describes her feelings about her husband's culinary demands, Meg drastically undercuts her earlier expression of the desire to leave ("I'm so *damn mad* I could just— *storm* out of here in the *car*") by rewording it as past hypothetical ("If I *wanted* to leave"). In doing so, Meg implies that she did not want to leave.

"Try" Constructions

Meg also diminishes herself as a potent agent or actor by frequently using the verb *try*. As every speaker of English knows, stating that an agent or actor "tried" implies that the attempt was unsuccessful. Meg uses "try" when recounting the actions she undertook in response to panic, for example, in response to feeling anxious following her thirtieth birthday:

> I was trying to escape the scary *feelings* I was having, but the— the more I tried the worse it became.

and in response to feeling trapped on the freeway:

> And I was trying to preoccupy myself and *distract* myself by reading the *book*. But I was so anxious it was just *futile*.

Negation

Perhaps the most obvious grammatical resource for diminishing the role of agent or actor is *negation*. Negation frames the narrator or protagonist as failing to complete a given action. Meg's narratives of panic experience are threaded with negated attempts to act, based on Meg's perception that she is not capable. We have already pointed out one example of negation: when Meg recounts how she could not storm out of her house in response to her husband's frustrating culinary demands. She also uses "couldn't" throughout her telling of the panic attack she experienced following her thirtieth birthday:

Meg: And I couldn't seem to (.3 pause) *shake* this
Lisa: Um-hm
Meg: self-preoccupation.
       And that was *alarming* in *itself*,
       to think that I couldn't just carry on with my book and not
       (.6 pause)
Lisa: Uh-huh
Meg: stop obsessing about my rapidly beating *heart*, and how sweaty
       my hands were getting.

Intensifiers and Deintensifiers

Finally, Meg grammatically constructs a portrait of herself as helpless
by using *intensifiers* and *deintensifiers*. Meg uses intensifiers to amplify
her experience of anxiety and vulnerability. She uses deintensifiers primarily to dilute her experience of coping and being in control, present-
ing herself as neither able nor licensed to reach her goals. While certain
grammatical forms are recruited solely for intensification (for example,
"really," "so," "instantly," "very much," "a great deal of") and others for
deintensification ("like," "kind of," "sort of," "maybe," "some of"),
many grammatical forms may function in either capacity ("just"). Meg
uses intensifiers throughout her story of feeling trapped at the base of
Niagara Falls:

> And I *remembered* clutching on to my *daughter* and saying,
> "Beth I'm— *Mama's really afraid.*"
> (.3 pause) And— and um (.4 pause) and um (.4 pause)
> I— er I— I mean *instantly* regretted that I had (.4 pause) *told* her that I
> was afraid.
> But I— I *did.* I clutched on to her.
> And I remember asking her to *pray* with me because I was so *un-
> nerved.*

In a dramatic moment of realization in the wake of her husband's demands, Meg intensifies her sense of impotence:

And— and then I *realized*, "Well what can I—?" I felt *real helpless*.

And recounting the height of her panic on the freeway, Meg amplifies her sense of being unable to control her emotions:

And he goes, "Well I think she's just a little claustrophobic."
And (.3 pause) *meanwhile* I'm *just dying*.

It was *so* awful,
the *feeling* of that fear was *so* awful that (.4 pause)
um I think after that I would just do *anything*.

The intensifiers seem to magnify Meg's sensations of fear (*"really afraid*,*"* "*so* awful the *feeling* of that fear was *so* awful"), helplessness (*"real helpless*"), death (*"just dying*"), regret (*"instantly* regretted"), disequilibrium (*"so unnerved*"), and anxiety ("a great deal of my *anxiety*").

In addition, Meg uses a range of grammatical resources, especially "kind of," "sort of," "just," "maybe," and "like," that deintensify or hedge the sense that Meg accomplished her goal. After recounting her harrowing trip to the ski resort, for example, Meg comments,

That was kind of how I coped with the ski trip.

Meg does not make a straightforward claim that she managed to handle this difficult situation. Rather than patting herself on the back for this accomplishment, she presents a watered-down assessment that is self-effacing. In the Big Mama story, Meg also diminishes almost every aspect of her attempt to calm herself while panicking in the midst of the freeway traffic jam :

I remember clutching the *headrest* behind me,
just thinking if I (.3 pause) do *anything* to just sort of burn off some
of this nervous energy,
maybe I could get *through* this.

And when she recounts how she asks her husband to exit the freeway, Meg says,

And he turned around and looked at me.

And I said, "Can't you just like get on the *shoulder* and drive *off?*"

The deintensifiers in these passages present Meg as less than fully able to handle herself in stressful situations; she can't quite cope ("kind of how I coped") or relieve her nervousness ("to just sort of burn off some of this nervous energy"), and she doubts her ability to endure ("maybe I could get *through* this"). In addition, Meg uses deintensifiers to hedge her directives to others, in this case, to minimize her imposition on her husband William ("Can't you just like get on the *shoulder* and drive *off?*").

Meg is not alone in using these and other grammatical forms to weaken the force of their representations. These forms are used widely by speakers of English to convey politeness and modesty.[27] Researchers studying language and gender link this style of weakening claims and directives to women. When women and other members of society use these forms, they construct and present a relatively helpless, relatively powerless self to the world.

Meg also uses other linguistic devices that are not strictly part of grammar to intensify and deintensify actions and emotions. As mentioned in Chapter 3, to make it easier for readers to follow the transcripts, we have not represented all of these features in most passages within the text. But we include these features below, and in the final section of this chapter, to illustrate how Meg grammatically intensifies her sense of helplessness and anxiety through emphatic stress (indicated by *italic*), increased amplitude (indicated by CAPITAL LETTERS), stretched sounds (indicated by colons :::):

SO::: awful

just *DY::ING*

raised pitch (indicated by upward arrow ↑),

real ↑*HELPLESS*

Wh— what if that thing gets ↑*loose* and ↑*kills somebody?*

repetition,

It was *SO:::* awful, the *feeling* of that fear was so awful.

halting delivery, indicated by "um" and "er," deep in-breaths or inhalation (indicated by "hhh"), and pauses,

And— and um— (.4 pause) and um— (.4 pause) I— er I— mean (hhh)

as well as voice qualities of desperation and feebleness (indicated within double parentheses).

Building a Grammar of Panic

This discussion suggests that Meg draws upon a wide range of linguistic forms to verbally construct experiences of mild to extreme panic. We have seen how Meg uses these forms in diverse narratives. In the flow of narration, however, Meg packs these features densely together, creating a panorama of overwhelming anxiety. We reproduce and annotate an extended passage from Meg's story about her husband's culinary demands to illustrate how linguistic forms flood portions of a narrative to create a coherent grammar of panic experience. To facilitate analysis we parse this narrative passage into the relevant linguistic forms that together compose a grammar of panic:

Mental verb + Emphatic stress	And— and then I *realized*,
Voice quality	*((desperate, pleading tone))*
Present tense + Halting delivery	Well what *can* I—?
Intensifying adverb + Emphatic stress	I felt real *helpless*.
Mental verb + "Here" + Present tense + Stretched sound +	

Emphatic stress	I thought here I *a::m.*
Present tense + Intensifier + Emphatic stress	I'm so *damn mad*
Hypothetical + Intensifier + Emphatic stress + "Here" + Raised pitch	I could just— *storm* out of here in the *car* but
Halting delivery	(hhh)
Present tense + Negative modal auxiliary	*I can't leave.*
Halting delivery	I'm nine months preg— almost nine months pregnant
Negative modal auxiliary + Halting delivery	I can't—
Halting delivery Voice quality Hypothetical	(.4 pause) ((intensifies desperate tone)) If I ↑*wanted* to leave
Negative modal auxiliary + Raised pitch	I ↑*COU::LDN'T.*

Grammar plays a crucial role in Meg's construction and reconstruction of panic experiences. The sensations of heightened self-awareness, frustration, and impotence are verbally realized not only through the content of Meg's stories but also through their grammatical shape. In the span of the eleven short clauses that make up this brief narrative excerpt, Meg intertwines seven different grammatical structures (intensifier, mental verb, place adverb "here," present tense, hypothetical past, negation, modal auxiliary) along with variations in voice quality and delivery to construct an unhappy emotional portrait that continues to affect her. The mental verbs in this passage index her sense of self-preoccupation; the intensifiers amplify her anger and her escape dreams, which are only to be dashed repeatedly through negated modal auxiliaries ("can't," "couldn't"). Ultimately Meg dilutes the desire to escape itself by recasting it as an unlikely hypothetical condition ("If I *wanted* to leave").

At the same time, Meg's use of the adverb 'here' and the present tense verbally constructs her emotional predicament not as a completed narrative situation but rather as a preoccupation that is ongoing and close at hand. Finally, as noted earlier, certain grammatical structures, especially mental verbs and the construction "here I am," coupled with the clauses that follow them, glue interlocutors' attention to Meg's anxieties. Used in these ways, grammar serves to propel anxious thoughts and feelings over stretches of narrative discourse and into Meg's here-and-now consciousness. These grammatical forms work together to paint a coherent portrait of panic and person as irrational and helpless. Yet other features of the narrative paint quite a different picture. We now explore this alternative perspective.

5

Accommodation as a Source of Panic

> And all these questions, according to the Angel of the
> House, cannot be dealt with freely and openly by
> women: they must charm, they must conciliate, they
> must—to put it bluntly—tell lies if they are to succeed.
> Thus, whenever I felt the shadow of her wing or the
> radiance of her halo upon my page, I took up the inkpot
> and flung it at her. She died hard.
>
> —Virginia Woolf, 1929

Telling a story is not always easy. We often begin stories without knowing where they will take us. We become preoccupied with particular strands of the story and forget to mention a crucial detail. We need those around us to help thread bits and pieces of life experiences together, especially aspects of the setting that may explain what happened. It is particularly hard to tell stories about emotions and events that unnerve us and those we love. Our distressing sensations may eclipse our narrative vision. We find ourselves tongue-tied, unable to create a story line that makes sense. We hold back our stories for fear that they may distress our family and friends. When we initiate such stories, our interlocutors pull back, uncomprehending and apprehensive. We suffer the loss of co-authorship. And emergent stories, lacking the commentary and questioning that imbue an incident with motivation and rationale, never come to maturity.

Meg, like the rest of us, does not always unravel disturbing events, tracing what happened to a nest of background circumstances. Rather, she often begins with only the briefest of settings—when and where she was and what she was doing just before panic struck—and then plunges into the dramatic moments of her panic experience. While Meg's stories are lush with the details of the panic experience itself, their settings are skeletal:

> Um (.6 pause) I was just reading a book. We had gone out to dinner to celebrate my birthday. And um when we came home, and I was sitting on the living room sofa reading a book. And all of a sudden I (.4 pause) uh became aware of feeling (.4 pause) just *anxious* unaccountably.

Meg's first thought as she begins this story is what she was doing immediately prior to the onset of panic ("I was just reading a book"). She backtracks briefly to earlier that evening, reporting what happened in a single clause ("We had gone out to dinner to celebrate my birthday") before hastily returning to the scene immediately preceding her panic ("when we came home, and I was sitting on the living room sofa reading a book"). Meg never returns to this circumstantial setting. We don't know where the dinner took place, who was present, or what occurred during the dinner. We don't know how she felt about the dinner or about turning thirty years of age. The story becomes the story of panic and its aftermath, with Meg continuing to wonder about "feeling (.4 pause) just *anxious* unaccountably" even as the story winds to a close. Where does this anxiety come from, and why at this moment in her life?

At the time of her first panic experience as an adult, in the wake of her thirtieth birthday, Meg is unable to pursue these questions. Her sister, a pre-med student, tells Meg that she is having a panic attack. But this knowledge does not quell Meg's distress:

Meg: B— but it didn't— I still had the anxiety. And I—
Lisa: [Um-hm
Meg: [it was hard for me to get to sleep that night

In telling about subsequent panic episodes, Meg dwells on the panic experience and its outcome. Each time Meg describes her anxious feelings, she repeats that they came on "unaccountably," "suddenly," or "out of the blue." These expressions place roadblocks in the process of making sense of what has happened. Meg does not attempt to link panic to the settings of her stories once she begins to recount its distressing effects. Eventually she evolves a master narrative, a ritualized story plot that holds for all of her panic experiences, wherein anxiety is presented as an irrational response to being in an immediate activity setting—on the freeway, at the base of Niagara Falls, in the hospital, in an airplane or an elevator—in some past or imagined world. This dominating story line implies a world view or theory that links panic to place.

It may very well be that this master story line, that is, this theory linking panic to place, is what ultimately drives people like Meg to seek therapy. Therapeutic interactions may provide the opportunity to develop other narrative theories. Guided by psychological paradigms and intuition, therapists and clients collaboratively excavate events and construct contexts that might account for panic attacks. Psychotherapists working from psychodynamic orientations search for the roots of their patients' panic in childhood experience, while those with alternative perspectives, such as cognitive-behaviorists, strive to identify more proximal causal triggers.

We suggest that therapists and clients might benefit from gaining expertise in discourse analysis or from working closely with discourse analysts to articulate the hidden structure of a client's story. By "hidden structure," we mean the less obvious connections between events that hold a story together. The hidden structure is unobtrusive and subtle, calling for an interdisciplinary endeavor (psychotherapy *cum* linguistics) to mine story settings for crucial causal threads. These hidden elements, nestled in story settings, are less memorable than the climax of a story; they are often hurriedly mumbled *sotto voce* on the way to telling about a peak experience.

Downplayed as they are, the hidden parts of each story nonetheless are presented by a teller. The teller could have left out these parts. That the teller includes them at all suggests that he or she recognizes that these hidden story elements play a role in the narrated experience. That is, that the teller included them means that he or she has some awareness of their relevance to understanding what happened. In therapeutic encounters, it is often implicit that the client cannot access precipitant circumstances, which makes it necessary for the therapist to elicit new information.[1] In these cases the therapeutic interaction may take on an asymmetry of expertise, in which the client is the novice and the therapist is the expert on the client's life experiences.

We suggest that clients are considerably more articulate and expert than a first hearing of their stories might suggest, and that this expertise is captured by analyzing how they construct their stories. We offer this study of Meg's stories as an example of the technique and a testimony to the rich insights that abide in the teller's own words. Relistening to particular stories provides an opportunity to bring out the teller's expertise and to discuss theories and understandings hidden in his or her stories. In particular, therapist and client can profit from returning, with linguistically trained ears and eyes, to story settings articulated in clients' first or subsequent tellings of a life experience.

This view is based both on what we have found in returning to the story settings of Meg's narratives of panic and on the field of narrative analysis. Settings introduce characters. In the setting the storyteller builds an atmosphere. And on the basis of the setting, listeners or readers build first impressions of the protagonists and make inferences about upcoming events in a story. The setting, in other words, provides a frame for making sense of one or more focal experiences. It is in the setting that the storyteller articulates the circumstances that lead to a climactic event. The setting is also the structural locus for the storyteller's stance toward a climatic event—whether and why an event is problematic, for example. It is the setting that good writers and good storytellers manipulate to forge a dramatic story. In Alfred Hitchcock's film *The Birds*, the events are gradually and horrifyingly given meaning as the viewer is given access to more and more background concerning a pair of pet birds purchased by an unsuspecting family.

Unlike Hitchcock, who focuses his artistic attention on the setting in all of his films, Meg and others like her are less reflective in crafting the settings of their stories. At some level of awareness Meg knows that the elements she includes in her story settings are germane to her panic. Returning to story settings can potentially raise that level of awareness and bring to the surface understandings of panic that are hidden in the structure of the story.

When we follow the trail of Meg's stories of panic, we see a progression toward greater elaboration in their settings. Our technique has been to analyze the more elaborate settings for their relation to panic episodes and to return to more abbreviated settings to see if they also display similar features. Looking at a composite of story settings we find that most of Meg's stories include a recurrent circumstance that anticipates panic. Succinctly put, despite reservations, Meg accommodates to a proposed activity, participates, and panics. Accommodation is, in Meg's storytelling framework, the hidden *precipitant*—the backgrounded theory—of panic.

Our work with Meg and her family was not designed to identify the *cause* of panic and agoraphobia. As discussed in Chapter 1, many factors contribute to the onset of the disorder. This study seeks to illuminate the sufferer's own understandings of the environmental conditions and interpersonal dynamics that trigger panic, demonstrating the depth of insight that can be gleaned by looking at the grammatical and discursive architecture of stories. Whether the theories of panic conveyed in her narratives apply to the lives of other sufferers remains an open question. But the method we model in this book is reproducible to that end. We now elaborate this second narrative theory, which ties panic to accommodation, and in so doing we illustrate how to mine narratives for the hidden theories they contain.

Meg is not alone in her struggle between satisfying her own desires and accommodating to the desires of others. Accommodation is the unfortunate proclivity of women in many societies, including the United States. Women are socialized to be pleasers, often to their emotional disadvantage. The historical legacy of the "good woman" that lives on in the inherited collective image of the feminine became firmly formulated in the nineteenth century.[2] Women's social worth resided in their contribution to men and children, and hence to society, through unselfish goodness. For women it was not enough to be good in oneself; a woman had to have a positive effect on others to fulfill her true nature. In Virginia Woolf's words, "women must charm, they must conciliate, they must—to put it bluntly—tell lies if they are to succeed." These ideals continue to organize the expectations of contemporary Americans.[3] Woolf's struggle to battle this image of feminine goodness (the "Angel of the House") in order to express herself attests to its power in silencing the authentic voices of twentieth-century women. Meg's self-portrait depicts much the same struggle:

> I've always been one to *worry* more than others (.3 pause) about um what other people think of *me*. (.3 pause) You know? I'm more conscious of you know uh— (.3 pause) more needing to do the *right thing*, so people would *approve* . . . and certainly those kinds of— *that* kind of personality is a set-up for *anxiety*, because there are so many ways in which you can screw up and people won't like you.

This disposition may very well contribute to psychological disorders associated predominantly with women.[4] On the basis of her own research and that of others in the field, the psychologist Dana Crowley Jack describes how women suffering from depression acquiesce to the needs and desires of others, particularly their husbands, at the expense of their own well-being. She illustrates this behavior by quoting the words of a depressed woman:

> I don't really think about myself. I put myself as a person out of the picture and I just accommodate other people.[5]

We suggest, on the basis of Meg's stories, that accommodation contributes to her agoraphobia as well.

But we are getting ahead of ourselves. Accommodation is part of a more encompassing communicative dilemma that systematically appears in the setting portions of Meg's stories of panic. Meg makes this dilemma relevant because she expresses it as part of her story settings, the appropriate narrative locus for orienting the audience to the main narrative events. However, although she establishes an atmosphere in which she is caught in a distressing communicative dilemma, Meg never links this distress explicitly to panic. By the time that she recounts the onset of panic, she severs all connections with the communicative scene she previously established (and directs her audience to do the same). Up until the moment of the panic attack, Meg builds a narrative theory of distress as arising out of accommodation to an undesirable proposal. At the point of the story climax, her narrative switches to the theory of distress as an irrational response to being in a particular place. The settings of Meg's narratives offer new insights into her experiences and, perhaps, into agoraphobia more generally. By returning to these portions of her stories and examining how they scaffold both her tale and their grammatical form, we can teach Meg what she knows but does not fully recognize.

The Communicative Dilemma

What is this communicative dilemma? Our journey through Meg's narrative accounts finds her consistently following a path that leads into a communicative predicament. This path may be schematically summarized:

1. A family member or other intimate proposes a future activity involving Meg.
2. Meg has reservations about participating in the proposed activity but does not communicate them.
3. Meg accommodates by participating in the activity.

We now follow Meg, step by step, as she moves along this path to panic.

The Proposal

The first step involves a proposal by one of Meg's friends or a family member that she participate in some future course of action. In each of the story settings where Meg recounts such an interaction, she formulates the proposal using the same grammatical construction: all take the form of a "let's" imperative. When Meg begins a story of panicking in a swimming pool, for example, she quotes a childhood girlfriend who entreats her to jump into the deep end:

> I remember a friend of mine who was a *very accomplished* swimmer and a diver. She took me swimming one time. (.4 pause) And she said, "Come *on*. Let's jump in *here*."

Similarly, in the initial setting of the Big Mama story, Meg uses the same grammatical form to portray her husband William's proposal to join him in entertaining his visiting cousin Harriet. In a weary tone, Meg begins to recount William's proposal that they take Harriet to lunch. In this passage, she renders William's and Harriet's words in a sing-song voice:

> So in the *midst* of this, this long-lost cousin calls us and says, "I'm in Lomita staying at the Marriott." And my husband says, "Oh it would be so good to see you again *Harriet*. Let us come and take you to lunch."

On the way to lunch, Meg experiences anxiety akin to what she had experienced a week before when she was driving her friends home from a church brunch. Meg explains,

> So we drop everything and (.3 pause) head out this morning to the *Marriott* to pick up *Cousin Harriet*. And on the way there, I begin to feel those same trembly (.3 pause) scary feelings that I had had driving back from that *luncheon* that day.

In this passage, Meg uses the conjunction "and" to juxtapose accommodation ("So we drop everything . . .") with anxiety ("those same trembly (.3 pause) scary feelings . . ."), but she does not articulate a causal link between the two.

In the course of this story Meg recounts yet another proposal directed to her prior experience of panic, namely, that the whole family take Harriet to see William's father:

And it was after we'd finished the lunch, and we got— decided to go— "let's go take Cousin Harriet to visit William's *father.*"

Although Meg does not explicitly specify the proposer, the grammatical form of this directive parallels her rendition of William's prior and subsequent proposals, thereby implying his voice.[6] It is precisely in the execution of this proposal that Meg suffers the worst panic attack of her life, initiating the start of her agoraphobia.

Following this massive panic attack, Meg manages to get through the visit with William's father. She then insists that they avoid the freeway in returning Harriet to her hotel. Yet after dropping off his cousin, William once again tries to persuade Meg to travel home on the freeway in a final proposal. Again Meg formulates the proposal as a "let's" imperative:

William says, "Well *come* on. Let's take the freeway home. It's after rush hour, and there *won't* be any traffic."

The use of "let's" seems a friendly and communal way of engaging another in an upcoming activity. The speaker may use "let's" to establish what social scientists call "co-membership" with the addressee, that is, the speaker suggests to the addressee, "You and I are part of the same team."[7] "Let's" implies that the speaker and addressee will be engaging in the activity together; they will take joint responsibility and/or derive shared benefit from it. Yet the "let's" imperative *is* an imperative. The speaker is not *asking* the addressee if she is able to or desires to participate in the proposed activity, as would have been the case if he'd asked, "Do you feel like taking Cousin Harriet to lunch?" Rather, the speaker includes the addressee as part of a group of persons willing to undertake the activity that the speaker favors. It is almost as if to reject the proposal entails rejecting membership in this group. To say "no" to any kind of solicitation is difficult, but to say "no" to a "let's" imperative may make Meg feel as if she is dissolving a friendship or a marriage. The proposals put forward to Meg may not have had this grammatical shape; what is significant is that in Meg's ruminations about past panic experiences, she formulates these proposals consistently in this manner.

The pragmatic assumptions that accompany "let's" imperatives are relevant to current conceptions of agoraphobia. When Meg quotes her husband or her friend as saying "Let's . . . ," she couches communication about upcoming activities as (1) joint undertakings (encoded through the first-person plural pronoun "us") that are (2) desired by intimates and (3) imposed upon her (encoded through the imperative verb "Let"). These pragmatic assumptions correspond to the view that (1) agoraphobia is a relationship-based disorder, and (2) persons with agoraphobia are dissatisfied with this relationship, yet (3) they feel unable to negotiate or escape it. In this perspective, agoraphobia develops as a costly and extreme solution to a communicative dilemma: it provides a reason for staying in the immediate vicinity of spouse and family and curtails any thought of leaving. If we graft Meg's narrative world view of agoraphobia onto existing accounts of the disorder, communication seems to be the crux of a relational explanation of agoraphobia. The architecture of Meg's narratives embodies the view that agoraphobia is a communicative problem that is not tied to any single relationship, but spans a range of interpersonal interactions. We turn now to how Meg feels about the proposals put to her.

Meg's Reservations

Each time that Meg mentions that someone has issued a proposal to her, she also describes how she feels. She lists reasons why she should not participate in the proposed activity. In telling about her childhood friend's proposal to jump into the deep end of the pool, for instance, Meg explains to Lisa that she did not know how to swim well enough to comply:

Meg: My mother never bothered to give us swimming lessons
      [until I was thirteen
Lisa: [Aw

Meg: And so I had a fear of water
Lisa: Um-hm
Meg: I liked to *swim*, but I would never go in the deep end. And I was
      okay as long as I stayed *out* of that deep end.

Similarly, in telling the Big Mama story, Meg constructs a setting
replete with a litany of reasons why she was reluctant to take Cousin
Harriet out to lunch. For one thing, it was Christmas-time. She had
twelve dozen cookies to bake for a Christmas cookie party and presents
to wrap to send to relatives, and there was very little time left. On top
of this, the son of her estranged half-sister had recently appeared unin-
vited on their doorstep, asking to stay with them indefinitely. His presence in their small house was getting on her nerves. In the midst of
these overwhelming circumstances, Cousin Harriet telephones to say
that she is in town, and William says he can't wait to see her:

Meg: And I *remember* (.6 pause) not really *wanting* to go (.3 pause) that
      morning, feeling some like some *foreboding*, some feeling that
      um— (.4 pause) For one thing I had a lot on my *mind*. It was
      Christmas-time, I had presents to *wrap* and cookies to *bake*. It
      was an inconvenience t— . . . I knew— I knew that I had *more*
      than I could— I had bit off more than I could possibly chew. I
      had something like *twelve* dozen *cookies* to make that night, and I
      knew I should have been staying home (.3 pause) baking *those* for
      this Christmas cookie party. And I had presents to *wrap* and—
      and get mailed off to Oregon for Christmas-time.
Lisa: Um-hm
Meg: I had a *lot* on my mind. And *Robert* was staying with us, this
      (.3 pause) *stranger*.
Lisa: Um-hm
Meg: And the stress of trying to (.4 pause) maneuver around him in a
      small house with one bathroom was *getting* to all of us. (.3 pause)
      You know? And uh (.8 pause) he'd come and go at late hours
      and— (.5 pause) *I* don't *know*. It was just *stress* and all around.

Lisa: Um-hm

Meg: So in the *midst* of this, this long-lost cousin calls us and says, "I'm in Lomita staying at the Marriott." And my husband says, "Oh it would be so good to see you again *Harriet.*"

Other stories display similar settings with lists of complicating circumstances. In telling the story about her husband's culinary demands, for example, Meg includes in the setting that she was almost nine months pregnant and not in a position to satisfy his whims. In recounting the story about her panicky feelings on the road to the ski resort, Meg opens by stating that she was reluctant to go in the first place. Similarly, in telling about her anxiety at the base of Niagara Falls, Meg first reveals her extreme hesitation to take the elevator that goes down a shaft through the rock. These settings build up the view that Meg should not undertake the activity being proposed to her.

Accommodation

Although Meg expresses her reservations in telling stories to Lisa, she does not say that she communicated these reservations at the time the proposal was formulated. In these pre–panic attack scenes, Meg accommodates rather than supplying reasons against the proposal and/or declining. For example, although Meg recites a litany of reasons for not taking Cousin Harriet to lunch, she goes on to report that she simply drops everything and complies with her husband's proposal to that effect. Lisa asks Meg if she and William fought about the proposal to take his cousin to lunch:

Lisa: Did you fight with [William about it?

Meg: [No we weren't *fighting*. But I just— I did— my *heart* wasn't in it.

Lisa asks a question that to her seems a logical possibility, given the multitude of countervailing reasons that Meg has articulated. However, Meg responds that rather than confront William, she accommodates without conviction or enthusiasm ("my *heart* wasn't in it"), suggesting that her body participates but her anima resists.

Meg portrays herself as someone who, like most people, is reluctant to disappoint those who want her to participate in an upcoming activity. Generally persons who receive proposals feel awkward issuing rejections and try to put off the bad news.[8] They deliver negative responses hesitantly, interspersed with moments of silence or with delaying fillers such as "um," "uh," "er," and "well." Often those delivering disappointing responses first say how much they would like to accommodate and then go on to reject the proposal (for example, "I would love to go, but . . ."). When delivered, negative responses are usually laced with justifications that make them appear understandable or necessary (for example, "I would love to go, but I have twelve dozen cookies to make tonight, and I have presents to wrap and get mailed off to Oregon for Christmas-time").

Yet Meg's narratives indicate that she delays expressing negative feelings about a proposed activity for an extremely long period of time. The delay is not a matter of few seconds of hems and haws and beating around the bush. Rather, Meg delays communicating her displeasure about the proposed activity until after it is well under way and she is participating, and after she is drowning in panic. This analysis of her panic narratives suggests that Meg and perhaps other persons with agoraphobia may display an extreme reluctance to produce negative responses to proposals that affect their well-being, and that this reluctance contributes to the onset of panic.

6

Nonaccommodation as an Outcome of Panic

> When you're lying awake with a dismal headache, and
> repose is taboo'd by anxiety,
> I conceive you may use any language you choose to
> indulge in, without impropriety.
>
> —W. S. Gilbert, *Etiquette*, 1882

Meg's storytelling constructs the theory that her agoraphobia is rooted in an inability to produce negative responses freely and effectively to such an extent that she becomes ensnared in activities that compromise her sense of well-being. Although most Americans typically delay negative responses such as refusals, rejections, and regrets, these delays are usually brief, lasting from a fraction of a second to a few minutes. In her narrative accounts, however, Meg delays negative responses far longer, usually until after the onset of panicky feelings.

Viewed through the architecture of Meg's stories, panic is part of a communicative sequence that spans events both before and after panic sets in. In terms of story structure, the communicative sequence encompasses the setting, the central problematic event, and its aftermath. In other words, there is a communicative leitmotif that runs through Meg's stories. A communicative predisposition to withhold expressing reservations gives rise to actions, which in turn have immediate and long-term consequences. In this way communicative interaction binds the elements within Meg's stories. Returning to Toni Morrison's perspective that "narrative is radical, creating us at the very moment it is being created," we propose that the communicative patterns that lend coherence to stories simultaneously lend coherence to lives. The recurrent communicative predicament that gives shape to Meg's stories gives shape to Meg's life.

Meg's narratives reveal a characteristic communicative pattern that precipitates Meg's panic and agoraphobia. In Chapter 5, we outlined the first three steps of this communicative sequence. All three anticipate the onset of panic in Meg's stories:

1. A family member or other intimate proposes a future activity involving Meg.
2. Meg has reservations about participating in the proposed activity but does not communicate them.
3. Meg accommodates by participating in the activity.

How does this communicative sequence play out in the remainder of Meg's stories? We can codify the emotions and actions that, according to Meg, ensue after she accommodates to and participates in the proposed activity:

4. Meg experiences feelings of panic.
5. Meg directs others to take her elsewhere, communicating her distress as a warrant.
6. Meg identifies herself/is identified by others as agoraphobic.
7. Meg avoids the location of the panic attack and other locations she deems similarly threatening.
8. When faced with a proposal involving traveling to distant locations, Meg declines, citing her agoraphobia as a warrant.

Communicating Distress

Analyzing Meg's stories in terms of these eight steps, we see that a proposal (step 1) may initiate not one but several reactions from Meg, some of which remain unexpressed and others which are communicated publicly. As Meg narrates the situation, she reacts first with private doubts (step 2) but accommodates nonetheless (step 3). While participating in the proposed activity, she experiences panic (step 4), and only then tells others how bad she feels being "here" in the ongoing activity, and of her urgent need to escape (step 5).

Meg builds a portrait of her behavior after the onset of panic—her outbursts of agony and her demands to be elsewhere—as an inversion of her prepanic responses to participating in the proposed activity. Whereas prior to panicking Meg holds back her feelings (step 2), after the onset of panic, Meg communicates her feelings (step 5). Whereas earlier Meg accommodates to others' wishes by participating in the activity they favor (step 3), after the onset of panic Meg refuses to accommodate, issuing immediate cease-and-desist orders to co-participants in the ongoing activity (step 5).

Meg's communication of agony and her plea to be taken elsewhere can be understood as a greatly delayed communication of negative reactions to the idea of participating in an undesirable activity. In this sense, these postpanic responses constitute a second round of displayed reactions to participating in an activity. At the time of the first round of displayed responses, the activity is being proposed; at the time of the second round, the activity is going on. We schematize the sequence of emotional and communicative displays as they unfold in her telling:

Proposal → Display positive response toward activity
(accommodating actions with silent reservations)

Onset of Panic

→ Display negative response toward activity
(nonaccommodating actions with public display of distress)

The Big Mama story illuminates this sequential dynamic. In previous chapters, we isolated pieces of the story to highlight particular points. Here we present story excerpts to provide a more integrated analysis of Meg's communicative problem:

First proposal:	And my husband says, "Oh it would be so good to see you again, *Harriet*. Let us come and take you to lunch" . . .
Silent reservations:	I *remember* (.6 pause) not really *want*ing to go (.3 pause) that morning, feeling some— like some *foreboding*, some feeling that um— (.4 pause) For one thing I had a lot on my *mind*. It was Christmastime, I had presents to *wrap* and cookies to *bake*. It was an inconvenience t— so I went *unwillingly* . . .
First accommodation:	So we drop *everything* and (.3 pause) head out this morning to the *Marriott* to pick up *Cousin Harriet* . . .
First panic: (inklings of panic on way to Harriet)	And on the way there, I begin to feel those same trembly (.3 pause) scary feelings that I had had driving back from that *luncheon* that day . . .
Second proposal:	And it was after we'd finished the lunch, and we got— decided to go— "let's go take Cousin Harriet to visit William's *father*."
Second accommodation:	So we got on the Lomita Freeway to head up to um (.8 pause) t— to Westland . . .
Second panic: (full-blown attack taking Harriet to William's father)	And all of a *sudden*, all of the *symptoms*, the *worst symptoms* I've ever had *of anxiety* just overtook me. And I felt like I I was—if I didn't get out of that (.4 pause) *car*, and out of that freeway, that I bet something *terrible* was going to happen to me.
Nonaccommodation:	And I remember telling William, "William can we get *out* of here?" And he

	said, "What do you *mean*, Can we get out of here? Uh you know we're in *traffic*." He goes, "We just have to *wait*."
Nonaccommodation and Display distress:	And I go, "Well can't you get on the shoulder?" And he turned around and looked at me.
Nonaccommodation:	And I said, "Can't you just like get on the *shoulder* and drive off?" And he goes, "Well *no*. There *isn't* any shoulder here." And— and he goes, "Are you all right?"
Display distress: (cited as warrant)	And I go, "Well I— I— I'm not *doing* very good." And— (.3 pause) and he goes, "W— well what *is* it?"
Display distress: (cited as warrant)	And I go, "Well— well you know I just—(.3 pause) I'm feeling *anxious*."

Panic as Pivotal to Nonaccommodation

Looking at the communicative sequence within Meg's story, we see not just one but several communicative missteps. Meg's first misstep is not voicing her reservations but keeping them to herself. Her second misstep is accommodating by dropping everything she had to do and participating in the proposed event. Meg's third and fourth missteps repeat her earlier communicative pattern. In response to a second proposal, which extends the ongoing activity, making further demands on her, Meg again withholds her reservations and accommodates. We suggest that these communicative dispositions lead to the emotional turmoil of panic, which in turn Meg cites as warranting her abrupt communicative about-face, that is, her expressed misery and resolute determination to end her entanglement in the ongoing event.

This communicative path (Accommodation → *Panic* → Nonaccommodation) illuminates the dynamics of panic. Meg's narratives compose a sequence in which panic is a pivot point between accommodation—actions that are preferable to another but distressing to oneself—and nonaccommodation—actions that are unpreferable to another but crucial to one's own sense of well-being. Tragically, Meg—and likely other persons with agoraphobia—often appears to be able to display and act on reservations about an activity only after the onset of panic. As discussed in Chapter 4's analysis of the grammar of panic, panic gives an imperative quality to Meg's expressed negativity; that is, panic is seen as a warrant for her displeasing acts and words.[1]

Saying "No" Resolutely

As Meg tells it, the Big Mama story displays a progression from accommodation to highly delayed nonaccommodation. Ultimately, Meg produces nonaccommodating responses to her spouse despite his confrontational reactions to these communicative acts. This communicative progression continues throughout the remainder of the Big Mama story, as Meg portrays herself as resisting further undesirable proposals explicitly and promptly.

As noted earlier, the Big Mama story involves two further legs of the journey beyond taking Harriet to lunch and to William's father. They deliver Harriet back to the Marriott following their visit and then return home. Each of these legs forms a separate episode in the saga Meg recounts. In each episode, Meg portrays herself as able to express dissent against William's proposals about the route to take. In each episode, Meg voices her disagreement *before* the proposed course of action is under way. And in each episode, Meg sets the agenda; that is, she gets her way. We now examine how Meg narrates her response to William's proposal concerning the route from his father's house to Harriet's hotel.

Response
(to proposal):   Meg: I *begged* William,
                                  "*Don't* get on the freeway when we

take her back to the Marriott. Let's
just take surface streets. Please. I
can't *risk* that we might"— (.4 pause)
. . . I said I just can't. I *cannot* live
through another episode like what
I just *endured*. And if we get on that
freeway, and we get stalled again in
traffic— (.4 pause) I— I just can't
bear— I just can't *bear* that.

Lisa: Um-hm

Meg: *So*

Lisa: So you took [sur—

Meg: [We took like Lomita
Boulevard or Atlantic Boulevard—I forget which—*all* the
way down. And it took us *for-
ever* to get there. But we deposited her at the Marriott.

In this passage Lisa helps Meg to construct the outcome of Meg's resistance, namely, that the family drove on surface streets to deliver Cousin
Harriet to the hotel. Having dropped her off, William proposes taking
the freeway back home. In the following passage, Meg portrays the proposal and her response. She delivers a calm, soothing rendition of
William's voice, while articulating her own in pleading, desperate
tones:

Proposal: William says, "Well *come* on. Let's take
the freeway home. It's after rush hour,
and there *won't* be any traffic." And
(.8 pause) he said, "Come on, honey." You
know, (.4 pause) "Snap *out* of it."

Response: And I go, "I just *can't*. *Please* humor me.
Indulge me. Let's just (.6 pause) go surface
streets." So we *did*.

In this final episode Meg recounts in full detail exactly what William said in his proposal, how he tried to cajole her into accepting. She dramatizes her determined resistance, although all the while she paints herself not as sensible but rather as someone who needs to be "indulged" and "humored." Meg then turns the tables and directs a "let's" imperative to her husband ("let's just (.6 pause) go surface streets"), complete with its pragmatic implications. And it works.

Pathologizing "No"

Meg presents herself as able to express her feelings more explicitly and more elaborately as she faces each new proposal. As the narrative progresses, Meg articulates fuller representations of the confrontations between her and her spouse. In narrating the leg of the Big Mama story in which they deposit Harriet back at the Marriott, for example, Meg does not make explicit William's proposal to take the freeway. But she does make explicit his proposal to take the freeway in narrating the final leg of the journey, their return home. Similarly, although Meg expresses her resistance to the implied proposal, she does not articulate a counterproposal, as she does when resisting William's final proposal.

While this progression might be seen as a positive step, in that Meg expresses her feelings to her spouse, Meg herself frames these communicative encounters in highly pathological terms. She likens her assertiveness to symptoms of neurosis, labeling herself as agoraphobic (step 6). After narrating how she successfully challenges William over the route to Harriet's hotel, for example, Meg recasts this communicative act as a sign of her psychological decline.

Meg: I *begged* William, "*Don't* get on the freeway when we take her back to the Marriott. Let's just take surface streets. Please I can't *risk* that we might"— (.4 pause) And that was just the beginning right *there* of my *agoraphobia.*
Lisa: Um-hm
Meg: Because right there I avoided the freeway for the first *time.*

Meg recasts the confrontational act itself ("I *begged* William, *'Don't* get on the freeway' ") as the hallmark symptom—avoidance—of agoraphobia ("Because right there I avoided the freeway for the first *time*"). Meg focuses on *what* she was saying, namely the proposition to take surface streets in order to avoid the freeway. Meg dwells on the unreasonableness of her nonaccommodating stance and does not acknowledge that she has successfully looked out for her best interests.

Meg pathologizes her nonaccommodating communication more than once. In the final leg of the Big Mama journey, she equates her confrontive response to her husband as a sign of impending doom:

And I go I just *can't. Please* humor me. *Indulge* me.
Let's just (.6 pause) go surface streets.
So we *did.* (.6 pause) And that was like the beginning of the *end.*

In this passage, we see how the words Meg uses and the connections she forges between events construct her identity as powerless, irrational, and agoraphobic. In asking to be humored and indulged, she renders herself debilitated and pitiful. In declaring, "And that was like the beginning of the *end,*" she translates her success in getting what she wanted into a failure that extends into the present moment.

In Meg's mind and in the minds of many practitioners and researchers, agoraphobia is associated with avoidance of the location of panic (step 7). For example, just after Meg casts her assertive demands as "the beginning of the *end,*" she goes on to spell out the genesis of her avoidance:

Meg: It was *so* awful, the *feeling* of that fear was so awful that— (.4 pause)
       um I think after that I would just do *anything* [to avoid having to
       experience that again.
Lisa: [Um-hm yeah
Meg: So the freeway was the first thing that I began to avoid . . .

Here Meg vows that she "would just do *anything*" to avoid reexperiencing panic. She deems avoiding physical locations as the crux of her remedy. Meg's plan favors one of her narrative theories of panic—which ties panic to place—over the other—which ties panic to a communicative predicament. In so doing, Meg bypasses what may be the communicative core of her problem. By focusing on locations, Meg fails to see how her propensity to accommodate undesirable proposals contributes to panic, and misses the opportunity to alter her communicative style.

Agoraphobia as a Warrant for Nonaccommodation

In attempting to understand and treat psychological disturbances, clinicians ask how a client may be benefiting from a particular disorder. What is the payoff? The notion that symptoms serve controlling functions is a central feature of psychodynamic theories that derive from the work of Freud.[2] Freud felt that the control that neurotic persons gain over others by means of their symptoms represents a secondary gain of the disorder, an advantage that limits the phobic person's desire to change his or her behavior pattern. The primary gain, in Freud's view, was the reduction of the anxiety that had overwhelmed the person's defenses. Secondary gain refers to the control neurotic persons exert by restricting or otherwise determining the activities of family members owing to their symptoms. An agoraphobic person's avoidance behavior might result, for example, in shifting the responsibility for shopping onto her children or husband. Identifying the payoffs or secondary gains is a central part of mastering resistance to change in psychotherapy with agoraphobic persons and their families.[3]

More recently, some clinicians and researchers have suggested that a principal payoff of agoraphobia is that it provides a medical reason for not leaving an undesirable marital relationship.[4] Meg's narratives suggest that for her there may be a more fundamental, pervasive payoff, a payoff that spans a wide range of interpersonal relationships. Meg's narratives suggest that agoraphobia provides a medical reason for neither accommodating nor even negotiating demands and desires imposed or promoted by others. Following this line of reasoning, agoraphobia spares her from having to say "I would rather not," or "I can't, for these reasons," or "I have other obligations or priorities at this time." More crucially, Meg does not have to engage in the usual give-and-take negotiations that characterize decision making about plans. She does not have to explain herself or lobby for engaging in a joint activity when or where it is more convenient for her. In this perspective, agoraphobia is a warrant for avoiding confrontation and disappointment, and not having to accommodate. By defining herself as agoraphobic, for example, Meg declines rather than accommodates a friend's invitation to attend her graduation. She also resists persistent urgings from her mother to visit her. Although Meg expresses sadness about missing these occasions, she does not internally negotiate the limitations she has set for herself or discuss them with others in her life:

Meg: Like for instance the other day I got an invitation um (.3 pause) in the mail to attend a friend's *graduation* from State College. And (.4 pause) I'm thinking, well that's out of my safety— safety zone. I can't go over there because— (.4 pause) There again it's another one of those *can'ts*. I *can't*. [I can't drive to Hamilton.
Lisa: [Um-hm
Meg: It's out of my boundaries and (.3 pause) [I'll just have to find a way to explain.
Lisa: [What will you tell her?
Meg: I think she knows um she's not a real real close friend that I've confided in a *lot* about this. But I think she knows I have some anxiety problems.

In this passage, Meg implies that she will not try to figure out a way to go to her friend's graduation. She portrays herself as constrained by the rigidity of her physical boundaries to "have to find a way to explain" why she "can't" go, rather than talking through her doubts and reservations with her friend. When Lisa asks, "What will you tell her?" Meg has no ideas. Instead she counts on her friend's prior knowledge that Meg has "some anxiety problems." As Meg narratively represents her physical boundaries, their rigidity parallels the rigidity of her communication, in particular, her style of decision making: just as Meg bars herself from entering particular places, she does not allow herself to engage in open-ended negotiations.

Following her narrative sequencing of events, we see that an enduring consequence of her expressed refusal to accommodate proposals is that family members and friends become more reluctant to address proposals to Meg. Even those intimates who are unaware of her anxieties come to assume that Meg prefers not to participate in activities that take her outside of her home. And those who do know of her anxieties come to consider this condition preemptive of their wishes to involve Meg in collective activity. Meg's stories show how the label 'agoraphobic' constitutes a useful, enduring warrant for refusing to accommodate proposals and for discouraging their formulation in the first place.

Yet Meg's narrative travels ultimately reveal that this warrant's usefulness is far outweighed by the devastating effects of restricted mobility and labeling oneself as disabled. By providing a generic warrant for not accommodating, agoraphobia may temporarily resolve Meg's difficulty communicating particular reservations about a given proposed activity. The generic warrant masks and perpetuates Meg's communicative problem, however, as she avoids both communicating any reservations she may have about a specific proposal and navigating a solution with her interlocutor.

Agoraphobia as a Communicative Disorder

Meg's stories link her panic to an inability or unwillingness to communicate reservations about a proposed activity until that activity is under way. This perspective is relevant to the dialogue among researchers about the roots of agoraphobia. Although individual predispositions and life conditions contribute to this disorder,[5] Meg's narrative constructions suggest that she is suffering from a fundamental communicative handicap, namely, a difficulty in communicating negative reactions in a timely, effective, and appropriate manner. In this sense, for Meg, and perhaps others like her, agoraphobia may be critically a *communicative disorder*.

We are not the first to consider psychological problems to be communicative disorders. Breuer and Freud[6] and later Szasz,[7] for example, proposed that symptoms of anxiety form indirect communications. Szasz notes that in Freud's account of Frau Cacilie's hysterical facial pain, Freud described both the overt and the covert message content of her symptoms. The overt meaning was "I am sick. You must help me. You must be good to me"; and the covert meaning, directed principally to a specific person, was "You have hurt me as if you have slapped my face. You should be sorry and make amends." A central feature of the indirect communicative function of symptoms is that the sufferer is not responsible or accountable for the messages conveyed.

Building on Freud, Szasz explains that people use the symptoms of their disorder as a kind of language because they are not able to or find it undesirable to use ordinary language to convey these messages.[8] Indirect messages permit communicative contacts when, without them, the alternative would be (1) total inhibition, silence, and solitude or (2) communicative behavior that is direct, offensive, and hence forbidden.

The vast majority of studies linking psychological disorders to communicative dynamics has focused on interactions in the families of persons with schizophrenia. Gregory Bateson[9] suggests that schizophrenics are repeatedly caught in a "double bind," a situation in which another person (the mother) expresses contradictory messages, for example, "if you do not do X, I will punish you; and if you do X, I will punish you."[10]

Meg builds her narratives in a way that suggests that agoraphobia is a communicative disorder characterized by extreme avoidance of negative responses to undesirable proposals. When faced with such proposals, most people typically soften disappointing responses. We decline hesitantly, gently, politely, and/or warmly. In this way we are able to protect the sensibilities of our conversational partner at the same time that we preserve our own well-being.[11] Persons suffering from agoraphobia, however, may be either reluctant to or incapable of balancing their own want to disengage from a proposed activity with the wants of their conversational partners. Meg's narrative accounts suggest that she may initially prioritize the desires of her conversational partner until she is engaged in the activity and is fueled by feelings of desperation to prioritize her own well-being. This dynamic may characterize the communication of other persons with agoraphobia as well.

This communicative explanation of agoraphobia is more general than those focusing on a particular distressed relationship, for example, a distressed spousal or parent-child relationship. Communication is at the heart of all relationships. Relationships are complex social processes and structures that are themselves constructed through actions and demeanors toward other persons. In her narratives, when Meg accommodates rather than declines or renegotiates the terms of undesirable proposals, she constructs a particular kind of relationship with the person who issued the proposal. If Meg's narratives suggest that she does so in relation to one person who presents undesirable proposals, then they provide evidence of the roots of agoraphobia within that particular relationship. If Meg accommodates against her better judgment with a *range* of persons, however, then her agoraphobia is better explained by this communicative impasse. Indeed, in her life story as she tells it, Meg's communicative problem exists across relationships—with childhood mates, church friends, husband, parents, in-laws, and physicians.

7

Paradoxes of Panic

Every individual, completely vanishing and reduced to
nothing in a boundless world, nevertheless makes
himself the center of the world.

—Arthur Schopenhauer, 1966

When one of the authors, Elinor, was carrying out language and culture research in a Samoan village,[1] she heard this folktale:

> Once there were two brothers, *Leaga* 'Bad' and *Lelei* 'Good.' One
> day *Leaga* discovered that *Lelei* had been stealing from his taro
> patch. *Lelei* became ashamed, because he was bad and Leaga was
> good. That is why Samoans say *leaga lelei* [literally, "bad good," or
> "Good is bad"].

Leaga lelei, "bad good," is a paradox. Samoans tell their children *leaga
lelei* to socialize them into the idea that sometimes to be good is bad and
sometimes to be bad is good.[2] Being Samoan is knowing when to be
good and when to be bad.

Paradoxes such as "bad good," "less is more," "all men are created
equal, but some are more equal than others," and the paradox in
Schopenhauer's juxtaposition of the invisibility and centrality of hu-
manity are products of wise elders, philosophers, mathematicians, sati-
rists, witty conversationalists, and poets with epigrams at the tip of their
tongues. Because paradoxes are only apparently self-contradictory, they
capture our attention. They force us to look into their messages for

105

deeper and richer turns of meaning beyond the literal. Paradoxes entail a complex process of revelation, and as such lend an aesthetic to a statement. For lovers of poetry and indirection, paradoxes are a delight for the mind and the ear.

Paradoxes are also at the heart of psychological disorders. As noted in Chapter 6, Bateson proposes that schizophrenia is fueled by an environment of paradoxical messages that place a person in a double bind. Further, Freud's distinction between the primary and secondary gains of a neurosis parallels the distinctions between the literal and conveyed, denotative and connotative, and referential and emotive[3] aspects of a message. In many ways the relation between primary and secondary gain is a paradox. A symptom that cripples simultaneously supports the sufferer's well-being. For example, agoraphobic persons' restricted lifestyle renders them at once relieved and distressed.

To understand the paradoxes inherent in language and life we must transcend the literal and straightforward. It is precisely because paradoxes have meaning on multiple planes that they are potent. Literal paraphrases of paradoxical meanings are less penetrating in part because they circumvent the interpretive journey that paradoxes entail.

Paradoxes are also potent in that they allow their authors to communicate certain meanings without being held accountable for them. Because paradoxes are cryptic, they lend themselves to multiple interpretations. Poetry is rich with paradoxical meanings, but the hearer cannot pin any one meaning on the poet. Listening to poetry is a process of self-discovery, in which the poet affords but does not determine the emergent meaning. Minimalist aesthetic forms such as the Vietnam Veterans' Memorial similarly derive power as viewers discover paradoxical meanings. Walking alongside the Memorial, viewers may juxtapose paradoxical elements such as the towering, white, erect form of the Washington Monument with the sunken, black, sloped form of the Wall. The Wall's designer, Maya Lin, did not conceive of each viewer's interpretations. She designed the Memorial in a way that would compel internal dialogue, giving rise to a multiplicity of meanings. Paradoxical messages emerge as each viewer engages with the Wall and juxtaposes elements in different ways.[4]

In much the same way, the language of symptoms is a powerful mode of communication. The sufferer may display a behavior that conveys contradictory messages—for example, "I am helpless" and "You must do as I wish"—yet not be aware of them. Those listening to the language of symptoms may respond in ways that imply a sensitivity to paradoxical meanings, yet they do not necessarily hold the symptom bearer responsible for authoring them. Instead both sufferers and those in their lives attribute the perplexing contradictions as an effect of a medical condition, a symptom rather than an intention.

In a traditional village, members can draw on parables and other traditional genres to unravel the cryptic meanings of a paradox. And literary critics draw upon the tools of their trade to illuminate the paradoxical juxtapositions that imbue a poem or novel with power and beauty. But those of us who are locked into the paradoxes of our own and others' neuroses are not so endowed. We have no parables to ease our task. Unlike written texts, the texts of our lives are fleeting and not readily stayed for multiple interpretations and repeated readings. But through electronic recordings, we can capture words and actions from a "strip of happening"[5] in life experience. We have captured such strips from Meg's daily existence and turn now to linguistic and psychological analyses of paradoxes therein.

We identify contradictions on three communicative planes: semantic content, linguistic form, and communicative action (both linguistic and gestural). Paradoxes may exist within and across these planes. The paradox "less is more," for example, operates solely within the plane of semantic content. The apparent contradiction is between the literal meanings of the lexical items "less" and "more." Similarly the paradox "all men are created equal, but some are more equal than others" juxtaposes propositions with contradictory meanings. Although most paradoxes rest on apparent contradictions between literal meanings,[6] more broadly considered, a paradox may operate on more than one linguistic plane. One person may say to another, "I want you near me," but deliver the message with hostile intonation while increasing the physical space between them. In this case, one message is communicated through propositional content and a contradictory message is communicated through phonological form and communicative action. Many paradigms used by family therapists, including the double bind theory, focus on precisely these cross-modal contradictions.[7]

Paradox 1: Out of Control Is in Control

I was like I was just out of control and I didn't know why.

And I . . . felt real *helpless* . . . and trapped.

And I was afraid, you know? I thought, "What's happening?" You know? And I felt real helpless there too.

I could almost feel like my teeth were going to chatter if I didn't get this (.3 pause) feeling of shakiness under control.

I kinda tried to get a grip on myself but I— I— by that time I was— I was *visibly*, physically just shaking.

Meg's words paint a portrait of herself as helpless and out of control. She enhances this portrait by drawing from a palette of grammatical forms that render her a helpless victim of panic. Meg presents herself in sentential roles where she is not the agent. Strong feelings and other persons act on her rather than the reverse. She uses "try" constructions and negatives to color her attempts as failures. She imagines herself as an actor in hypothetical worlds but uses hypotheticals such as "even if," which render them improbable. Meg sweeps across her grammatical repertoire, bypassing modal constructions like "want to" or "would like to" and selecting instead "have to" and "got to," which cast her actions as imposed rather than willfully desired and in her control. Adverbial intensifiers such as "real" (for example, "real helpless") and a hesitant style of delivery are also favored in building this emotional self-portrait. Finally, in her stories of panic experience, Meg augments hues of helplessness with a portfolio of communicative acts in which she accommodates the wishes of others despite deep reservations.

This composite of helplessness dominates Meg's narrative ruminations. Helplessness is the most salient quality she attributes to herself as a protagonist moving through a panic episode. As Meg builds this image of herself as out of control, however, she builds a discrepant image of herself as in control, creating a narrative paradox. Meg's accounts of herself as feeling and acting out of control in the throes of panic contradict the communicative acts she carries out as protagonist. After the onset of panic, which she explicitly associates with a loss of control, Meg depicts herself as controlling the actions of others to meet her needs. When Meg produces directives such as

I've got to get out of here. I'm not— I'm not *feeling* good.

I've got to get *out* now. I feel *terrible.*

William, can we get *out* of here?

Can you *please* get off here?

she imposes her own agenda on others. She initiates a radical about-face in the ongoing course of action. By stating her wants and needs and requesting to "get out of here," Meg attempts not only to disengage herself from the current activity but to close down the activity for everyone. Getting Meg out of 'here' entails getting all co-participants out as well.

That the panic-stricken protagonist exerts power over others at the same time that she declares herself powerless is a paradox of panic. In other words, Meg's panic stories reveal a paradox between loss of control over oneself and gain of control over others. Meg resolves this paradox in part by relegating the control she exerts over others to the force of panic. Meg portrays panic as coming out of the blue and blindsiding her. In Meg's narrative frame, panic exerts control over her, and she, in turn, is driven by this force to exert control over others in an effort to escape the grip of panic.

The paradox of being at once out of control and in control characterizes Meg not only as a protagonist in some past circumstance but also as a narrator telling a story in the present. In telling about past experiences, Meg routinely uses grammatical forms that render her still overwhelmed by feelings of panic. She constructs panic with present-time vividness, as an entity not contained in the past, but which continues to invade her life. Meg often frames past experiences of panic in the present tense ("I'm just *dying*"), for example, and frames physically distant locations of panic using the place adverb "here" ("Here I am. I'm so damn mad"). In these ways she portrays panic as continuing to control her. Panic is part of her emotional here and now that she is still unable to escape.

What is paradoxical is that the very same grammatical structures that Meg uses to paint herself as a protagonist out of control allow her to exert considerable control over her interlocutors in her role as a narrator. Although Meg's use of the present tense signals that she remains in the clutches of panic, the vividness of the present tense controls interlocutors by immersing them more deeply in the tale. Like good storytellers everywhere, Meg shatters the temporal distance between the world of the interlocutor and the world of the tale: the tale is now. Similarly, when Meg says, "here I am," she both points to her dire existential predicament and controls her interlocutors by making them wait for subsequent information that clarifies this predicament. "Here I am" is only a preface; it is an attention-grabber that requires the interlocutor to listen further to unpack its meaning. In these ways, Meg uses grammar to build a portrait of herself as a panicked protagonist who remains out of control and, paradoxically, as a narrator who is very much in control of her audience.

Paradox 2: It Is Rational to Act Irrational

Meg's stories yield a further paradox. Meg treats her panic experiences as episodes of irrationality (for example, "All of a sudden I (.4 pause) uh became aware of feeling (.4 pause) just *anxious* unaccountably"). Yet Meg's stories show that it is precisely during such panic episodes that she finally acts to promote her well-being. Recall Meg's account of how she was able to turn events her way in the final leg of her freeway nightmare:

And I go, "I just *can't*. *Please* humor me. *Indulge* me. Let's just (.6 pause) go surface streets." So we *did*.

Hearing these words one could reasonably infer that Meg's so-called irrational conduct was rational. Indeed in *Critique of Practical Reason*, Kant posits, "To be happy is necessarily the desire of every rational but finite being."[8]

The way Meg links her communicative actions to desired consequences leads the listener to interpret her acts as reasoned. It is not only the listener but Meg herself who sees rationality in her non-accommodating stance. Although Meg explicitly states that her panicky conduct is irrational (for example, "*Please* humor me. *Indulge* me.") and uses grammatical forms that reinforce this perspective, she builds a story plot that casts her panicky conduct as logical: given that she has ignored reservations articulated in the settings of her stories and participated in an undesirable activity, her panic is plausible. Though an extreme reaction, panic makes sense because it brings her closer to her goal of exiting her present circumstances. Meg presents panic as providing a rationale for her communicative assertiveness. Meg's stories thus frame panic as kindling an emotional logic that is otherwise unobtainable in her 'normal' course of events.

We have suggested that emotions and actions Meg deems irrational possess their own rationality. What about emotions and actions Meg deems rational? In story settings leading up to panic episodes, Meg depicts herself as normal and rational. However, she also recounts that it is precisely in these prepanic circumstances that she acts against her better judgment: she ignores her reservations. Recall Meg's litany of reasons for refusing William's proposal to take his cousin Harriet to lunch and her decision to accommodate nonetheless:

It was Christmas-time. I had presents to *wrap*, and cookies to *bake*.
It was an inconvenience t— so I went *unwillingly*.

In this manner, Meg constructs a narrative in which accommodating an unwanted proposal is at once rational and irrational. Meg treats such accommodations as expected, as what normal people do. But when Meg comments, "I went *unwillingly*," she recognizes that normal, rational people also try to act in their best interests. Meg presents but does not reconcile this contradiction.

The world views of what it means to be 'normal' or 'abnormal,' 'rational' or 'irrational,' that are nested in her narratives have implications for Meg and perhaps other persons experiencing panic. Meg reports that when she is in a state of panic, she struggles to recover by thinking about or actually carrying out actions she deems ordinary and normal. She states, for example, that when she is in the grip of panic on her thirtieth birthday, she thinks of following her normal bedtime routine. Speaking rapidly, as if to convey agitation, Meg recalls:

> The *more* I tried to um (.5 pause) *put* myself out of mind, the harder that was to do. And I remember thinking, "Well I'll just go *do* something normal. D— you know? I'll go *upstairs* and I'll brush my *teeth*, and wash my *face*, and get ready for *bed*."

Meg's narratives suggest that such attempts to act 'normal' exacerbate rather than alleviate her panic, because acting normal involves silencing rather than communicating her distressing feelings. This dynamic can be couched as a logical syllogism:

If, in a normal state,

(i) Meg does not acknowledge nor communicate her needs and wants, and

(ii) not acknowledging and communicating such needs and wants precipitates panic,
     then

(iii) attempts to reassume a normal state fuel further panic.

And indeed it does, as reported in the continuing portions of the Thirtieth Birthday story:

> But really it was a form of— I was trying to *escape* the scary *feelings* that I was having. But the more I tried to *escape* it, the worse it

became. And— (.4 pause) and finally we— I told William, "I don't *feel* right. Something's— I feel *strange* and I feel really scared."

Meg's narratives reveal a corollary of the paradox that rational conduct is irrational, namely, that efforts to mitigate panic by acting normal may have the opposite effect of intensifying panic. Indeed, as a protagonist, the only way Meg mitigates panic is by communicating her distress to others. In the Thirtieth Birthday story, for example, Meg fails to quell her panic by contemplating normal actions but finds some relief when she communicates her feelings to her husband. Her relief is enhanced when she subsequently telephones her sister and obtains her counsel:

Meg: At one point then we called my sister and— (.4 pause) who was uh at *that* time a first- or second-year pre-med student— and we thought somehow she might be able to shed some *light* on it, which in a *way* she was. She said she thought maybe it was a *panic* attack and it (.3 pause) sounded like some things that she had seen in the *emergency* room, you know people thinking they're having heart attacks [and

Lisa: [Um-hm

Meg: And it was just anxiety. (.5 pause) And yet (.3 pause) I don't know— in a *way* that alleviated my *worry* because I— at least I was able to put a *name* to it.

If Meg were in a traditional village, she might have the luxury of a parable to guide her through the paradoxes of panic. We have used the tools of discourse and grammatical analysis to craft a possible parable:

Once there were two Megs: Good Meg and Bad Meg. Good Meg thought she was rational, and Bad Meg thought she was irrational. When Good Meg was being rational, she helped others but neglected herself. When Bad Meg was being irrational, she helped herself to the neglect of others. Both Good Meg and Bad Meg suffered. Good Meg did not give importance to her suffering until she panicked and became Bad Meg. Bad Meg did give importance to her suffering. Because she was suffering, she tried to become Good

Meg. She too did not give importance to Good Meg's suffering. She too did not realize that Good Meg's suffering kindled panic. When she became Good Meg, she panicked even more. Good Meg and Bad Meg still suffer today, because Good Meg still thinks she is rational, and Bad Meg thinks she is irrational.

8

Constructing the Irrational Woman

> These are not natural silences, that necessary time for
> renewal, lying fallow, gestation, in the natural cycle of
> creation. The silences I speak of here are unnatural; the
> unnatural thwarting of what struggles to come into
> being, but cannot. In the old, the obvious parallels:
> when the seed strikes stone; the soil will not sustain; the
> spring is false; the time is drought or blight or
> infestation; the frost comes premature.
>
> —Tillie Olsen, 1978

Our journey into Meg's tales of panic has illuminated how she narratively portrays herself as a woman plagued by irrational responses to normal events and experiences in the world. In her accounts of interactions with others in which she felt overwhelmed by inexplicable emotions and sensations, Meg frequently attempts to mask these feelings from other people in her midst. This is the case, for example, when Meg panics while driving a carpool back to the church after a holiday luncheon:

I was *driving*, and halfway back to the *church*—we had all met at the church and carpooled, . . . and then I started when I started having (.6 pause) those weird just ph— *pure physical* anxiety. I began to feel shaky inside, like a (.6 pause) like a— (.5 pause) like a *motor* was vibrat-

115

ing inside me . . . And then a feeling of impending *doom*, just—
that's the only way I can describe it— it's just afrai— just af— just
pure fear. And I— (.3 pause) I just felt afraid. But I didn't want to tell
anybody in the car because I wasn't sure *myself* what was *wrong* with
me. I just knew that I didn't *feel* right, and I just felt afraid but I
don't know *why*. And this is so *stupid*. Uh I can't tell them . . . I
remember being a little bit worried that um (.4 pause) that I would
appear abnormal to our house guest at that time, our— (.3 pause)
um (.3 pause) my half-sister's stepson who I'd just met. I remember
being a little worried that (.4 pause) that if I didn't get these *feelings*
under control I might (.3 pause) appear strange to him. And how
would I explain to *him* that um (.3 pause) what was *happening* to me
when I wasn't even sure myself?

At this point Lisa asks Meg if she eventually did mention this to anyone,
to which Meg replies,

No, I don't think I did. I remember struggling through a conversation with the pastor, and trying to act *normal*.

When Meg articulates her understanding of panic as an irrational response to routine events, she locates the problem within herself. In
what sense is Meg the author of this perspective? Meg's voice resonates
with authoritative accounts of agoraphobia that define it as a problem
that "lies in the patient herself."[1] Similarly, in telling about her life, Meg
borrows words like "agoraphobia" from the lexicon of mental health
professionals; she is not the sole author of her stories.[2]

The notion that words are not monologic or singly voiced but are the
products of previous, current, and hypothetical dialogues with other
speakers is taken up in literary theory by members of the Bahktinian
circle, especially Mikhail Bahktin himself.[3] In discussing the dialogic
nature of language, Bahktin explains that "prior to the moment of ap-
propriation, words do not exist in a neutral and impersonal language,
but in other people's mouths, in other people's contexts." The language
we use in telling our stories is a product of our contacts with others in
society.

The composer Luciano Berio describes musical compositions and the instruments that perform them in much the same way. Like words, "musical instruments are not just neutral tools. They are the concrete depositories of historical continuity, and like all working tools and buildings, they have a memory. They carry with them traces of the conceptual and social changes through which they were developed and transformed."[4] Like the music that flows when instruments are played, the stories that emerge when words are spoken are collaboratively constructed. They form a dialogue between past and present.

From this perspective, each word, each utterance, each story can be seen as a co-authored product of the speaker's voice and voices of the past. In parallel fashion, words, utterances, and stories can also be co-authored products of the speaker's voice and the voices of persons presently interacting with the speaker. The fusion of voices within the collaborative construction (co-construction) of stories takes place on interactional as well as historical planes.[5]

When we speak of co-authorship and co-construction of stories, we do not mean that the co-authors necessarily share the same or even a compatible perspective. Similarly, the identities of protagonists and tellers that are co-constructed during storytelling are not always those that a protagonist/teller intends or desires. Storytelling can stimulate interlocutors to misunderstand, disagree, and argue; nonetheless, the interlocutors are co-producing the stories and identities that emerge.[6]

Although there may be a principal narrator or an initial teller who introduces a story into ongoing conversation, everyone present plays an essential role in shaping the story as it unfolds. Co-participants may make verbal contributions to the story, eliciting or supplying information in ways that amplify, corroborate, reframe, challenge, or dispute the preceding talk. In addition to asking questions, they contribute information that is critical to interpreting the significance of the events under consideration. Co-tellers influence the direction the story takes not only through the words, phrases, and clauses they utter but through nonverbal expression of attention and stance—through pitch, intonation, vocal intensity, laughter, overlap and its resolution, unfinished and suppressed syllables, silence, eye gaze, facial expression, gesture, body positions, and orientation to surrounding objects.[7] Although Meg does much of the talking in her interactions with Lisa, for example, Lisa shapes the stories that unfold by asking questions, nodding, encouraging Meg to continue, and displaying understanding through nods and vocalizations such as "uh-huh."

Stories, then, are far more than the sum of their words. They comprise a complex interplay of sound and silence, eye gaze, facial expression, and body position. Each aspect is relational. The sounds of one's voice, the meaning of one's words, change in resonance depending on relational acoustics—whether one is heard or not heard, how one is responded to verbally, visually, physically. Like sound and silence, movement and stillness, each person's contributions defines the others'.

Again, stories resemble compositions, and tellers resemble orchestra members playing their instruments. In discussing his musical composition "Notturno," Berio explains the title:

Notturno because it is silent . . . Notturno is silent because it is built in unspoken words and on unfinished discourses . . . of open spaces that fail to get filled, propositions that aren't taken up. The most conspicuous of these propositions comes as a line from the viola a little way into the piece. Nobody else in the quartet seems to be hearing it, and it fizzles out into the inevitable shiverings. When, nearly twenty minutes later, the viola tries again, that's the signal to quit.[8]

Like members of an orchestra, William, Meg, Beth, and Sean play different instruments in the narrative compositions that emerge as they talk over dinner. Within each composition, each instrument plays a different part—sometimes dominant, sometimes muted, sometimes silent, sometimes in harmony, sometimes dissonant. Just as the sound of any instrument in an orchestra depends on those of the rest, each member's contributions to the story are shaped by those of the other participants. And as the viola in Berio's "Notturno" has shown us, each part is crucial to the composition—the story—that emerges.

Orchestra members' parts vary depending on the compositions being performed. Similarly, family members play different parts in different storytellings—sometimes as initiator, sometimes as recipient, sometimes as protagonist, sometimes aligning with and sometimes challenging the perspectives of other members. Each family member is focused on at different times, in varying degrees. But just as there are more solos written for strings than for woodwinds, frequency of prominence varies among family members.

Orchestras play pieces that reflect their structure, displaying the strengths of their most talented members. Similarly, the structure of relationships, distribution of power, and identities of members within the family shape the stories that are told. In the same way that musical selections reinforce the orchestra's structure and the identities of individual members, stories that are told reinforce the roles and identities that give rise to them. The complex choreography of every storytelling is part of an ongoing pattern of interaction that unfolds over and over again. Every storytelling is both responsive to its immediate interactional environment and the product of a history of interactions and relationships. Whether symmetrical or asymmetrical, such relationships are reproduced through co-constructed interaction. What is crucial is that reproducing or challenging any social order and the identities of members therein is a coordinated, interactional achievement.

Storytelling creates a rich nexus around which participants' identities and world views are instantiated and challenged. It forms a unique dialogue between past and present by involving participants in the past realm of the story and the present realm of the telling. Tellers attempt to establish their identities and world views through the way that they portray themselves as protagonists acting in the past. Yet the identities and world views that emerge are also shaped through the organization and negotiation of participants' roles in the telling. For example, Meg may attempt to construct herself as a rational woman by portraying herself as a rational protagonist in a story about a past event. At the same time, she attempts to construct herself as a rational narrator acting in the present. Yet, as we shall see, Meg cannot single-handedly define her identity, nor can any teller. In both story and storytelling realms, such attempts require ratification from other participants.

Co-participants ratify and refute tellers' narratives through verbal and nonverbal communicative channels. Their responses to a story—whether with words, intonation, eye gaze, body position, or lack thereof—display varying degrees of alignment with the teller's portrayal of the situation. In these ways they either validate or repudiate the teller's rendition of the narrated scenario. Simultaneously, such responses validate or repudiate the teller's authority as narrator. Constructing an identity as rational involves obtaining ratification for portrayals of oneself as a rational protagonist acting in the past and as a rational teller acting in the present. To be rational is to have the authority to reframe experience in a way that is legitimized by other rational people. Part of the benefit of therapeutic dialogue stems from the creation of an empathic environment in which patients' accounts of inexplicable behaviors and feelings are regarded as valid. The collaborative effort to understand particular actions and emotions presupposes a legitimate reason for their occurrence, and the interactional environment constructs the patient as a competent, rational narrator.

Our narrative odyssey continues as we join the Logan family at dinnertime, with a particular interest in the co-construction of Meg's identity as an irrational woman. As we have seen in previous chapters, Meg frequently portrays herself as a protagonist whose responses to situations are unaccountable and therefore irrational. We focus now on how this identity might be perpetuated through family members' joint participation in storytelling. This endeavor takes us from the narrated scenarios of panic that Meg constructs while sitting on her sofa to the kitchen, where Meg has prepared dinner, William and Beth have just finished setting the table, and Sean can be heard through the window, racing his Big Wheel up and down the sidewalk. Beth takes her place at the table, while William summons Sean. The screen door slams behind father and son. Sean, still panting, sits down by Beth as Meg finishes positioning dishes of food on hot plates at the center of the table, before she and William seat themselves.

For the Logans, like many American families, dinner is a special time of day.[9] The meal begins with grace, after which family members share events and experiences from their lives. During dinner Meg introduces stories more often than any other member of the Logan family. These stories typically focus on her own experiences, although she also guides Beth and Sean in telling William about an incident in their day. A great majority of the stories Meg initiates about herself and a significant percentage of the dinnertime stories in general portray Meg as a protagonist wracked with anxious feelings.

In building such stories Meg does not explicitly define her actions and emotions as irrational. Rather, she attempts to portray her responses as sensible in light of the narrated situation. Yet Meg's accounts of anxious experiences convey the sense that her anxious feelings continue up through the present moment of the telling. Like most people, Meg uses narrative to make sense out of unnerving events and experiences in her life. She portrays happenings and emotional responses she is unsure of in an effort to obtain validation from other members of her family, particularly William, and to develop a more coherent, legitimate perspective.

Meg seeks validation from William by directing her stories to him, particularly those about her own experiences.[10] In so doing Meg opens her own emotions and actions for his review and sanction. Together family members assume narrative roles that implicitly establish William's position as "'panopticon'—the all-seeing eye of power."[11] As used by Foucault, 'panopticon' refers to a type of institutional architecture, exemplified in prison architecture, in which spaces both confine inhabitants and expose them to surveillance from a central watchtower. Elinor and her colleague Carolyn Taylor,[12] applying the notion of panopticon to narrative structures, suggest that storytelling arranges protagonists and tellers in relations of power and lays out the lives of protagonists for inspection.[13] The term panopticon applies to a dynamic they have observed in extensive study of dinnertime interactions in American families, in which the majority of stories were directed to fathers and centered on the lives of children, establishing fathers' position as central watchtowers and children as monitored subjects.

By laying out her stories of anxious experience for William's inspection and commentary, Meg sets herself up as monitored subject. This narrative organization may *reflect* Meg's sense that she is irrational and needs validation from others for her understandings of events in her life. It may simultaneously *perpetuate* Meg's identity as irrational in that she presents herself as lacking internal access to the voice of reason, both as a protagonist and as a narrator, and attempts to obtain it through William. In this way she constructs William's authority as a rational, reasonable person and renders herself vulnerable to his judgment.

In examining family interactions, it is important to remember that Meg considers William her greatest ally in her struggle against anxiety: he consistently encourages her to participate in activities outside the home that bolster her self-esteem; he is supportive of her therapy, driving her to her weekly sessions when she so desires; and he offers compassion and understanding each day. Yet, for reasons about which we speculate at the end of this chapter, William does not provide the responses to Meg's stories that she actively solicits and desperately desires.

We now delve into three storytelling interactions of the Logan family at the dinner hour. We select three stories with a common leitmotif. This trilogy illuminates an array of narrative routes to the construction of the irrational woman. The first story is initiated by Meg, directed primarily to William, and centers on an anxiety-provoking encounter she had earlier that day. The second is initiated by William and directed at the entire family, but incites anxiety in Meg over the course of the telling. The third is initiated by Meg and directed primarily to William, but centers on another female protagonist's anxious experience. The three stories are thematically related: each is oriented around pit bulls. Together they provide the opportunity to observe continuity within and across storytelling sequences as they occur moment by moment, night after night.

Meg begins the first pit bull story by casually mentioning that she stopped by William's father's house earlier that day:

I stopped by your dad's today to get the movie. They were showing me their *garden* and—

Meg's tone of voice intensifies:

> I saw the pit bulls. Oh my gosh! I— I was standing there talking to
> your *dad* by the back *wall*. And I just happened to remember these
> *dogs*. I looked over the wall and this dog, it— it *came at* me.

Meg drops her fork, turns her face toward William, pauses for half a
second, inhales, and continues:

> I mean thank *God* it was *attached* but— to the *chain*. But I went,
> "*Eeyow!*" And I jumped back off the tree stump.

At this point Meg excitedly flings her arms up over her head. The children are mesmerized, their eyes fixed on Meg. She pauses, looking at
William, who continues to eat, then at Beth and back at William, and
proceeds to describe the dogs:

> The dog was snarling. And you've seen these pictures of these—
> these these big um heavy leather collars with metal studs? These—
> these collars that they have on? This is what he was wearing. And
> the links on that chain must have been— (.4 pause) I don't know
> how— Uh at least this big.

Meg joins her thumb and index finger, positioning her hand for
William's viewing.

> Now the *female*, she didn't do *anything*. She just kind of sat there.
> But that— that *male* pit bull, he looked at us. And the *weird* thing
> was, while he was growling and barking at us he was wagging his
> tail, and he had the most *wicked* expression on his face. And your
> dad said if he ever got *loose*, you know that'd be the *end* of us. He
> could scale this wall and kill us.

As Meg continues her story, she increasingly stresses her psychological responses to the dogs. She builds a portrait of herself as protagonist
that highlights not only *what* she was thinking and feeling, but *that* she
was thinking and feeling. In this way she opens herself up to others'

assessments both of the content of her thoughts and feelings and of her having been engaged in thinking and feeling at the time. For example, Meg describes her father-in-law's attempt to calm the dog:

> You know how your dad could charm just about any animal? He was talking to their dog and it was *wagging* its tail. And yet its expression looked like it was sort of snarling and ready to bare its teeth. And your dad the whole time was saying, *"Good boy, good boy."* You know how your *dad* is. He can make any animal his friend.

Reorienting her body toward William, she adds,

> But I couldn't help but wonder what would happen—

William, looking down at his food, nods briefly, and leans back in his chair away from Meg. Looking up at William, Meg pauses and continues, "You know?" Still oriented toward William, Meg waits another half second. She scratches the top of her head and looks down at her plate, at which point William mutters, "They'd be in big trouble." Meg then completes her account of her wondering: "if he really did get into your dad's yard."

Shortly thereafter, in a somewhat louder voice, Meg continues, "I got to thinking." After a half-second pause, looking straight into William's face and shaking her head emphatically, Meg states, "These aren't *pets*." After another half-second pause, William looks up from his food, and then back at his plate as Meg continues: "Nobody would treat a *pet* like that." Flashing a glance at William, her voice even louder: "They're strictly there to chew up *anybody* who might come into their yard." At this point William looks up again, not at Meg but at Beth. He then glances at Meg, and, turning toward Sean, he mutters, "Sure they are."

Meg's eyes follow William's to Sean, and she says, "Wh— what?" Returning her gaze to William's face, she completes her thought:

> What? What if that thing gets *loose?* And *kills* somebody? I think they ought to be outlawed.

When Meg reports *what* she was thinking and feeling and *that* she was thinking and feeling, she brings her consciousness of her mental and emotional activity into focus. Although she associates this activity with a past episode, her narrative gives the impression that her absorption with thinking and feeling did not end when she left her father-in-law's yard, but continues through the moment of the telling. She voices her thoughts and feelings in the present tense, depicting them as current, enduring concerns. Meg asks, "What *would* happen?" rather than "What *would have* happened?" and "What if that thing *gets* loose?" rather than "What if that thing *got* loose?" Through repeated use of these grammatical forms, Meg indexes over and over again that she remains caught up in a web of worries. In this way she opens herself up to family members' assessments of her current as well as her past concerns about the dogs.

So far, our analysis has focused on the first pit bull storytelling as it unfolds in Meg's words. We now attend to the interweaving of words, silence, eye gaze, and body movement that tell the story. These dimensions offer penetrating insights into the construction of rationality and irrationality. In particular, not only does Meg open herself to others' evaluations of her thoughts and feelings, but she constructs the story in a way that actively elicits feedback, particularly from William. Meg delivers the parts of the story that convey her thinking and feeling with hesitations, pauses, and rising intonation, which are conversational strategies for soliciting responses. And she frequently orients her body and eye gaze toward William, singling him out as preferred responder.[14] This pattern of pausing, body orientation, and eye gaze suggests that Meg may be seeking validation for the content of her thoughts, if not for being legitimately preoccupied. Validation, however, is weak at best.

For example, when Meg presents statements about her thinking, such as "I couldn't help but wonder . . . ," William nods his head. Yet his gaze remains fixed on his food and his body oriented away from Meg. After a short pause, Meg, who is looking at William, solicits additional feedback from him by asking, "you know?" William withholds feedback through a lengthier pause. In response to his silence—which is generally taken as a sign of disagreement or nonalignment[15]—Meg, still gazing at William, amplifies her display of confusion by scratching the top of her head, thereby more strongly soliciting a response. At this point William speaks up.

The same dynamic emerges shortly thereafter, when Meg presents additional statements conveying her thinking about the pit bulls:

Meg: And they look so *barbaric* the way they're tied up with these
          big chains. I got to thinking, These aren't *pets*. (.3 pause) No-
          body would treat a *pet* like that. They're strictly there to chew
          up *anybody* who might come into their yard
William: Sure they are.
Sean: Well wh—? Mom?
Meg: What if that thing gets *loose?* and *kills* somebody?

Although William stares at Meg as she begins to relate her thoughts ("I got to thinking . . ."), he does not provide verbal feedback after her first predicate ("these aren't *pets*"), after she looks straight into his eyes and intensifies her message by shaking her head, or after a subsequent half-second pause—which constitutes a lengthy conversational invitation to take the floor. William continues to withhold substantive response during Meg's second thought ("Nobody would treat a *pet* like that"), even though she flashes a glance at him. This prolonged lack of response can be taken as a strong sign of nonalignment. As Meg goes on to express a third thought ("They're strictly there to chew up *anybody* who might come into their yard"), William looks up, not at Meg but at Beth. He glances at Meg momentarily, en route to fixing his gaze on Sean. At this point, William offers a verbal response ("Sure they are"). But his eyes, remaining focused on Sean, signal that his attention is divided.

Further, William's assessment does not match the intensity of Meg's portrayal. Because it is downgraded it tends to undermine rather than ratify the world view Meg is attempting to construct. Meg goes on to express her fourth and most potent thought ("What if that thing gets *loose?* and *kills* somebody?") as a direct question to William, clearly soliciting a response. Yet William remains focused on Sean and does not acknowledge Meg's question.

Although William helps Meg to overcome her fears in a range of social situations in and outside the home, William's responses to Meg's stories at the dinner table help perpetuate her panicky thoughts and feelings. In response to silence, low-affiliative, or downgraded responses, tellers typically escalate the intensity of both the narrated situation and their bids for alignment from others.[16] In the pit bull story, William's limited responsiveness, signaling a lack of alignment with Meg's portrayal, seems to lead Meg to increase the frequency of her bids for a response. She does so by describing her experience in progressively more self-threatening and anxious terms. Meg intensifies the danger of the situation by amplifying the vicious nature of the dogs and by heightening the relevance of her narrated predicament to other family members.

Meg develops hypothetical scenarios that expand the scope of the threat to people other than herself, including the neighbors' grandchildren as well as generic anyones and someones. For example, after describing the dogs' partial destruction of the fence separating them from the rest of the neighborhood, Meg adds,

> Ed and Bonnie [neighbors] don't want to let their *grandchildren* in the backyard with this dog because if this dog ever got loose it could just—

Meg's voice trails off. Although Meg does not articulate the final outcome of this hypothetical scenario, its relevance to Beth and Sean, her father-in-law's grandchildren, is clear.

At this point Meg launches a dramatic rendition of her thoughts about the dogs. As we have seen, she begins this portrayal by characterizing the pit bulls inversely, in terms of a category they are not members of ("pets"), and describes how a negative set of persons ("nobody") would act with respect to that category. She then describes the animals as more threatening: as creatures who exist for the sole purpose of mauling anybody in the vicinity. Finally, Meg asks her half-attending husband to ponder with her the possibility that the one particularly menacing pit bull, which she emphatically describes as a "thing," could "get loose and kill somebody." Meg's portrayal of the dogs increases the scope of the threat to include not just herself but "anybody" and "somebody." In so doing, Meg unleashes the relevance of the scenario from its location in the past realm of the story to the present time of the telling.

This progression can be viewed as an attempt to engage William's participation by drawing him into the story. By casting the scenario with "grandchildren," "anyone," and "someone," Meg entreats members of her family to put themselves in her shoes. At the same time, Meg constructs her actions and emotions as what would be expected of "anybody." She thus attempts to fill her shoes with rational feet and, in this way, to legitimize her psychological responses as protagonist and her voice as narrator. But to no avail.

When they are not ratified by her husband, Meg's attempts to portray her actions and emotions as what would be expected of normal, rational persons may leave her feeling abnormal and irrational. This dynamic illustrates the collaborative construction of narrators' and protagonists' identities and world views. The outcomes of storytelling interactions are collectively, not single-handedly, achieved. How Meg portrays her thoughts, feelings, and actions is largely influenced by William's responses or lack thereof and by her desire to obtain validation from William. It is important to remember that Meg delivers the story in a way that establishes William's authority to confer or deny her rationality, both as protagonist and as teller. The story that unfolds, with her emergent character as protagonist and narrator, is a function of the roles that are established in the telling. Further, this narrative sequence is part of an overarching choreography that has been established through recurrent family interactions. It is replayed night after night in various narrative scenarios.

Pit bulls return to the Logan dinner table a few weeks later in the second story in the pit bull trilogy. Following the death of Rex, one of the Logans' beloved dachshunds, the Logans consider getting another dog. In the context of this discussion, William reports:

I got to *tell* you what they were advertising in Glenview, on Glenview Boulevard on the way home.

All eyes on him, William proceeds, elongating each word for dramatic effect, ending his remark with hearty laughter:

We could *have* a *pit bull* and *shepherd* and part-*rottweiler* puppy. *Ha Ha Ha Ha!*

Meg responds by jerking back in her chair, away from William, and nervously saying, "Oh yeah." Beth reiterates William's proposal as a question: "a pit bull shepherd and rottweiler?" The story concludes quietly as Meg looks down at her plate and philosophizes, "Who needs a gun with a dog like that."

Narratives have a family history in the sense that the meaning of each story is shaped by and shapes those that precede and follow. This second pit bull storytelling is not initiated by Meg, nor is she a narrative protagonist. Yet despite changes in storytelling roles, the choreography of the story—how it unfolds—perpetuates relationships and identities among family members. This storytelling harks back to the first both thematically and interactionally. William's report of the advertisement he has seen invokes and counters Meg's earlier rendition of the pit bulls, as he makes light of a situation she has portrayed as threatening. In so doing, he simultaneously discredits Meg as a protagonist and as a narrator. William's proposal to bring a pit bull mix into their home can be seen as a more extreme version of Meg's worst-case scenario: that a pit bull might enter her father-in-law's yard ("I couldn't help but wonder what would happen if he really did get into your dad's yard"). Further, William's suggestion that they adopt the dog as a pet directly opposes Meg's world view of pit bulls, conveyed in her emphatic statement, "these aren't *pets*."

These two pit bull stories are also similar in that both portray Meg as having irrational thoughts and feelings. William's light-hearted report can be seen as an invitation to laugh at the thought of adopting a pit bull as a pet. It also can be seen as poking fun at Meg for being mired in anxiety about the dogs. Yet Meg's response demonstrates that she does not share the sentiment that pit bulls are a laughing matter.

The third pit bull story in the trilogy is immediately touched off by the second. Following William's lead, Meg jokingly relates an incident in which a neighbor's mother-in-law unwittingly locks herself in the backyard with a ferocious pit bull. In this sequence Meg portrays a ridiculous, if not irrational, woman protagonist whose distress over the pit bull is laughable. Looking at William, Meg announces,

> Joe and Charlotte have a pit bull. And he said his mother-in-law got *locked out*—the door to the backyard locks automatically when it closes behind you.

Infusing her words with laughter, she continues,

> And and she went out in the backyard. She was visiting them and they didn't know that (.3 pause) she was back— in the backyard with the *pit bull*. And all of a sudden she yells, *"Charlotte! Charlotte! Open this door!"*

Laughingly heartily, Meg covers her mouth with her hand. Nobody else laughs. Their silence, more palpable than Meg's lone voice, is excruciating. Like William's silences in the first pit bull storytelling, this silence is akin to that Tillie Olsen speaks of: the silent "thwarting of what struggles to come into being, but cannot."

Instead of laughing, Beth, looking at Meg, loudly asks, "What?" Meg repeats herself:

> Joe's mother-in-law got locked out in the backyard with their pit *bull*, and he said it would *eat* anybody.

Beth laughs as Meg continues, looking down at her plate, her body oriented toward William:

> She didn't know they had the door that would—

William finally joins in, not with laughter but with disapprobation:

> I'd be afraid to have it— to have that *dog* around the *kids*.

Beth, appearing confused, asks,

What dog?

William and Sean, looking at Beth, simultaneously reply,

The pit bull.

Beth, still confused, asks,

Oh. Across the street?

Meg and William both respond, "No." William subsequently clarifies, "Joe and Charlotte's," while Meg concludes, "Any pit bull actually."

Despite changes in the cast of narrative protagonists, this storytelling sequence harks back to the previous pit bull storytellings, and like the others it perpetuates family members' roles and identities. In developing the scenario, Meg locates Joe's mother-in-law in the place she herself initially imagined and most feared being: in the yard of an unleashed pit bull. Yet by casting Joe's mother-in-law's distress as laughable, Meg places the protagonist of her joke in the position she occupied over the course of William's joke telling: they are both women with irrational fears that are comical to others.

In telling a joke, Meg may be attempting to align with William's light-hearted stance toward pit bulls. Yet Meg continues to display anxiety. As in the previous two pit bull stories, she describes the dog as threatening not only to her but to everyone ("it would *eat* anybody"). This portrayal converges with her depiction of the pit bulls in the first story, as being "there to chew up *anybody* who might come into their yard." She expands the scope of the threat to include not just Joe and Charlotte's pit bull but all pit bulls ("Any pit bull actually"). Rather than being confined to a particular dog in a particular yard, the threat is now universal, extending to any pit bull, any time, and any location. As in the progression in the second pit bull storytelling, by the end of her "joke," Meg portrays the scenario as no longer laughable, but menacing.

William's comment, "I'd be afraid to have it—to have that dog around the *kids*," helps construct this shift in tone. Although he is perhaps attempting to validate Meg's fears, his comment pushes Meg further into the chasm of expressed anxiety that is gradually overwhelming the particulars of her story. Furthermore, William's comment frames the scenario as threatening to *"the kids."* Using these words, he does not align with the protagonist's (the mother-in-law's) fears or, by extension, Meg's fears. Instead, he differentiates himself from the two women who are afraid of the dogs, articulating his fear for the safety of the children. This response is reminiscent of William's response in the first pit bull story to Meg's fears about pit bulls entering his parents' yard. Referring to his parents' vulnerability (rather than to Meg's), William comments, "They'd be in big trouble." Framing fear of pit bulls as valid for children and the elderly, but not for competent adults, William's responses may insinuate that Meg's fear is groundless or that she is like a child or an old person.

Meg frequently directs stories about anxious experiences to William. In this way she establishes him in a key position to evaluate her rationality and competence both as a protagonist acting, thinking, and feeling in the past and as a narrator acting, thinking, and feeling in the present. These interactions rarely help her to make sense of confusing and distressing experiences. More often family storytelling leaves her with the sense that her point of view deviates from the norm, that she is an irrational woman.

The pain and isolation that accompany mental illness are partly attributable to loss of the authority to reframe experience. Meg's view of herself as irrational and abnormal leads her to avoid places outside the home in which she fears the pain of inexplicable sensations and emotions and, ultimately, to label herself agoraphobic. This outcome sheds light on the self-portrait Meg constructs in her narratives of panic experience. When unratified portraits of herself as rational (that is, like anyone else) give way to enduring portrayals of herself as irrational or agoraphobic, Meg gives voice to the sounds and silences of collective experience. The voices of the Logan family, embodied in its stories and its interactions, tell us that psychological dispositions exist not in the isolated mind of an individual—between the ears and beneath the skin[17]—but rather are constructed in interactions between people.

Why doesn't William empathize with Meg's anxious narrative recollections and speculations? And why does he initiate stories that undermine her world view? He may wish to curtail her panic. Intimates listening to Meg's accounts of past anxieties may withhold feedback for an extended period of the narrative to avoid validating her apprehensions or to avoid aligning themselves with her anxiety, because they fear it is mushrooming out of control. William's desire to diminish the anxiety level of family members may also motivate his light-hearted narrative reframings of Meg's fearful experiences. When Meg recounts prior anxiety-ridden scenarios for her family, she brings her past anxieties into present collective consciousness. William may display only minimal responsiveness to such recountings to discourage Meg from continuing this process and perhaps from involving their children in experiencing these same fears. William's minimal displays of involvement may be attempts to quell narrative emotionality before it gets out of hand, develops into full-blown panic, and sweeps the family into submission. Unfortunately William's low affiliative responses have the opposite effect, leading to the escalation of anxiety not only for Meg but for everyone at the table.

9

Socializing Emotion

> Closed spaces emanate from a whole web of circum-
> stances. A sense of space grows out of the society in
> which you are born and the way you are socialized to
> move through that society, and that movement or lack
> of it determines who you are, how you see the big you
> when you look into a mirror.
>
> —Gloria Naylor, 1990

$\mathbf{B}$eth and Sean are also drawn into the rising tides of emotion that engulf the family. They participate again and again in stories that in turn shape their identities and world views. These moments of listening and contributing to storytellings with recurrent emotional themes and formats create critical socializing experiences.

Storytelling interactions between anxious parents and their children provide a window into understanding the development and perpetuation of anxiety in families. Children of anxious parents are known to be at risk for developing anxiety disorders themselves,[1] and children of agoraphobic parents appear to be most vulnerable.[2] Despite strong support for a familial component in the development of anxiety, particularly among children of agoraphobic parents, relatively little is known about interfamilial transmission. Although genetic factors clearly play a role,[3] genetics account for relatively little of the variability in outcome. First, not all children of anxious parents develop anxiety disorders, even within the same family. It is often the case that one of two identical twins develops an anxiety disorder while the other does not. And among identical twins studied, no two who developed anxiety shared the same disorder. These findings suggest that if anxiety is passed from parent to child, a predisposition for anxiety in general rather than for a particular disorder is inherited.[4]

To understand the perpetuation of anxiety in families, we must take genetics into account. But there is more to the story. Knowing that there is a genetic component does not tell us what is passed on in families, nor about protective factors. Although we are learning more about physiological predispositions that children may inherit from parents that render them vulnerable to anxiety and panic,[5] much less attention has been paid to environmental influences that exacerbate or ameliorate these processes.

There has been a great deal of speculation about socialization experiences that may contribute to the development of anxiety among children of agoraphobic parents. One hypothesis is that agoraphobic parents model a cautious, fearful stance toward objects (including people) in the world, and that their children internalize this stance.[6] A variation on this perspective suggests that children of agoraphobic parents observe their parents' behavior and adopt the tendency to respond to fear through avoidance, which eventually results in an array of phobias and anxieties.[7] This view is supported by studies finding positive correlations between the number of situations agoraphobic parents avoid and the severity of anxiety in their children.

Another conceptualization suggests that interacting with an agoraphobic parent who feels out of control and copes with these feelings by avoiding situations outside the home undermines the *child's* sense of control, generating feelings of anxiety and helplessness.[8] This perspective is backed up by evidence that children of agoraphobic parents perceive themselves to have less control over events and experiences in the world than do children of nonanxious parents.[9]

Psychoanalytic models of the transmission of anxiety in families highlight a dynamic in which agoraphobic parents depend on their children to alleviate their fears of being alone. Such models hold that the children are socialized into caregiving roles in which they assure their parents that they will not become autonomous and leave. It follows that these socialization experiences create conflict and anxiety in children who are increasingly faced with situations requiring separation from their parents.[10] This perspective is supported by studies finding higher rates of separation anxiety in the children of agoraphobic parents in comparison with not only children of nonanxious parents but children of parents suffering from other forms of anxiety as well.[11]

Each of these models is substantiated by research that identifies correlations between characteristics of anxious parents and their children on the basis of their responses to questionnaires, highly structured interviews and, occasionally, the observation of children in experimental situations. Without observing anxious parents and their children, however, especially in natural settings such as the home, we can only speculate about the dynamics that underlie the correlations that have been documented. In addition, whereas highly structured measures limit the scope of investigation to a predetermined set of questions, observation in natural settings opens new, often unanticipated avenues of inquiry.

Lisa became aware of the need for observational research and its promise as an approach to understanding the socialization of anxiety during her first visit to the Logans' house. Although Beth's responses to the questionnaires and experimental procedures in Lisa's dissertation study were interesting, it was the way Beth engaged in the tasks that was most striking. From start to finish, she had difficulty making decisions. Before beginning the first task, which required estimating the prevalence of twenty-five maladies by circling stick figures on a stack of pages, Beth was given the chance to choose from a box of colored marking pens the one she wanted to use. She labored over the decision for nearly fifteen minutes before developing an elaborate rotation system: she used each pen once, moving forward through the box, and again, moving backward. Beth then arranged the pens in the box "so they'd be more color coordinated" before moving through the forward and backward progression again, this time using each pen twice. She expressed frustration with herself for not having decided to rearrange the pens before beginning the task.

Beth displayed similar degrees of indecisiveness while proceeding through the measures themselves. After Beth estimated the prevalence of various risks and maladies, Lisa asked her to sort cards labeled with the same maladies into two baskets: things that were serious and things that were not so serious. Beth belabored each decision, separating the cards into several small stacks on the carpet around her. She then moved the baskets together, placing seven cards in the baskets and the remaining eighteen on top, straddling the two. She reviewed this stack several times, paring the number of cards in her "undecided" pile from eighteen to twelve. Beth used the same approach in sorting the cards on the basis of degree of perceived control over the risk condition, although she eventually distributed all but four items.

Beth also displayed this decision-making style in responding to multiple choice and true-false questions about frightening and anxiety-provoking experiences:[12] she made an initial pass at the items, leaving many unanswered. When she went back to those she'd left blank, Beth frequently changed her response to the questions she'd already answered.[13] Ironically, one of the items she changed from "True" to "False" read, "I have difficulty making up my mind."

Beth's behavior provides interesting information about children's beliefs, fears, and anxieties about themselves and the worlds they inhabit. Such information is often helpful in identifying children who may be in need of intervention. Our aim is to show that children (and adults) reveal who they are not only through the content of their responses to questions—*what* they say and do—but through how they go about responding—*how* they say and do it.

Beth's approach to tasks tells us something important about her sense of control beyond what can be gleaned from her ratings of the controllability of various situations. Similarly, how she completes the questionnaires—the caution and indecisiveness she displays—reveals sides of herself that are not captured by her responses to the items and are often inconsistent with the self-portrait she articulates. Such inconsistencies are not unique to Beth. They are universal. Each of us shapes our own identity and those of the people with whom we live through a multiplicity of communicative channels. That these channels often produce discrepant messages attests both to the many ways in which we affect each other and to our limited awareness of the nature of our influence.

Meg expressed concern about her influence during a conversation with Lisa:

> There's *nothing* I want more than to protect my kids from the kind of agony I go through. I try not to say anything to them, you know, or to say the right thing. I try not to let on when I'm feeling anxious or upset. But yet I'm still afraid that somehow they'll know that something's wrong with *Mom*. And I worry that maybe something I'm doing is affecting them somehow, you know *negatively* affecting them, either now or in the long run.

Meg's children—like all children—pick up socializing messages as they participate in storytelling interactions. These interactions are fleeting, and many aspects lie beneath conscious awareness, but their cumulative effects are powerful and lasting.

Socialization

Just as identities and world views are manifest both in *what* people say and in *how* they interact with others, the socialization of identities and world views occurs on both planes simultaneously: what and how are inseparable. Socialization refers to the processes, both overt and covert, by which novices such as children become competent members of a society or culture. These processes take place over the course of daily social life, through interactions in which more experienced, expert members display to novices culturally expected ways of thinking, feeling, and acting. Children are socialized into particular family cultures that are embedded in broader sociocultural norms and values. These societal structures include formal institutions, such as economic, political, educational, medical, and religious systems, as well as more informal, habitual relations between people and common knowledge about the way things are done.[14]

Novices learn through explicit instruction and by observing and modeling the behavior of more competent members of society. In focusing on the former, we tend to overlook the numerous implicit everyday opportunities for children to gain skills and understanding of the world around them. Though not often intended as instructional, the routine and recurrent interactions between parents and children provide powerful socialization experiences. Through guided participation in everyday activities, children are socialized into particular ways of acting, talking, thinking, and problem solving that allow them to enter into the culture in which they live.

Lisa observed many such interactions during her visits to the Logan home. One day, while Lisa and Meg were talking, Sean entered the kitchen carrying a dead bird:

> *Mommy! Look!* I found a dead bird. It was right outside by the *tree* and I think maybe *Rex* killed it.

Meg quickly led Sean out the back door and into the garage, saying,

> We don't bring dead things into the house. *Okay*, Honey? We don't bring dead things into the house.

Sean explained, "I was gonna put it in the trash." Meg replied,

> Well that's fine, Honey, but we want to wrap him up first. And then we'll put him in the big garbage can outside.

Meg wrapped the bird in newspaper and sealed the paper with masking tape. Together they walked toward the big plastic garbage cans near the back fence, away from the house. Meg removed the tightly sealed lid and asked Sean,

> Do you want to drop him in?

Sean nodded, reaching for the fragile bundle with both hands, and carefully placed it in the can. Meg replaced the lid on the can, securing the seal. As they returned to the house Meg reached for Sean's hand. In a soft voice she said,

> I don't think Rex could kill a bird like that. Maybe Rex found him after he was already dead. Maybe a *cat* killed the bird.

Again Sean nodded, his eyes downcast. He asked,

Do you think we can get me a popsicle now?

Meg responded in a soothing tone,

Sure we can, Sweetie. Come on. Let's go into the house.

This momentary, spontaneous interaction between Meg and Sean socializes him into particular ways of handling dead creatures and attitudes toward death. Meg provides explicit and implicit instruction. She explicitly articulates behavioral guidelines: "We don't bring dead things into the house. *Okay*, Honey? We don't bring dead things into the house." Meg then models the culturally appropriate solution to the problem, socializing a set of practices through her actions and involving Sean in the process: she securely wraps the dead bird in newspaper and invites Sean to deposit it not in any trash can, as he is wont to do, but in the can furthest from the house. Meg's careful handling of the dead bird differentiates it from other items she throws away, as does her bringing it to a can outside. Her thorough, thoughtful response distinguishes this situation from the many other occasions in which Sean's unsolicited announcements and requests are treated as interruptions and hurriedly dismissed. Meg's gentle, solemn stance socializes a particular orientation toward this situation and toward death in general, showing that it is to be taken seriously. Her suggestion that Rex may not have killed the bird reinforces the relevance of accountability, an issue Sean initially raised, and conveys the desire to absolve family members (including pets) of responsibility. Finally, by readily accommodating Sean's request for a popsicle, particularly since she had previously denied it, and addressing him as "Sweetie" in the process, Meg provides comfort. In so doing, Meg socializes the appropriateness of efforts both to seek and offer solace following encounters with death. Her actions differentiate this and like situations both from those that can be dismissed as trivial and from those involving grave danger. Her response identifies the incident's place within the ongoing flow of daily life.

Language Socialization

As illustrated in the interaction between Meg and Sean, language plays an essential role in socialization.[15] Children and other novices in society develop cultural skills, systems of belief, and knowledge in large part through participation in language-mediated activities—through communication with others. Language is a major tool for conveying sociocultural knowledge and a powerful medium of socialization. Language socialization refers to both socialization through language, which has been our focus so far, and socialization to use language. Through social interactions involving language, more competent members of society show novices how to do things with words. Every utterance displays a set of linguistic forms that members of a social group use to construct stances, identities, relationships, and social actions. These forms mark the type of social situation that is or may be taking place.

Cultural skills and knowledge are often socialized through the message content of communication. This is the case, for instance, when Meg tells Sean, "We don't bring dead things into the house." Yet sociocultural information is also encoded in the delivery, in the *form* of the message. Many features of discourse carry sociocultural information, including phonological and syntactic construction, word choice, type of speech acts, conversational sequencing, interruptions, overlaps, gaps, and turn length. Experts make use of these features of language in socializing children and other less competent members of society.

Drawing from the interaction between Meg and Sean, we see that *how* Meg uses language plays a crucial role in the socialization of a set of practices, embedded in a particular world view of death. For example, Meg grammatically marks that she is delivering a norm and an edict to Sean through the inclusive, authorial form of the pronoun "we" together with the negative auxiliary "don't" and the simple present tense of the verb "bring" ("We don't bring dead things into the house"). This use of "we" not only refers to Meg and Sean but includes the collective members of decent society as well. In using "we," Meg speaks with the authoritative voice of full membership status and in addition incorporates Sean in this social group. The use of the simple present-tense form of "bring" marks the action as habitual, generic, or normative (for example, "We eat with forks").

Meg uses other linguistic means to convey appropriate behavior to Sean. She conveys a solemn stance toward the situation paralinguistically, by using a hushed, reverent tone of voice, and through her quiet use of repetition, coupled with a term of endearment ("Honey"), when providing guidelines for Sean. Meg's choice of words communicates important information, constructing the identities of participants in the interaction and relationships between them. By using endearments in addressing Sean ("Sweetie" and "Honey") Meg also offers comfort. This act establishes a particular relationship with him, modeling the appropriate way of relating to people who are coping with death. In addition, whereas Sean refers to the bird as "it," Meg refers to the bird as "him," humanizing the animal. Meg's language constructs the animal not as an object but as kin, heightening the relevance of the bird's life and death.

In this interaction with Sean, Meg uses language to socialize an understanding and an associated set of practices, embedding the situation within a particular sociocultural world view. At the same time, her use of language socializes an understanding of how to do things with words. When Meg lowers her tone of voice to construct a solemn, reverent stance, she both communicates a particular orientation to dead animals and demonstrates how members of the culture use language to be solemn and reverent. Similarly, when she softens her voice, uses terms of endearment, and readily agrees to Sean's request, she both communicates the relevance of comfort during encounters with death and demonstrates how to comfort—the sounds, references, and speech acts that make up comforting relationships. And when she suggests the likelihood that a cat, rather than Rex, killed the bird, Meg not only conveys the relevance of accountability and absolution but demonstrates how to propose a hypothetical scenario that mitigates family responsibility. The interactions between expert and novice members of society simultaneously organize the roles and relationships between participants and socialize the sociocultural meaning of situations and ways of using language.

Both aspects of the socialization process are manifest in an interaction between Sean and his friend Raymond that took place some hours after the dead bird incident. Lisa and Meg were talking in the living room, where they could see through the patio doors into the backyard. They watched as Sean and Raymond approached the garbage can that contained the bird and quietly slid open the glass to overhear their conversation. Sean explained,

> I can show you the bird I found. He can't be in the house, so me and my mom wrapped him up and put him in here.

Removing the lid from the can and placing it on the grass, Sean continued, in a low, serious tone of voice,

> You have to wrap him up because he's *dead*. And he needs to be *outside*.

Sean gingerly removed the bundle from can. Seeing only newsprint, Raymond protested,

> I didn't get to see! That's no *fair*.

Sean conceded,

> You can hold him. But then we have to put him back.

Raymond reached for the bird. Fingering the tape that sealed its packing, he asked,

> *Can't* I just *look?* Just for a *second?*

Sean sighed, responding,

> Okay, but then we have to put him right back. Here. I'll do it.

Sean lifted the bird from Raymond's hands, and struggled to remove a piece of masking tape without tearing the paper. He looked at Raymond and said,

> I think it's too hard. Maybe next time I'll show you first.

Raymond vigorously nodded in agreement, saying,

Okay. Put it back.

Echoing Raymond, Sean replied,

Okay. You get the lid.

Sean carefully placed the wrapped bird in the can. Raymond then set the lid on the rim, joining Sean as he pounded around the perimeter with his fists to secure the seal. Sean said, "There." "That's enough," Raymond added. Then Sean proposed, "Let's go get our Big Wheels." And off they went, down the path alongside the fence and out the gate into the front yard.

In this interaction Sean communicates his newly acquired understanding of how to treat dead animals to Raymond. He voices and enacts the knowledge and skills he has learned. Sean rephrases instructions his mother provided, such as, "He can't be in the house." In addition, he articulates parts of the process he observed his mother carry out, as when he explains that the bird needs to be wrapped; and he reenacts others, as when he makes sure to reseal the garbage can lid. Sean also mirrors his mother's use of language. He lowers his voice, speaking in hushed, solemn tones. His manner is gentle relative to the rough-and-tumble demeanor that he and Raymond typically display.

In this encounter, Sean uses grammatical forms in ways that parallel those used by his mother earlier that day. For example, parallel to his mother's use of the inclusive, authorial "we" in "We don't bring dead things into the house," Sean uses an impersonal form of "you" in "You have to wrap him up." Similarly just as Meg uses "do's" and "don'ts" to convey normative standards, Sean uses auxiliary forms such as "have to" and "can't" to convey a similar message to Raymond, continuing the socialization process. Sean's language and behavior in relating to his friend demonstrate a sociocultural understanding of the situation and of how to use language to construct actions, relationships, and stances that can be traced back to his interaction with his mother.[16] Through participation in language activities with more expert members, children and other novices develop concepts of a socioculturally structured universe and their roles and identities within this universe.

As Gloria Naylor remarks, "a sense of space grows out of the society in which you are born and the way you are socialized to move through that society, and that movement or lack of it determines who you are, how you see the big you when you look into a mirror." Her words apply to other senses as well. The ways we see, hear, feel, and give voice to the worlds we inhabit is embedded in the culture in which we live and how we are socialized within that culture. And the way we are socialized determines who we are and how we see ourselves.

The Child as Apprentice

Socialization can be seen as a "cultural apprenticeship," an apprenticeship in which children and other novices gain the cultural skills and understandings of members of their society.[17] Cultural apprenticeships take place as children participate in daily activities with more experienced members. Traditionally, we tend to think of apprenticeships in skilled crafts and trades. We imagine young Ben Franklin working alongside his mentor at the printing press, and Paul Revere seated at his workbench as an apprentice to his father, a silversmith.

Apprenticeship is a fitting metaphor for socialization because it highlights the active role of learners within a community of people who guide their participation in skilled, valued sociocultural activity.[18] Apprentices actively attempt to make sense of new situations by observing and participating, while their more expert partners support and structure novices' efforts, passing on skills and knowledge through tacit and explicit communication as they go about their work. The participation framework is a medium for learning.[19] The apprentice starts out as a peripheral participant, and through increased participation strives to occupy a position as a legitimate participant with full membership status.

Apprenticeships provide beginners with access to both the overt aspects of skills and the more hidden inner processes of thought.

Through close collaboration with a more knowledgeable person, one who has a broader vision of the activity at hand, the novice acquires not only a set of skills but the sociocultural world view in which these skills are embedded. Becoming a silversmith involves more than learning how to cut copper plates and cast church bells; it involves developing an understanding of the world of commerce, ranging from knowledge about how to attract business to opinions about appropriate levels of taxation. Through direct participation, the apprentice is situated at the intersection between actions, technologies, ideas, beliefs, and world views. In this way apprenticeships cultivate a depth of understanding that may be difficult to articulate for mentor and apprentice alike.[20] The apprentice appropriates these skills and knowledge, often in new ways.

Irving Stone's account of Michelangelo's apprenticeship to the painter Domenico Ghirlandaio displays essential features of apprenticeship:

There was no formal method of teaching at Ghirlandaio's studio. Its basic philosophy was expressed in a plaque which Ghirlandaio had nailed to the wall alongside his desk: "Continue without fail to draw something every day" . . . Michaelangelo . . . moved from table to table doing odd jobs, all the while observing those around him . . . Not looking up from the canvas Ghirlandaio declared, "Never try to invent human beings; paint into your panels only those whom you have already drawn from life" . . . Ghirlandaio cleared his desk and set up two corresponding sheets of paper. He handed Michaelangelo a blunt-nibbed pen, picked up another for himself, and started crosshatching, saying, "Here's my calligraphy: circles for the eyes, angular tips for the nose, like this; use the short nib to render a mouth and score the underlip." Michaelangelo followed the older man with quick movements of the hand, noting how Ghirlandaio in sketching a figure never bothered to finish the legs but tapered them down to nothing . . . Michaelangelo spent hours at this work desk with pen in hand, redrawing Ghirlandaio's models from hundreds of different angles, dialoguing with Ghirlandaio's pen and mind, probing his head, searching his heart for what he felt and his hand for what it could disclose about the object before him.[21]

The apprenticeship model applies not only to skills and knowledge specific to a trade or art but also to ways of thinking and acting that enable us to maneuver through daily life. Barbara Rogoff suggests that cognitive development can be viewed as an apprenticeship in thinking.[22] This apprenticeship takes place as parents guide children's participation in routine daily activities. Through guided participation, children appropriate ways of thinking and acting in the world. This perspective highlights the interactive roles of children and other people in children's acquisition of new skills and knowledge. It also locates cognitive development within a sociocultural matrix rather than within the isolated mind of the individual. The psycholinguist Dennie Wolf comments on this change in perspective: "Since psychology began in this country, the dominant metaphor for a learner has been something between Rodin's thinker and Huck Finn heading off to the territories—a singular, lone figure arm-wrestling the world, some conundrum, or a conceptual matter to the table. We are at long last learning to question the singularity, even the isolation, of that figure."[23] The apprenticeship model includes more than a single expert and a single novice; it involves a group of people who serve as resources for one another, such that all participants continue to develop breadth and depth of skill and knowledge.

Just as Ghirlandaio structured and simplified aspects of painting for Michelangelo, caregivers organize daily interactions with children to help them develop new skills and understandings. Across stages of development, caregivers guide children in navigating physical, psychological, and social terrain by structuring situations in ways that enable them to carry out tasks they would be incapable of otherwise. Experts assist children in building and combining skills, allowing them to solve increasingly complex problems. Psychologists refer to this process as "scaffolding."[24] In scaffolding a novice's problem-solving efforts, experts first recruit interest in the task. They then simplify the problem, guiding the child step by step toward its resolution, helping the child stay focused and directed, and working to minimize the child's frustration. Experts also scaffold novices' efforts by pointing out discrepancies between what the novice has done and more effective alternatives, and by demonstrating or modeling ideal solutions.

Like the notion of apprenticeship, scaffolding is typically discussed in relation to the socialization of cognitive skills or task competence. Our focus, however, is on the socialization of emotion. We propose that apprenticeship models apply to emotional as well as to cognitive development. That is, children's guided participation in daily activities and interactions can be viewed as an apprenticeship in feeling as well as in thinking. Interactions with caregivers socialize children into particular ways of feeling. Children learn how to express and interpret emotion. They learn how to present emotional portraits of themselves and others. They develop expectations about how others will feel and act toward them, and beliefs about the meaning of various emotional experiences. Through participation in social interactions, children adopt a system for navigating and understanding the world of emotion.

Language provides a uniquely powerful medium for the socialization of emotion. Learning to express and interpret emotion is tied to learning how to use particular kinds of language. Returning to the interaction between Meg and Sean over the dead bird, we can see that Meg's use of language is central to Sean's apprenticeship in feeling. Through her words or, to borrow Toni Morrison's phrase, through "how she does language," Meg socializes particular ways of feeling. In so doing, she passes on a particular set of linguistic tools for building and communicating feelings and for constructing the emotional identities of objects and people in the world, including one's own.

Our interest in the socialization of emotion is guided by the desire to understand how anxiety is passed on in families over the course of routine interactions. But before we explore the socialization of emotion in the Logan family, one point bears emphasis: through guided participation in the activities of daily life, children appropriate their parents' practices and beliefs for better or for worse. Children are socialized into problematic as well as adaptive practices, attitudes, emotional dispositions, and world views. It is apparent in the intergenerational continuity of child abuse, alcoholism, and even anxiety that parents socialize children into maladaptive practices, attitudes, emotional dispositions, and world views in spite of their strongest desires and best efforts.[25] Meg comments:

I don't think anybody is as worried about their child becoming agoraphobic as agoraphobics themselves. We agoraphobics, more than anyone, would do whatever we could to stop it from happening.

Despite Meg's heartfelt desire to avoid passing on the fears and attitudes that confine her to her home, her children are at risk, as are those of other sufferers.

We endeavor to illuminate the socialization of emotional fragility and vulnerability within the context of one routine language activity: storytelling. Since ancient times, storytelling has played an important role in home life, communal or group work, religious and social gatherings, and in marketplaces. Ovid's *Metamorphoses* (7 C.E.) depicts a scene that would be found later throughout Europe and the British Isles: that of women sewing or spinning and telling tales to make the time pass more swiftly.

One of the women says: While the others are deserting their tasks . . . Let us lighten with various talk the serviceable work of our hands, and to beguile the tedious hours, let us take turns in telling stories.[26]

The historian Strabo (7 B.C.E.) implies that telling tales is a common human experience:

Man is eager to learn and his fondness for tales is a prelude to this quality. It is a fondness for talk, then, that induces children to give their attention to narratives and more and more to take part in them.[27]

Storytelling in the home is one of the most universal of human experiences.[28] Many cultures consider storytelling to be of utmost importance to children. Children of the Ewe people of Ghana, for example, are not considered educated unless they have repeatedly heard the *gliwo*, animal stories that are intended to teach basic lessons in obedience, courage, honesty, and other virtues through indirect example.[29] Storytelling is also of great significance among Native Americans. In the words of Yellowman, a Navajo Indian: "If my children hear stories, they will grow up to be good people; if they don't hear them they will turn out to be bad."[30] This view is supported by accounts of storytelling gatherings in which children are present and expected to listen attentively and, as they grow older, to participate as tellers.[31] Storytelling is also an integral part of the practice and promulgation of a wide range of religious traditions, including Buddhism, Christianity, Hinduism, Islam, Jainism, and Judaism.[32]

In considering the socializing impact of storytelling, most observers focus on the message or the moral of the stories themselves. Bible stories, for example, are evaluated in terms of what children learn about God and about how to live their lives according to a moral code. Similarly, analyses of the socializing force of storytelling generally focus on the appropriateness of various topics.

Yet from our perspective children are not only socialized into the attitudes and beliefs contained in the messages of stories; they are also socialized into constructing these messages themselves. By listening to stories and contributing to their telling, children learn how to organize their own life material in story form. They are socialized into particular ways of narratively connecting emotions and events; they are socialized into particular ways of narrating their lives. When parents or other experts tell children a fable or religious parable or relate an experience from their own lives, they not only relate a particular moral or lesson; they show children how to build an understanding of their own experiences. Similarly, when Meg tells her children about her encounter with the pit bulls, she not only offers a lesson in coping with dangerous dogs, but more generally models ways of interpreting emotions and events.

From birth, children overhear and contribute to jointly produced narratives. Collaborative storytelling is a powerful way in which families co-construct the emotions, actions, and identities of members.

Parents' responses to their children's emotions and actions as protagonists and tellers influence not only children's interpretations of particular past events but their attitudes, beliefs, and identities more generally. In this way storytelling interactions simultaneously shape the physical and psychological spaces members have inhabited and those they will inhabit in the future.

By listening and contributing to stories with more experienced tellers, children are apprenticed to structure their own stories.[33] Children are unwitting novices in these storytelling interactions: they are drawn into storytelling realms when others tell stories to them, about them, with them, or simply in their presence. Even stories not directed primarily to a child, those a child merely overhears, may be highly influential. Stories told around the dinner table, for example, may draw the child's interest in several ways: some stories contain an unresolved problem that the child is inspired to tackle; some are dramatically recounted, using animated gestures and punctuated by moments of escalating intensity; and some are fascinating to the child because he or she is involved as a protagonist.

As addressees, protagonists, narrators, and over-hearers, children become co-authors of the stories that unfold. It is precisely this co-authorship that renders storytelling such a powerful medium for socializing knowledge and emotion. Children are not passive recipients of stories; rather, they contribute to the direction that these stories take. Their questions, their reactions, their additions to the storyline make them active partners with their parents or others in the development of their understandings of events and emotions. When we look at storytelling as an instrument of socialization, we discover yet another aspect of Toni Morrison's claim that "narrative is radical, creating us at the very moment it is being created." In telling stories to, about, with, and in the presence of children, we not only (re)create ourselves, we create storytellers out of our children. By telling our stories, we show children how to tell their stories—how to "do language." And as Morrison reminds us, doing language "may be the measure of our lives." In socializing the telling of stories, we socialize the constructing of lives. We offer the tools for designing and building, for maintaining and transforming, who we have been, are, and will be. Perhaps this is part of the meaning in Leslie Marmon Silko's remark, "Stories . . . aren't just entertainment. Don't be fooled. They are all we have. They are who we are, and all we have to fight off illness and death." Stories conceive, sustain, revitalize, and transform emotions, events, persons, and relationships. Through participation in storytelling, novices learn to give meaning to their experiences—to create and re-create their lives.

10

Socializing Anxiety

> It is the early formative years and the enclosure of the
> family that provide the encoded pain, violence, and
> loneliness, or the well of security, love, and possibility,
> that feed the imagination. The territory that we claim
> with our earliest selves is somehow so deeply imprinted
> in the brain that I think anything else could go and
> you'd still have that; you'd still have this great reservoir
> of emotion.
>
> —Joyce Carol Oates, 1990

Agoraphobia is intimately tied to a deep sense of the absence of control over one's feelings and actions. We are interested in how children come to know particular theories about control, about how emotions arise, and why events occur. Storytelling interactions can "encode" the feelings Joyce Carol Oates depicts: "pain, violence, and loneliness, or the well of security, love, and possibility, that feed the imagination." Through storytelling practices, we are apprenticed into an emotional logic we rely upon to navigate "the territory that we claim with our earliest selves" and inhabit for the rest of our lives. Storytelling interactions also socialize us into ways of using language to construct enduring portraits of ourselves and our relation to the world. In storytelling interactions between members of the Logan family, feelings of anxiety, especially the absence of control, may be socialized when:

1. A parent portrays a protagonist unable to control or explain actions and emotions, and
   • a child expands on this portrayal
   • a child repeats or reenacts this portrayal, or
   • a child suggests a way to control a narrated predicament, which is subsequently rejected as ineffective;
2. A child portrays a protagonist unable to control or explain actions and emotions, and
   • parent affirm(s) this portrayal; or
3. A child portrays a protagonist in control, and
   • parent challenges this portrayal.

Parent Portrays a Protagonist Out of Control

Meg frequently introduces narratives in which she and other adult protagonists are overwhelmed by uncontrollable fears and anxieties. In the telling of the first pit bull story, for example, Beth and Sean are closely attending to Meg as she portrays her strong emotional response to the unexpected advance of two ferocious dogs:

> I— I was standing there talking to your *dad* by the back *wall*. And I just happened to remember these *dogs*. I looked over the wall and this dog, it— it *came at* me. I mean thank *God* it was *attached* but— to the chain. But I went *"Eeyow!"* And I jumped back off the tree stump.

In reporting this incident, Meg dramatizes her distress by flinging her arms above her head, intensifying the sense that she is off balance and out of control. Such storytelling moments socialize children by modeling uncontrollable emotional responses to life events.

In some stories Meg not only depicts herself as unable to cope but also describes recruiting her children to help alleviate her anxiety. Meg portrays herself as feeling trapped and panicky at the bottom of Niagara Falls, for example, and as imploring her daughter to pray with her. In telling this story to Lisa during one of their conversations, Meg explains how awful she felt:

> When I got down there I became *claustrophobic* . . . And I— I realized there's no way out but through that *darn* elevator.

Lisa empathizes with her realization, commenting, "That's right." Meg continues,

> And I re*mem*bered clutching on to my *daughter* and saying, "Beth I'm— *Mama's* really afraid." (.3 pause) And— and um (.4 pause) and um (.4 pause) I— er— I— I mean *instantly* regretted that I had (.4 pause) *told* her that I was afraid, but I— I *did*. I clutched on to her. And I remember asking her to pray with me because I was *so unnerved*. (.8 pause) And I— I said, "I wanna go *up* now."

In that Beth is called upon to protect her mother, this story is consistent with the notion that agoraphobia involves the inversion of parent-child relationships. Such dynamics are thought to perpetuate agoraphobia across generations by creating in children a sense that their parent cannot survive without them, thereby making it conflictual to separate and become autonomous beings. As we will explore in more detail later, the scenario of a child helping a distressed parent is not limited to Meg's accounts of past anxious experiences. Meg also relies on her children in dinnertime interactions to help her resolve disturbing problems that continue to plague her in the present.

Meg narratively crafts menacing scenarios based not only on distressing encounters but also on seemingly benign events in the lives of one of the children. For example, when Sean lightheartedly produces a piece of tin foil wrapped around a bit of plastic and says, "Look at my cigarette lighter," family members, especially Meg and Beth, develop a hypothetical scenario in which a child may innocently bring this object to school and be suspended. Upon seeing Sean's contraption, Beth immediately instructs him,

> Well *don't* take that to school.

Turning to her, Sean asks "Why?" to which Beth responds,

You could get in *big* trouble. If I took something like that to school? And the teacher thought it was a cigarette lighter? She'd—I'd get suspended.

While William and Sean downplay the menacing potential of Sean's contraption, Meg takes up Beth's construal of this object. Meg compares the resemblance between the piece of plastic and tin foil and a real cigarette lighter to the resemblance between a toy gun and a real gun, and goes on to liken the negative consequences that might ensue. She launches into an account of innocent people who are arrested for bringing toy guns into banks.

Like that toy *gun*. I was telling Sean the other day that people have been *arrested* for pulling out toy *guns* in *banks*, because sometimes the bank teller thinks it's a *real* robber.

Beth completes her mother's projection, adding,

With a *real gun*.

Whether stated explicitly or implied, these storytelling interactions socialize the view that there is a fine line between menacing events that have actually happened, those that might have happened, and those that could happen in the future.

As we saw in Chapter 8, Meg tells stories in ways that solicit validation from her spouse. Similarly, she actively recruits her children's attention and participation by regularly directing her gaze, body, and utterances toward them; monitoring their comprehension; and responding to verbal and nonverbal reactions, including assessments, solutions, and signs of confusion. In these ways, Meg solicits validation from her children for her perception of uncontrollable danger in the world. Further, as discussed in Chapter 8, Meg seeks ratification of her sense that her fears and anxieties are rational—that they would be expected of anyone in the same situation.

In general, Beth and Sean are more responsive to Meg's tales of anxious experiences than is William. As we speculated at the close of Chapter 8, this may reflect William's desire to rein in Meg's anxiety and diffuse its effect on everyone. In any case, Beth and Sean gaze more consistently at Meg during the course of the storytelling, they answer her questions, and they provide consistent, often escalated assessments of the events. In these family storytelling moments, Meg's children display empathy with her narrated predicaments through several channels. In recounting the pit bull story, for example, Meg presents a continuing problem—that pet pit bulls threaten the safety of members of the neighborhood. She says, "They're so str— they have such *strong jaws* that if they attack somebody they could just— . . ." Beth, who has been closely attending, is moved to complete her mother's thought. She presents the unresolved neighborhood threat of these pit bulls in the emphatic comment, "*One bite*, that's just about all it would take."

In telling of the ever-present threat of pit bulls, Meg dramatizes her rendition by emphatically stressing certain words and stretching out the vowel sounds, as in *"stro::ng ja::ws."* Meg furthers stages her delivery by reenacting the menacing movements of the dogs' jaws: she juts out her chin, moves her jaws forward and back, furrows her brow, and frames her face with her hands, like a portrait. Sean is mesmerized by this storytelling display and mimics his mother's portrayal of the dogs' jaws by opening his mouth and jutting out his chin as he listens.

The children also attempt to assuage their mother's anxiety (and likely their own) by offering solutions to a story's problematic event. As we have seen, Meg raises a number of unresolved, anxiety-provoking problems related to encountering pit bulls. Although these concerns are primarily directed to William, it is the children who are most responsive. For example, when Meg begins to ponder,

I couldn't help but wonder what would happen if you know—

William preempts Meg's formulation of the problem by offering a consequence of what he imagines she's wondering. He concludes,

They'd be in big trouble.

Meg, however, goes on to complete her formulation of "what would happen," adding,

> if he really did get into your dad's yard.

At this point the children collaboratively construct a solution to their mother's expressed concern. Beth proposes,

> *I'd* call the pound.

and Sean enthusiastically concurs,

> Me too . . . to come get him.

In proposing solutions, Beth and Sean attempt to show that they are capable of handling such enduring problems. Meg, however, along with William, negates the efficacy of these solutions. In so doing, the parents undermine the children's efficacy as agents. Meg quickly rejects the viability of calling the pound as a solution, reinforcing the inevitability of harm. Looking first at William and then at Beth, she says,

> Well the problem is, you can't report them until they actually *harm* somebody. But by then it's too *late*.

After Meg renders this judgment, Sean turns to his father, who in turn affirms Meg's position ("Yeah"). This family interaction demonstrates how parents may collaboratively undermine their children's sense of control.

Analyses of storytelling at dinnertime show how children and parents construct and inhabit perilous, uncontrollable worlds that extend from the past into the present and future. In the Logan family, when past problems are given story form, their telling often kindles present anxieties about future experiences, which precipitate the support of the children as co-authors of insoluble predicaments. As we observe these children offering candidate solutions to stave off mounting distress, we are reminded of the little Dutch boy who notices a hole in a dam and sticks his thumb in it to stave off a flood that threatens his community. Like the boy whose thumb becomes stuck in the dam, the children become mired when their solutions are deemed inadequate. These interactions socialize not only a view of the vulnerable individual in the uncontrollable world but the psychological and communicative processes through which this view can be sustained and reinforced.

Child Portrays a Protagonist Out of Control

Although children of both sexes are affected by parental anxiety, girls are most likely to develop agoraphobia as adults. At the time of our study, Beth shared some of her mother's difficulties with anxiety, particularly anxiety about separating from other members of her family.[1]

The stories Beth tells about her life experiences often parallel Meg's accounts of distressing events. Beth depicts herself as carrying out actions and experiencing emotions without reason and as the innocent victim of others' aggressive acts. Just as Meg describes her panic as coming on "all of a sudden" or "unaccountably," Beth draws on a similar set of grammatical forms, including "for some reason" and "just," in building narratives of inexplicable emotions and actions. In telling a story about her baby doll, for example, Beth describes strong feelings coming on "for some reason":

I— for some reason I would like love her for a while . . . and then I'd get *mad* at her and I'd put her in the closet— I'd *lock* her in the closet.

Later in the story, Beth uses "just" to convey her impenetrable emotions and actions:

It was the only doll I ever really hated.

Lisa asks, "Do you remember why you hated her?" And Beth replies,

No. I'd just get *mad* at her. I'd go, "Shut up! Be Quiet!" And I'd shake her . . . I'd just go "Be Quiet! Be Quiet!" I'd grab her and hold her up, not knowing what to do with her.

In addition to using "for some reason" and "just," Beth laces her narratives with indirect and rhetorical questions to which the answers are beyond her reach. In talking about her doll, for example, Beth remarks,

> I don't know *why* I used to hate that doll that talks though. She was *expensive* too.

In formulating these questions Beth emphasizes not only that she cannot account for such feelings and actions, but that she is engaged in wondering why. This self-reflective stance mirrors Meg's prolific use of mental verb constructions such as "I couldn't help but wonder." In the clinical literature, as well as in Meg's narrative accounts, one of the hallmark features of agoraphobia is a preoccupation with feelings one cannot explain or control.

Meg's contributions to stories that feature Beth as a protagonist may also reinforce and even augment a view of people in general, and Beth in particular, as lacking control over their emotions and actions. In telling about her frightening encounter with a boy with a shaved head, for example, Beth frequently uses grammatical forms that emphasize the inexplicability of her feelings and actions. Beth draws on phrases and words such as "for some reason" and "just" to imbue her rendition of this experience with a sense of bewilderment:

> For some *reason*, it just scared me.

Throughout this account, Beth also ponders the source of this boy's behavior and of her own fear at the sight of him. Why would anyone shave his head? Why did I feel that way? But she does not come up with answers to these questions. After much deliberation, at the end of this lengthy story, Beth turns to her mother for help:

> Why would anyone do that?

Meg at first laughs and then offers the following response:

> I don't know.

Meg's response perpetuates Beth's wondering and aligns their world views. Together Meg and Beth construct the perspective that people behave in ways that are incomprehensible.

Alternatively, Meg's narrative contributions may socialize Beth into a view of the world as uncontrollable by constructing a fatalistic Weltanschaaung. In this Weltanschaaung people's actions and emotions are determined by either (1) generic properties of human behavior or (2) enduring character traits of individuals. Meg frames such properties and traits as absolute, thereby negating individual responsibility and influence. In responding to narrative predicaments, Meg often appeals to fate as a categorical explanation for circumstances rather than to individual agency or will. No one is at fault; this is the way things are. Further, no one can do anything to control circumstances.

Meg's generic explanations routinely make use of a set of linguistic forms that includes universal and inclusive quantifiers, such as "everybody" and "most"; normalizing adjectives, such as "natural" and "normal" ("it seems very natural"); and phrases that presuppose a generic kind of day or time of life ("these days," "those days," "at that age"). When Beth portrays herself as liking to lay down her Tiny Tears doll (not, incidentally, the doll she hated) and watch the pee leak out of her, for example, she frames her behavior as bewildering, even to her. Meg responds by offering a normative, generic explanation. Beth describes what used to happen:

> I'd lay her down and I— I didn't for some reason— I didn't— I didn't— (.3 pause) I'd take off her clothes.

Meg starts to say something but Beth continues along the same path, laughing nervously at the end of her account:

> So I could watch her pee. And I'd just feed her, and I'd watch it come out. (.3 pause) And it was funny (laughs).

Meg at first tells Beth that she is silly. Beth agrees, and continues to laugh, yet does not stop wondering why she did these things:

I know I am (laughs). I'm weird. I don't know *why* I did that when I was little. I'd take off her dress, and lay her on the towel, and go get her bottle.

Before Beth completes this thought, Meg comes in with a generic rationale for Beth's conduct:

I think— (.3 pause) I think *most* kids do that. They like to *see*.

On other occasions Meg takes an alternative tack when Beth describes experiencing and acting out inexplicable anger toward a doll. Meg responds with explanations that attribute her behavior to enduring psychological traits:

I didn't know you had these sadistic tendencies.

And, albeit laughingly, Meg recasts Beth's behavior as potentially transferable to a more extreme case:

Well I think it was a good thing you had her. If you had a baby sister or something you might have beaten up on her instead (laughs).

Meg reframes this story about Beth's unaccountable aggressive acts in a way that links Beth's behavior with an unbridled, enduring character trait, the expression of which is both inevitable and uncontrollable.

By appealing to enduring conditions or human character traits, Meg builds explanations that simultaneously suggest lack of culpability and lack of control. In the interactions we have tracked so far, Meg relates such conditions and traits to Beth's actions and feelings. She portrays Beth as like "most kids" or as having lasting "tendencies," which are difficult to control in particular situations.

Meg's narrative reframes also characterize the actions and feelings of *other* persons as inevitable, particularly the behaviors of persons Beth identifies as her persecutors. When Beth describes a boy who "ended up being a jerk," for example, Meg offers a generic overview justification:

He had a hard life. There were a lot of kids in that complex that didn't have dads.

Beth responds by reiterating her negative appraisal:

He ended up being a jerk.

But Meg also sticks to her ground, augmenting her normative explanation:

He was only five or so. Five-year-old boys can be kind of jerky anyway.

Beth and Meg go back and forth, disagreeing with each other in this way. Beth emphatically insists,

No. I mean he was a *jerk.*

Then Meg begins to challenge Beth's memory of her relationship:

You think so? For a while there you used to get . . .

As the story unfolds, Beth eventually backs down and agrees that the boy was not a jerk at five years of age. But she insists that he did become a jerk at an older age. This time she provides circumstantial evidence to support her claim and, adopting Meg's strategy, questions her mother's memory of past events:

Actually he was a *jerk* when we moved *out.* Don't you remember? He said some nasty words.

At this point, Meg renews the generic explanation she had previously offered to account for this child's conduct:

Well *again* (.3 pause) that's because he doesn't have— didn't have real good leadership in his home not having a daddy.

In the end Meg and Beth finally come to a truce, as Beth portrays this boy's brother in a positive light:

His *brother* was nice though. He was shy. He liked basketball.

Meg and Beth take off in a new direction, remembering how they invited the brother over to their house to play.

In other cases, Meg responds to Beth's tales of her aggressors by proposing hypothetical generic explanations for their behavior. Beth often joins Meg in building these accounts. In telling a story about being bullied by a girl at school, for example, Beth collaborates with Meg in constructing a hypothetical general rationale for the girl's behavior. Meg begins,

> So she's a little older maybe she was held back . . . That could make her especially sensitive or uh (.3 pause) You know—

Beth confirms this generalization, "Yeah." Meg continues her point:

> To think that somebody is doing better than her.

Beth again agrees. Meg goes on to point out some general properties of Beth's status that might make the girl unhappy, such as her grade level. Meg and Beth then conclude that Beth did nothing to provoke the girl's behavior toward her, rendering Beth innocent yet helpless—a description that forms the core of Meg's emotional self-portrait. Meg comments,

> I don't think it was anything you *did*. It was just—

At this point, Beth completes this explanation by supplying an enduring condition:

> being *me*.

And her mother quietly affirms,

> Yeah.

This type of exchange, in which one person begins to articulate a thought and another completes it, is common in interactions between intimate members in mainstream American society.[2] Husbands and wives, parents and children, and close friends may collaboratively construct an idea in this way. These collaboratively built judgments provide an important means of building world views of selves and others.

In their storytelling interactions, Meg and Beth construct a view of the world in which people are victims of their own and others' uncontrollable emotions and the actions they inspire. This world view is instantiated and socialized not only through Meg's appeals to enduring circumstances and generic conditions as a warrant for unprovoked actions and emotions, but through her repeated and persistent use of the question "Why," particularly in relation to story events Beth has deemed inexplicable. Throughout storytelling interactions that involve Beth's victimizing and victimization, Meg directly elicits reasons from Beth (for example, "Why do you think these people's parents did this to these two girls?"). Similarly, she suggests that Beth must wonder why she was delivering or receiving such treatment ("Didn't you wonder why she was being so mean to you?"). And she articulates these questions herself ("I wonder why?"). As noted earlier, Beth also repeatedly poses such questions to herself and Meg. The question "Why?" plays a salient role in collaborative storytelling at dinnertime as well. In these interactions, such questions simultaneously mark the importance of knowing why and the inevitable conclusion that "it was nothing you did." Whether constructed by Meg and Beth or the entire family, these narrative renditions typically attribute actions and emotions to preexisting characteristics of the person or situation.

Paradoxically, categorical attributions can be seen as an effort on Meg's part to exert control by limiting the unforeseen, unpredictable aspect of life events, a most extreme case being her own experiences of panic. Her appeals to categorical explanations supply an answer to the question "why me?" that both mitigates the responsibility of the victim and casts her plight as not unique but pandemic. Yet by reinforcing the notion that nothing could have been done, or can be done, to stave off victimization, this narrative reframing further cements the individual's vulnerable position in an uncontrollable world.

Categorical attributions are similar to the label of agoraphobia in that both circumvent the execution and negate the utility of particular communicative responses to particular situations. Such reframing, though perhaps intended to protect Meg's children from future devastation in the face of inevitable uncontrollable negative experiences, undermines the child's sense of control by casting her as a potential victim of enduring conditions of life, which neither she nor anybody else has hope of overcoming. Through participation in these storytelling interactions, children not only develop interpretations of particular events but, more enduringly, are socialized into a particular way of experiencing themselves and others in the world.

Child Portrays a Protagonist in Control

When Meg narrates distressing situations, her children, especially Beth, often offer strategies for controlling similar situations. We have seen, for example, how Beth and Sean provide solutions to the threat of the pit bulls in the first pit bull storytelling by suggesting that they call the pound to capture the hypothetical pit bull on the loose. We have also seen how both parents may subsequently weaken these acts of control by pointing out their loopholes. Meg displays similar responses in narrating with Beth when Beth frames herself as a capable agent acting in some past distressing circumstance: Meg frequently reframes these narrated events in ways that undermine Beth's control as protagonist.

One way Meg does this is by casting doubt on the credibility of Beth's memory of the story events and on her legitimacy as narrator by suggesting that she does not recall an event well. When Beth introduces a story about how she managed to stop taking the ski lessons she despised, for example, Meg remarks,

Boy this is ancient history. I— I don't remember.

Similarly, Meg states that she cannot remember a story Beth tells about being chased by her uncle during a camping trip:

Meg: I don't remember that.
Beth: *I do.* (laughs)
Meg: You do?
Beth: Um-hm

Meg: I don't remember that.
Beth: He was chasing us. And he came, and he goes *"Rrrr!"*
Lisa: Oh
Beth: And we're under the *blanket*, and we're all peeking out.
Meg: I don't remember that. I think I've heard—

These storytelling interactions undermine Beth's attempts to construct herself as a capable protagonist and ultimately render her as a somewhat unreliable narrator.

In addition to challenging Beth's memory of an incident, Meg recasts Beth's portrayal of the threatening circumstances she has overcome as nonthreatening. In judging the incident to be nonthreatening, Meg portrays Beth as not truly surmounting danger. Meg revoices Beth's accounts of serious threats as "pretend" or "teasing," for example, and thereby not only challenges Beth's portrait of herself as overcoming negative circumstances but suggests that she misread the situation in the first place.

Meg also reframes threatening incidents as nonthreatening by trying to elicit Beth's sympathy toward her tormentor. When Beth portrays a protagonist as menacing, Meg often portrays the same protagonist as an object to be pitied rather than feared. In the narrative about the boy with a shaved head, for instance, Beth describes herself as terrified at first, but then as overcoming her fear of this person:

And I ran away from him. And it was just *funny*. (.3 pause) I turned around and started *laughing* because I realized he was just a kid.

Meg responds by suggesting that the boy may have been undergoing treatment for cancer, thus casting him as vulnerable rather than frightening. Meg at first queries,

Do you think he really did shave his hair off?

Meg's question steers the conversation off the topic of Beth's accomplishment. Veering from her account of realizing she had no cause for fear, Beth admits,

I don't know.

Meg continues,

> Maybe he had cancer treatment or something, you know how some
> kids go through?

Beth resists this point of view, however, and pursues her earlier charac-
terization of this boy, this time supplying evidence:

> No. It looked like it was *shaved*, because he had something weird
> around here.

Beth enacts her claim by circling the side of her head with her index
finger.

During other storytelling episodes, Meg responds to Beth's accounts
of herself as capable of overcoming problems not by challenging the
existence of a threat entirely, but by limiting the extent of the distressing circumstances. When Beth describes obtaining assistance after
being attacked by a bully who "bites, kicks, scratches, and punches," for
example, Meg narrows the physical and temporal scope of the threat.
She first asserts that he "does not bite," then deems such attacks rare,
and goes on to provide counterexamples of the bully's sociability.

Meg also scales back the severity of a problem that Beth handled during a family ski trip. Throughout this story, Beth portrays herself as
overcoming the entirely negative experience of her ski lessons by refusing to continue:

> Dad had signed me up for these skiing lessons and I *hated* them . . .
> I went, "Well I don't *want* to *learn*." It's like, "I *hate* this!" . . . And
> I hated S'mores, and I thought that the hot cocoa tasted awful. So
> I *sat* there and went, "I'm not going to eat this!" I told Dad I was
> *mad*, and I didn't want to have these stupid lessons . . . "I can ski
> with *you*. I don't want to— (.3 pause) I don't want to take these *dumb*
> *lessons*."(.3 pause) So that's what I ended up doing . . . He would he
> would hold me in front of him and get me by the shoulders and
> around the waist and we'd ski down the hill.

Throughout the Ski Lessons storytelling, Meg mitigates Beth's account of the situation. Upon hearing Beth's negative appraisal of the marsh-mallow and chocolate S'mores, Meg offers a challenge and laughs:

That doesn't sound like such a cruel punishment (laughs).

She also implies that Beth was too little at the time to pass judgment on the lessons. In a series of responses to Beth's negative comments, she points out, "Well you were pretty little" and "Yeah you were *real* little. You were only like three."

In addition to challenging Beth's memory of story events, recasting threats as benign, and mitigating the intensity of distressful circumstances, Meg undermines Beth as a capable agent by attributing the resolution of a negative circumstance to a protagonist other than Beth. In the story of the ski lessons, for example, Meg attributes the end of Beth's dreaded lessons not to Beth's actions but to a parental decision. At the close of the story, Meg concludes,

You didn't have to go back after that.

In using the modal auxiliary "have to," Meg frames the achievement of Beth's goal as a consequence of forces outside Beth's agency and voli-tion.

Similarly, in another storytelling interaction, Beth recounts how she squarely confronted a girl who was bullying her in chorus:

And I would *tell* her, "I'm not going to *take* it."

She adds that she obtained assistance in handling the matter from the vice principal:

Finally I had to take it to the principal, and he had to have a *talk* with her.

Meg, in contrast, reframes the cessation of the girl's actions as a product of the vice principal's agency. Moreover, Meg portrays Beth not as a hero but as culpable, along with the bully. She says of the vice principal:

Actually he had you both in there talking.

But Meg does not always undermine Beth's control as a protagonist and teller. We now turn to moments when Meg does acknowledge Beth's success in controlling a bad situation. While Meg displays pride in some of these moments, at times she recasts Meg's controlling moves in a negative light. This is particularly true when Beth portrays herself as controlling a difficult situation by communicating her negative feelings to others. Each time Beth reports directly expressing her anger or distress, Meg renders this conduct embarrassing. In telling the story about her ski lessons, for example, Beth reports that she handled her problem by clearly articulating her negative feelings ("I told Dad I was *mad.* And I didn't want to have these stupid lessons"). Meg and Lisa respond to this portrayal in diametrically opposite ways:

Meg: She's always spoken her mind.
Beth: (laughs)
Lisa: That's great.

In contrast to Lisa's "That's great," Meg deems this communicative act to be the sign of a somewhat disagreeable trait, Beth's outspokenness. Albeit less potent, this stance is reminiscent of Meg's evaluations of moments when she herself confronts others with her negative feelings in the throes of a panic attack, which she portrays as the "beginning of the end." Meg's narratives render both her own and Beth's outbursts as inappropriate, if not emblematic of a character flaw.

As a coda to this story, both Beth and Meg point out to Lisa that Beth can no longer go on skiing trips because she has developed an allergy to cold climates. In harmony, they collaboratively construct this outcome:

Beth: Nowadays I wouldn't survive in *any* cold.
Lisa: No?
Beth: I'm allergic to the cold. (.3 pause) I get a *rash.*
Meg: She does.
Beth: I break out.
Meg: Her skin gets sort of blotchy *red* when she gets cold. Isn't that *weird?*

In this interaction, Beth and Meg forge a possible link between outspokenness and persistent negative consequences. They construct a pathological ("Isn't that weird?"), enduring condition that warrants Beth's avoidance of any cold place.

The story they collaboratively construct about Beth's ski lessons bears a remarkable resemblance to the plot structure of Meg's panic attack stories. First, in both cases, the protagonist feels she must engage in an activity in which she does not want to participate. For example, note how Beth describes being roped into taking ski lessons:

I had to take those ski lessons.

She says, "I had to," not "I wanted to." Similarly, later in the story she makes clear whose idea motivated this activity:

Dad had signed me up for these skiing lessons.

Second, in both stories the protagonist experiences heightened frustration in participating in an unwanted activity. Beth repeatedly comments on how much she hated these lessons, even the snacks. Third, in their respective roles as protagonists in the Ski Lessons story and in the panic attack stories, Beth and Meg vent strong negative feelings toward those who proposed the activity in the first place: Beth tells her dad and Meg tells her husband. Finally, the coda to Beth's Ski Lessons story parallels the eventual outcome of Meg's panic attack stories. In both sets of narratives, the protagonist is seen as developing a debilitating medical condition. In each case, the condition is associated with a physical property of the world: Beth's condition is narratively linked to cold temperature and Meg's condition is tied to locations distant from home. In turn, these associations and medical conditions are seen as precluding the protagonist's participation in any future activities that take place in the physical settings in which they arose.

In all of these ways, Meg's children join her in constructing treacherous, uncontrollable worlds. In their roles as protagonists and co-tellers, Beth and Sean participate in storytelling interactions that may socialize anxiety: sometimes by validating Meg's recurrent, often frantic assertions that her and her children's distress is a fundamental property of life on this planet; sometimes by searching for solutions, only to find them dashed; sometimes by offering up for family approbation parallel portrayals of themselves as victims of indiscriminate actions and uncontrollable emotions; and sometimes by offering portrayals of themselves as competent problem solvers, only to find themselves recast as protagonists who are either not truly in control of the situation or in control but rude. Meg's contributions to the stories are likely designed to protect her children from future devastation in the face of uncontrollable negative experiences—experiences she deems inevitable. As we have seen, however, these storytelling interactions may unwittingly undermine Beth's and Sean's sense of control by implying that even if they overcome a particular trial, the world in general cannot be controlled. Particularly for children, such interactions give rise to emotions that endure long after the stories end. Joyce Carol Oates reminds us, "It is the early formative years and the enclosure of the family that provide the encoded pain, violence, and loneliness, or the well of security, love, and possibility, that feed the imagination . . . anything else could go and you'd still have that; you'd still have this great reservoir of emotion."

11

Therapeutic Insights

For the real question is whether the "brighter future" is
really always so distant. What if, on the contrary, it has
been here for a long time already, and only our own
blindness has prevented us from seeing it around us and
within us, and kept us from developing it?

—Václav Havel 1987

When people seek therapy, they have a story to tell. For Meg, and
perhaps others, the story is one of inexplicable, unforeseen experiences
that undermine her sense of well-being and self-satisfaction and her
knowledge of how the world is or ought to be. Meg explains her decision to enter therapy:

And finally, after the Big Mama, when my agoraphobia had gotten
to the point where it was completely unmanageable I started seeing
a therapist. I had tried talking to the pastor and the pastor's wife.
I'd prayed about it, you know that things would get better for me—
that I'd be back to my old self again . . . It just got to the point
where I was *beside* myself. I didn't know what to do, or what to
think, really. Nothing made sense. I'd try to figure out why this was
happening to me. You know, maybe it was a test, or maybe there
was a purpose. But it just didn't make sense, you know? I just
couldn't understand *why*. You know why these things were happening to *me*. And my agoraphobia seemed to be getting worse and
worse . . . I guess I'm not entirely sure, but I think it's helped. I

173

think I've learned a lot about myself. Maybe it's just having someone to talk to who understands.

At the time of the study, Meg had been seeking counsel from a local
psychotherapist for three years. Lisa assumed the role of participant ob-
server rather than therapist throughout her visits to the Logan home,
during which Lisa recorded Meg's tales of panic experience and her everyday interactions with family members. We now explore the relevance of our analysis of Meg's narratives of anxious experiences to therapeutic interactions. Although our study applies to the construction of
emotions, actions, and identities in any environment, it may be most
relevant to those interested in understanding psychological disorders,
particularly panic and agoraphobia.

How might insights into the grammatical and discursive shaping of
life stories enhance therapeutic encounters? Although we locate our approach within the discussion of narrative therapies, we are by no means
proposing a new form of psychotherapy. Further, we are not implying
that this book will sufficiently equip readers to carry out the depth of
analysis demonstrated herein. We offer this study of Meg's stories as an
example of what can be done when psychologists and discourse analysts
work together to mine the architecture of sufferers' stories for their understanding of their experiences. We encourage psychotherapists to explore linguistic perspectives through cross-disciplinary collaboration
and training. At the same time we encourage linguists to work with clinicians to develop more acute understandings of the interface of language and emotion.

Psychotherapy as Narrative

From its inception as a profession, psychotherapy has been closely
linked to narrative analysis. Since the time of Freud, psychologists have
published case studies of individuals, connecting events, physiological
conditions, and emotions within paradigms of the human condition.[1]
Freud wrote that "clinical psychiatry troubles itself little about the actual form of the individual symptom or the content of it; but that psy-

cho-analysis has made this its starting point, and has ascertained that the symptom itself has a meaning and is connected with experience in the life of the patient."[2]

More recently, clinicians from diverse theoretical backgrounds have renewed interest in the relation of narrative to therapy by visualizing, in a postmodern framework, therapy as discourse, in particular narrative discourse. In this perspective, psychotherapy is a process through which individuals and families tell and revise their life stories. This orientation is pursued by both family therapists[3] and psychoanalysts[4] who view therapy as the collaborative reauthoring of lives and relationships. These conceptualizations are grounded in the postmodern notion that we create meaning as we narrate our lives with others. Every time we tell a story, we create for ourselves and for others one or more versions of experience. Each version we present brings to life a view of ourselves and others in our world that carries us into the future. All human beings are guided by the stories they construct. Unfortunately, people often construct stories that seriously impair their ability to cope with circumstances, events, and relationships. Some of us tell story versions that oppress us (and perhaps others as well); others of us generate versions that lack coherence.

Events in our lives that are consistent with what we believe to be true about ourselves and the world can be easily talked about and seamlessly integrated into our life story. Many experiences, however, are more difficult to resolve narratively because they do not easily fit, or may even contradict, the identities and world views we wish to maintain. Indeed such episodes may not receive a narrative voice until they can be integrated in a way that preserves the coherence of our ongoing narrative. Meg, for example, in describing her panic experiences to Lisa during one of their first conversations, comments,

It's sort of strange talking about these things, you know? I mean it took me quite a while to even begin to put it into words for other people, you know people who hadn't experienced panic themselves, because these *attacks* or whatever you want to call them were so strange.

Incomplete stories, stories that omit or fragment certain life experiences, and stories that resist articulation do not allow tellers to move on. Unincorporated, often distressing life experiences and the emotions they evoke remain an active threat to well-being. This is most dramatically apparent among sufferers of Post-Traumatic Stress Disorder, who, until they are able to work through traumatic events, are plagued by flashbacks—intrusive fragmented memories—that wreak havoc in their lives.[5]

Therapy provides the opportunity to develop alternative versions of stories. By telling and retelling experiences in therapy, clients and therapists collaboratively develop stories that create new understandings. Therapeutic storytelling generates insights that allow individuals to incorporate elements that, in Meg's words, "just don't make sense." These stories convey a revised view of self and others that not only reshapes the past but creates new paths for the future. The psychoanalyst Roy Schafer goes so far as to say that "so-called self-concepts, self-images, self-representations, or more generally the so-called self may be considered to be a set of narrative strategies or story lines each person follows in trying to develop an emotionally coherent account of his or her life among people."[6]

Client and Therapist as Co-Authors

Therapy is a dialogic process in which client and therapist collaboratively construct an emergent story.[7] Moment by moment, session by session, client and therapist co-author a series of successive versions of the client's life story. Life stories are not delivered *to* the therapist. Rather they evolve out of the client's and therapist's interpenetrating contributions. Even psychoanalysts, who may remain silent for much of the time, are engaging in dialogue with their patients; their silences as well as their utterances play a large part in the story that unfolds.

Therapists employ differing interpretive principles in their roles as co-authors. Therapeutic theories, whether behavioral, cognitive, humanistic, psychodynamic, structural, or systemic, contain story lines or master narratives about the locus of psychological disturbances (within the individual or a system) and their appropriate treatment. Well-developed, scientifically based narratives of the human psyche shape the stories initiated by clients. Therapists accentuate certain features of client-initiated narratives while relegating others to the background. The psychoanalyst Donald Spence comments,

> The therapist is constantly making decisions about the form and status of the patient's material. Specific listening conventions . . . help guide these decisions. If, for example, the therapist assumes that contiguity indicates causality, then he will hear a sequence of disconnected statements as a causal chain . . . If he assumes that the transference predominates and that the patient is always talking in more or less disguised fashion about the analyst, then he will 'hear' the material in that way and make some kind of ongoing evaluation of the state of the transference.[8]

From this vantage point, the therapeutic process involves a blending of the client's story with a story line adopted by the therapist. In therapy, the client's account may be reworked by the psychoanalyst into a tale of family romance, by the cognitive behaviorist into a struggle to overcome catastrophic thinking, and by the Rogerian into a battle against conditional regard, and so on.[9]

These interpretive frames can powerfully influence how people recall experiences in their lives. The psychologist Carol Feldman and her colleagues have studied how people who hear different story versions of a set of events—for example, one that emphasizes actions and another that emphasizes mental activity—recall different story elements. When tellers of different versions stop midway through the story and ask, "What do you think will happen next, and why?" their listeners make different predictions and different causal attributions.[10] Similarly, the co-telling of story versions in therapy can lead clients to differing logics of events, each of which affects their expectations about the future course of their lives.

Linguistic Tools

Because narratives form the core of therapeutic interactions, therapists and clients are in a position to capture clients' own theories of their experiences. Narratives that emerge in therapeutic interactions with persons with agoraphobia, for example, provide access to sufferers' multiple perspectives on panic experiences. However, although therapists rely on narrative accounts to formulate interpretations and derive clinical impressions, they tend not to focus on how clients build their own theories through grammatical and discursive structuring. As a result, therapists miss meaningful aspects of the way a sufferer represents and maintains his or her predicament. Grammatical forms fly by and are easily forgotten. Subtle links that the narrator may forge among narrative settings, problematic initiating events, psychological responses, attempts to resolve the problem, and their consequences are impossible to capture on one hearing.

Similarly, studies designed to gain insight into psychological dispositions based on narratives told in psychotherapy tend to rely on therapists' case notes. Though efficient given the exigencies of clinical work, such notes generally represent therapists' clinical impressions. In this sense they constitute impoverished accounts of what clients say and understand. Studies based on therapists' case notes do not have access to the multiplicity of self-understandings conveyed in the clients' own tellings. Although clinical impressions and case notes are a vital part of therapeutic practice, they are insufficient tools for positing claims about client awareness. By considering grammar and discourse—story structure as well as story content—therapists and researchers gain access into clients' sense of themselves and others.

Recently, interest in constructivist approaches to psychotherapy has spawned various narrative therapies. Grounded in the view that people construct themselves through language, these therapies promote attention to narrative and the dynamics of therapist-client co-authorship.[11] By and large, however, these constructivist approaches do not involve delineating how narratives are constructed. How exactly do narrators build settings and events and psychological demeanors? What linguistic resources do they habitually draw on to build narrative portraits and emotional landscapes? How do these narrative practices evolve over the course of a single therapeutic encounter? Over a series of encounters? The theoretical underpinnings of a constructivist perspective have been championed, but analytic methodology lags behind.[12]

Most constructivist therapies concentrate on revising narrative content. The family therapists Michael White and David Epston, for example, suggest that clients' agency and problem-solving ability can be enhanced in therapy by listening to their narratives of personal experiences, identifying "problem-saturated" descriptions, and redrafting the narratives in ways that relocate the problem in external circumstances rather than within themselves. White and Epston also propose that clients might benefit from audio-recording and relistening to alternative versions of problem-saturated stories, versions they call "success" stories.[13]

These undertakings do not involve sufferers in identifying habitual linguistic forms and discourse patterns that actualize debilitating portraits. To what extent can we change our life stories (and our lives) without accessing their formation—the rudimentary linguistic tools that we use to construct them? Substituting narratives of success for problem-saturated narratives may alleviate distress, and substitute versions may even provide a positive model for the interpretation of ongoing experience. Yet sufferers may not be able to sustain these models in their future lives when they tell stories to themselves and others. A missing piece of this therapeutic enterprise may well be apprenticeship into a "grammar of success." Ultimately, to paint a desired portrait, a narrator needs to recognize the properties of the paints on her communicative palette—those she habitually selects and alternatives within her reach. Narrators need to distinguish the emotional hues and textures rendered by particular linguistic forms—those that debilitate and those that empower. The apprentice teller learns how to apply these symbolic materials in varied combinations, with different strokes, to craft a phrase, an episode, a story, a life. The therapeutic translation of this apprenticeship awaits realization, but holds great promise.

Toward this end, Schafer articulates the importance of revising one's life story to place individual agency in the foreground.[14] He proposes a new "language for psychoanalysis," which emphasizes action. Schafer suggests that in the course of analysis, the patient learns to construct narratives of personal agency more readily, independently, convincingly, and securely as she linguistically shifts from a passive to an active stance.[15] This perspective highlights the significance of reflexive awareness of modes of talk and suggests that to change, we need to understand how we use language strategically, and sometimes irresponsibly, to shape our subjective experience.

Therapeutic dialogue about the grammatical and discursive practices a client habitually uses has the potential to empower the client as storyteller and as an ongoing protagonist in her life experiences. Analyzing narratives in terms of how tellers routinely link settings to more dramatic events can heighten awareness of hidden story lines that clash with more dramatic elements of a tale, revealing latent theories of events. Engaging in such dialogue invites tellers to identify master story plots that run through their stories. Similarly, analyses of the grammatical resources that tellers habitually rely on in crafting these narratives illuminates the fabric of their emotional worlds. Dialogue about linguistic practices may also illuminate alternative forms for constructing alternative emotional worlds, worlds that may be inaccessible to sufferers at the time of the telling.

Here we elaborate methods we have used in analyzing Meg's narratives that can be applied to illuminate other narratives as well. In retracing our steps, we point out that the discursive and grammatical forms prominent in Meg's panic narratives may characterize those of other sufferers and may play pivotal roles in constructing psychological dispositions other than agoraphobia. The ubiquity of these practices, however, remains open to investigation.

Relistening

The foundation for exploring narrative practices is listening to recordings of storytelling interactions between clients and therapists and/or clients with others. As noted earlier, the spoken word is ephemeral and difficult to recall if not to reproduce. An audiotape or, better yet, a videotape allows the therapist and the client to (re)listen to selected passages and stories.[16] This activity allows persons to review how they construct life experiences.

Collaborative relistening to story versions may be as important a therapeutic tool as collaborative retellings. In Sumerian the word for "ear" and for "wisdom" is the same: the ear, which is located mostly internally and is coiled like a spiral or labyrinth, takes in sound to transform the imperceptible into meaning.[17]

Relistening to a story is akin to viewing a film of one's everyday conduct. Both undertakings bring habits of action and feeling into focused awareness. When we slow down the film to view our expressions and our movements through physical space, we see emotions and motions that are otherwise invisible to us. The film allows us to attend, frame by frame, to the unfolding construction of each posture our bodies take, each flicker of emotion that crosses our faces. Relistening to a story utterance by utterance allows us to focus on the unfolding construction of symbols that we use in building the plots and characters that give shape to our lives.

Guided by one who is skilled in discourse analysis, clients can journey through their own stories and can formulate understandings of how they relate events and emotions and how they represent themselves. Meg, for example, might see in her stories *how* she constructs theories about her panic experiences, and she may gain insights by considering the theories that her stories hold. Meg's narratives might compel her— as they do us—to consider interpersonal dynamics before, during, and after panic sets in. Regardless of the nature of the insights that are gained, this therapeutic endeavor gives prominence to tellers' expertise as interpreters and theory builders. Although both therapists and clients have theories, at the start of therapy those of the therapist may be more accessible and explicit. Such asymmetry may exacerbate the client's sense that she doesn't understand herself. When provided with the tools of linguistic analysis, however, the client-turned-narrative-analyst becomes an authority.

Discursive Structuring

Once client and therapist are relistening to stories of perplexing experiences in the client's life, there are two planes of linguistic structure they might choose to explore: discourse and grammar. We turn first to the discursive structuring of storytelling.

Any story can be examined for its basic story structure. Stories told spontaneously often do not come out in smooth blocks, with one element logically flowing from another. Rather, stories that are difficult to tell or have never been told before unfold unevenly, with restarts and flashbacks and addendums. These qualities characterize not only stories about traumatic experiences such as panic—stories of the sort that emerge in therapeutic settings—but informal storytelling between friends and family as well. Most people, most of the time, tell stories not as a performance or an entertainment, but to seek advice or empathy about something that has happened to them. This process takes time. Sometimes important story elements are illuminated only after considerable talk with other people. Others not only ask questions but provide basic information, offer novel perspectives, and elaborate on story events, sometimes confirming and sometimes challenging a position put forward.[18]

Minimally, stories contain a sequence of temporally ordered events. They usually include the following story components:

1. *Setting*—the temporal, spatial and psychological context of events.
2. *Problematic event*—a predicament around which a story episode revolves.
3. *Attempt*—an action designed to resolve a problematic event.
4. *Consequence*—an immediate or enduring effect.
5. *Psychological response*—protagonist's emotional or cognitive stance.

In addition to these story elements, stories told in interactional settings may be punctuated throughout by feedback such as "uh-huh" or "um-hm," which signals attentiveness and encouragement to continue. Stories may be prefaced by a short abstract, which encapsulates the gist of what happened, or terminated with an explicit coda.

The way tellers organize these story elements constructs cause-effect relations between narrated events and emotions. With expertise in discourse analysis, therapists cum linguists can mine these causal relationships with their clients for the tellers' theories about themselves, their emotions, their relationships, and their life events.

Tracing the links of such causal chains may reveal a spiraling of problematic conditions and responses. We have seen in Meg's stories, for example, how a problematic condition (a traffic jam on a freeway) triggers a psychological reaction (panic), which in turn becomes a problem in itself that provokes a series of attempts to bring circumstances back to normal. These attempts fail, fueling more panic, which then gives rise to more confrontational attempts to resolve what is now an intolerable problem. Given the self-perpetuating nature of panic and other forms of psychological distress, it seems likely that other sufferers of agoraphobia and other syndromes might also construct spiraling accounts of perplexing experiences. Yet this remains to be seen.

In telling a distressing story, tellers tend to focus primarily on the central problematic event and the subsequent problems that ensue. Meg, for example, dwells on the panic episode itself to the neglect of other pieces of the story puzzle. This central climactic episode tends to be most memorable for listeners, as well, and most compelling as a topic for further discussion and problem-solving efforts. Rather than being swept up in the dramatic core, therapist and client might profit from a discourse-analytically informed return to the not so captivating portions of a story, namely, to the settings. As we have seen in Meg's tellings, story settings are rushed through, en route to the climax of the story. They may seem insignificant and may not even be noticed on the first hearing. Yet they are vital to unlocking panic. The following two approaches may be helpful in therapeutic encounters.

1. *Notice the degree to which story settings are elaborated.* Does the setting communicate psychological circumstances as well as the time and place of events? Recall that Meg's account of her first panic attack following her thirtieth birthday celebration relates the specifics of time and place but says nothing about her psychological state prior to panicking. Meg's sense of panic as unaccountable is reflected in the absence of this infor-

mation. Yet as she continues to tell such stories, Meg perpetuates the perspective that her panic is irrational. To break such a cycle, it may be useful to discuss the psychological climate prior to the onset of panic. We do not mean to suggest that this is a novel strategy; it is common-place in psychotherapy. A stereotypical therapeutic scenario pictures a client telling a story, and a therapist responding, "What were you feel-ing?" Indeed, being confronted with one's story—including what one did not say—is a powerful experience. Hearing her own words, the cli-ent may be sensitized to the kind of story-world she has built and may develop a more concrete sense of how to rebuild.

2. *Consider possible causal links between settings and distressing psychologi-cal responses.* Where stories do depict psychological circumstances that precede distressing psychological responses, therapist and client can ex-plore possible causal connections. For example, when Meg elaborates her settings, as in the Big Mama story, she articulates extenuating cir-cumstances that provide a rationale for panic. Recall how Meg's panic narratives routinely depict a communicative setting in which she ac-commodates to a proposal despite reservations and then panics. By jux-taposing these story elements, her narratives forge a causal connection between accommodation and panic. But Meg does not fully recognize the connection. She grammatically severs the causal link by announcing that panic came on "unaccountably," "out of the blue," and "for no rea-son." The task of the discourse-minded therapist and client can be to bring to light theories tucked away in those portions of a story that lead up to a distressing episode; and to identify how the hidden theories co-exist and conflict with more dominating and more explicit theories.

Discourse analysis brings new insights to light, insights that may give rise to change. As we saw in Chapter 5, for example, Meg structures her stories in a way that links accommodation and panic. She, like many women, may benefit from therapeutic dialogue about the sources and consequences of the proclivity to accommodate against her wishes and her better judgment. Although all of us wrestle with conflict between our own and others' wishes, women are especially vulnerable to expec-tations to accommodate. Such dialogue might address the importance of acting in one's best interests—that it is possible to express disagreement without rupturing a relationship with a friend or a loved one.[19]

When clients and therapists turn their attention to the psychological circumstances in story settings, they acknowledge the clients' own understandings of their suffering. The client is credited with insights that are reflected in the settings of her stories. She reaps the benefits of perspectives that might otherwise have been overlooked as prefatory details. Narrative validation of what the client knows is particularly important in understanding syndromes such as agoraphobia, given the notion that sufferers lack awareness of the interpersonal dynamics that contribute to panic. On the basis of his clinical practice and research, A. Giovanni Liotti writes,

> It is a widely diffused impression among psychotherapists and researchers, that the onset of agoraphobia may be related to life events that imply changes or expected changes in the network of the patient's affectional bonds . . . Yet many agoraphobics are not aware of the possibility of a relationship between these changes or prospective changes in their life and the appearance of their phobic disturbance, and insist that their distress is the result of some morbid process that could not possibly be related to their personal life.[20]

This conclusion is based on a limited notion of what constitutes awareness. In most studies, awareness is evidenced only by an explicit response to questions about relationships or by responses in paper-and-pencil surveys. Story structure, however, reveals other levels of awareness. Tellers may not have an explicit understanding of the dynamics that contribute to their distress, but they may display an implicit understanding through their structuring of stories. Although she does not explicitly voice this theory, Meg structures her stories in a way that encodes her awareness of problematic communicative dynamics and their connection to her panic. Narrative analysis illuminates such nuances of awareness, articulating the discursive structures that index levels of awareness and the particular insights so indexed.[21]

Grammatical Structuring

Meg's panic narratives, like many tales of distressing experiences, are tragedies. Aristotle described tragedies as poetic imitations of serious actions of magnitude that inspire pity and fear. Meg is a cross between an Aristotelian historian and poet in that she not only tells what happened but also "tells of such things as might happen, things that are possibilities by virtue of being in themselves inevitable or probable."[22] Tragedies involve reversals from one state of affairs to its exact opposite, such as transitions from normal, familiar circumstances to the strange or unexpected, or the passage from a rational state to one of irrational panic. Tragedies involve a protagonist who is essentially a virtuous person, as in Meg's portrayal of herself as self-sacrificing. A tragic heroine, she moves from a state of ignorance to a state of heightened awareness of her tragic situation about which she can do nothing; she suffers helplessly, evoking terror in herself and sympathy from those who hear her tale.

The tone of tragedy, especially the building of a tragic character, is largely achieved through the medium of grammar. Although story structure also builds character, grammar is the poet's essential tool. Story structure provides a blueprint of events that have resonance for protagonists, but grammar brings that blueprint to life by giving color, texture, and intensity to events and the protagonists who move through them.

In therapy, clients dramatize life experiences of varying tragic proportions. While language is the primary vehicle for these dramas, therapists and clients tend to look *through* rather than *at* its form. Informed attention to various relatively basic features of language can enhance existing strategies for apprehending life dramas in the making. We delineate these features to illustrate the potential merit of a linguistic approach. Attending to the form of utterances gets at the foundation of self-representation. Grammatical analysis is not a matter of sentence diagrams or tree structures as we may have learned in elementary school. Grammatical analysis of our own talk brings us into contact with the repertoire of grammatical forms we habitually use to create and re-create who we are.

Although we tend to think of grammar as arbitrary structures, in many ways grammar is iconic of ideas and emotions. Weakness and strength, for example, can be iconically represented by *sentential position*. Subject position gives prominence, whereas object position demotes the force of persons or other entities so represented. Oblique positions, such as indirect objects or objects of prepositions, even more dramatically sublimate the entities. With a grounding in linguistic analysis, client and therapist can focus on a small segment of a story and trace the sentential positions in which clients cast themselves and others. A guiding question might be, "How prominent is the client in different relationships and emotional contexts?"

Concomitant with tracking their sentential posts is the tracking of *semantic roles* protagonists assume. These semantic roles vary in control along a continuum from agent (one who acts on entities) to experiencer (one who feels or thinks), to the roles of patient (entity acted upon by agent) and recipient/goal (endpoint of action or experience). Tracking semantic roles can reveal the degree to which—and the contexts in which—clients portray themselves as agents in control of events and relationships in their lives. In parallel fashion, this process may illuminate the extent to which clients portray themselves as patients controlled by others' actions or as recipients of unwanted feelings and thoughts. More important, this endeavor makes the process of self-construction concrete, rendering it not just an abstract theoretical notion but a grammatical practice. Undesirable selves can be linked to grammatical habits and repertoires, which, with effort, can be modified.[23] In this way, attending to grammar provides a method of penetrating therapy as a reconstructive process.

Another grammatical resource for modulating the relative strength of a protagonist in a story is *ellipsis*, which is grammatically possible deletion of a component of a sentence.[24] In English, for example, it is grammatically possible to omit a large range of grammatical forms, including the would-be subject, for example, "Wonder how they are feeling" versus "I wonder...," or "Hope he's not mad" versus "I hope...." Ellipsis iconicity demotes the referent to the point of invisibility. As delineated in Chapter 4, our analysis of Meg's narratives shows that she favors this grammatical option for (not) representing herself, as when she narrates, "the *feeling* of that fear was so awful," rather than "the *feeling* of that fear was so awful for me." Meg is not alone. Grammatical forms such as ellipsis can be recruited to mitigate agency with respect to any number of emotions or situations. Speakers can avail themselves of ellipsis not only in constructing panic but in building a range of helpless identities.

Furthermore, there are alternative grammatical forms that speakers can use to make themselves or others invisible as participants in experiences. *Nominalizations* are one such invisibilizing tool. Meg, for example, uses a nominalization in the quotation: "the *feeling* of that fear." Alternatively, she could have said "I felt afraid," putting herself in the feeling experience. Likewise, Meg narrates, "And then a feeling of impending *doom*," rather than "I felt impending *doom*."

Paralinguistic features, in particular *intonation* and *voice quality*, also can iconically convey strength and weakness. But in tragic narratives like Meg's stories of panic, the strengthening effect may heighten tragic elements of a scene. This is the case, for instance, when Meg combines emphatic stress and elongation of sounds to strengthen the sense of "impending *doo::m*." Alternatively, speakers may iconically build a self-portrait of weakness by expressing ideas in a hesitating manner. Meg, for example, often delivers accounts of her emotions haltingly, as in the passage, "It's just afrai— just af— just *pure fear*."

Paralinguistic resources for conveying strength and weakness may be supplemented by *intensifying* or *deintensifying* adverbs that either amplify the protagonist's fear or mitigate the protagonist's ability to exert control. Amplifying adverbs include, for example:

"real" (as when Meg states, "I felt real *helpless*")
"really" ("*Mama's* really afraid")
"so" ("I was *so unnerved*")
"pure" ("*pure fear*")

Mitigating adverbs include, among others:

"like" ("Can't you just like get on the shoulder and drive off?")
"kind of" ("That was kinda how I coped with the ski trip")
"sort of" ("if I (.3 pause) do anything to just sort of burn off some of this nervous energy")
"maybe" ("maybe I could get *through* this")

The weakening and strengthening effects achieved through the manner of delivery in concert with (de)intensifying adverbs are similar to those of a class of verbs called *modal verbs*. These verbs depict a speaker's commitment to the truth of a proposition. Modal verbs indicate the extent to which the speaker believes an idea is possible, probable, necessary, or certain. Meg's narratives are replete with such verbs, including, for example:

"can" ("I tend to really believe that I can't go out of town . . .")
"will" (". . . or something terrible will happen")
"must" ("I must say it's pretty uh (.3 pause) tied up now with my identity")
"have to" ("How will I cope with (.3 pause) um just all the things you have to go through being pregnant?")
"got to" ("I told William I've got to get out of here")
"need to" ("if I felt real anxious and needed to leave the office")

Meg, and perhaps other sufferers of panic, habitually uses the modal constructions "have to," "got to," and "need to." These forms frame actions as required by external forces. By using these modals Meg depicts her actions as necessary, even urgent. By using them to describe her actions while in the grip of panic, Meg portrays panic as necessitating her behavior.

Therapists with linguistic training might guide their clients in identifying modals of extrinsic control, stimulating therapeutic dialogue about the consequences—possible payoffs or secondary gain—of using these constructions, and the motives behind them. Clients could be encouraged to imagine or even practice reconstructing their narratives using alternatives that render the client in control of her actions. Meg, for example, might substitute "want to" for "got to" or "need to," as in "I told William I want to get out of here" rather than ". . . I've got to get out of here." These grammatical alternatives are structurally essential in transforming narratives of helplessness into narratives of voluntary action.

Forms that depict actions as unrealized or failed, such as *try constructions* and *negation*, are additional grammatical tools for constructing helplessness. Meg repeatedly narrates her actions as unrealized or thwarted by talking about how she "tried" or "tries" to do something, or "couldn't" or "can't." She uses a try construction, for instance, to narrate her unsuccessful efforts to cope while panicking: "And the more I tried to um (.3 pause) put myself out of mind the harder that was to do." Toward the same end, she uses negation to convey her frustrated intentions to act while anxious: "I can't *leave* I'm nine months preg— almost nine months pregnant. I can't—(.4 pause) If I *wanted* to leave I *couldn't*."

When examined in a therapeutic context, such utterances might invite investigation of how clients portray themselves along a continuum of helplessness and control as they construct different logical worlds. As storytellers, clients depict not only actual worlds but worlds that are hypothetical, worlds that are only imagined. These latter worlds are the "if" worlds, as in "If I *wanted* to leave I *couldn't*." What is striking about the hypothetical worlds in Meg's stories—and what could very well be a hallmark of agoraphobia in addition to depression[25]—is that they are pessimistic. These constructions express improbability, conveyed by the use of a subordinate conjunction with a past tense verb, for example, "If I *wanted* to leave." Speakers use these forms to construct a hypothetical past that is not likely to be realized. In the above example Meg talks about her wishes, but because they are couched as hypothetical past wants, they are rendered unlikely, as if to say "even if I wanted to leave, which I probably didn't really." Examining these hypothetical constructions may enhance therapeutic interactions concerning how clients portray their wants and goals, the worlds in which they cast them, and their (frustrated) attempts to realize them.

Attending to grammar illuminates the construction of particular past, present, and possible worlds. Meg's panic stories, for example, grammatically distinguish irrational from rational worlds. As noted, Meg marks irrationality through *abnormalizing adverbs* (for example, "out of the blue"), *mental verbs* that place Meg outside of herself ("all of a sudden I (.4 pause) uh became aware of feeling (.4 pause) just *anxious* unaccountably") and the *place adverb* "here," which locates Meg in an unfathomable existential predicament ("I felt real *helpless*. I thought, 'here I *am*' "). Along with modal verbs of necessity such as "got to" and "have to," Meg uses these forms to portray the inexplicable loss of control she experiences in the throes of panic. This quality is a sine qua non of the irrational.

The grammatical forms Meg draws on in constructing her irrational experiences may be emblematic of panic narratives more generally. In addition, such forms may appear in narratives of other experiences tellers deem irrational, narratives of the sort that are likely to emerge in therapeutic contexts. In Meg's narratives, however, this irrational state of being often inspires rational attempts to secure her well-being. Attending to the shape of stories can reveal such paradoxes, providing grist for the therapeutic mill.

In narrating panic experiences, Meg portrays herself as having to suffer tremendously before meriting the right to take care of herself. But as in a classic tragedy, the sense of well-being she achieves during such episodes is short-lived and ultimately overshadowed as she brands herself with the label of an enduring disability—agoraphobia.

The Future around and within Us

Václav Havel writes poignantly of our relation to what lies ahead, telling us that the "brighter future" is not as distant as it may appear. Indeed this future has been with us for a long while, only we have not been able to see it. It is "around us and within us"; we have only to discover how to apprehend it.

Meg's words validate this reflection. Her words show us that the knowledge she needs to free herself from panic is around her and within her. With guidance, she can learn from listening to her own stories what she already knows. She can gain access to the insights that are hidden in the discursive architecture and grammatical coloring of her tales. These tales are not new; they have been rehearsed through silent ruminations and publicly voiced. They assume a story line that is worn and familiar and that helps to sustain Meg's psychological state. These stories contain important messages for Meg that hold a promise for a brighter future. Simple identification of these messages is not in itself a panacea. Nor will a change in the architecture of one's stories or in one's grammatical repertoire instantly transform the self. The therapeutic process is complex. We offer these linguistic practices not as a therapeutic alternative but rather as supplemental tools for developing mental health within any paradigm.

Whether the specific hypotheses and conclusions we have drawn apply to sufferers of agoraphobia more generally remains open to future investigation. The method we have used in constructing these generalizations, however, is reproducible to that end. Discourse and grammatical analysis is a rich resource for working with sufferers of psychological disorders such as agoraphobia both to elucidate their self-understandings and, we hope, to inspire changes in their self-construction through language practices.

Epilogue: Flying

Pegasus—so expectantly christened so long ago—is
gone now, yielding his ethereal wings to the realization
of wood and steel ones that fly as high and higher, but,
for all that, are never so buoyant or capable of bearing
such cargoes of hope.

—Beryl Markham, 1942

A few months after the conclusion of this study, Lisa tried to reach Meg
several times to find out about the latest events in her life. She left messages on the Logans' answering machine, but Meg did not return her
calls. This was not like Meg. She usually responded without delay.

Some weeks later Meg did telephone Lisa and made a momentous
announcement:

> I'm so sorry it's taken me so long to call you back. It's just that so
> *much* has happened in my life lately. I'm sorry to say my dad died.
> But I was able to make the trip to Oregon to be with him during his
> last days.

Lisa returned to the Logan home to hear Meg's story. On the way
there Lisa reflected on prior conversations with Meg that illuminated
the significance of Meg's journey. The inability to fly was central to
Meg's definition of herself as agoraphobic:

> I tend to really believe that I can't go out of town or something
> *terrible* will happen, or that— (.3 pause) or that I never *will* be able to
> fly on an airplane again. I guess I do sort of define myself as an

193

agoraphobic. And I don't— (.3 pause) uh I look at other people as normal.

In recounting a past period of remission, the first thing Meg mentions is being able to fly home to see her parents. Similarly, in describing the return of her agoraphobia, Meg focuses on her inability to fly to Oregon, rendering herself a disappointment, if not a disgrace, in her parents' and her own eyes:

> If I really cared, if I were really a dutiful daughter (.4 pause) I would— I would come home and *see* her and Dad before they die.

Meg greeted Lisa at the door: "Welcome back. It's been a pretty long time, hasn't it? Well anyway, like I said to you on the phone, a lot has happened around here since your last visit." As Lisa and Meg were seating themselves at the dining room table, Sean entered. Meg quickly ushered him back down the hall into his room. She seemed eager to begin her story.

Meg explains that when she first heard the news that her father was terminally ill, she became obsessed with the desire to fly home to see him one last time:

> I had some forewarning that Dad was going to die. I still felt that while there was time left (.3 pause) and I was able-bodied. (.3 pause) You know? I should try to *see* him. And so I really (.3 pause) I just *couldn't* get this out of my *mind*, that I *had* to do it. I had to do it. And it was getting to be almost an *obsession*.

Meg describes how she initiated a plan to prepare for the trip:

Meg: I decided to uh (.4 pause) at least make steps in that *direction*. So um we began by driving just to the nearest airport, which is in Lomita. So we made a couple trips down on weekends,

Lisa: Uh-huh

Meg: and watched airplanes come and go. But at some point I— I guess I decided to get some medication, which I'd never made use of before. So I went to a GP and told him I had agoraphobia.

Lisa: Um-hm

Meg: And he immediately prescribed Xanax. No problem . . . And
       then I began practicing taking minute amounts of it,

Lisa: Um-hm

Meg: as I made these *forays* to the— into the airport.

Lisa: Um-hm

Meg: And what not.

Lisa: Um-hm

Meg: And found that it wasn't as frightening as I thought it would be
       to take a medication, which was something I had feared.

The next step in Meg's plan was to board an empty plane "to get the
feeling of being on a plane before take-off."

   But time was running out. In a desperate tone of voice Meg recounts
that weeks after learning of her father's illness, she received word that
he was on his deathbed:

Meg: I uh— I got the call that this was the *end.* Dad's had a *stroke.* He
       probably won't live out the w— you know my sister told me that
       she felt it was a matter of *weeks* now. Not (.3 pause) even a *month*
       left.

Lisa: Um-hm.

Meg: And so that just threw me into a tailspin, a place where I just felt
       like this is *it.*

Meg quickly began to make plans, consulting with family and co-workers. Yet she weaves into her tale the fear that she would not be able to
board the plane and fly the distance:

   I felt a *hopelessness,* that there was no way I'm— (.4 pause) a person
   like me can *do* what I'm proposing to *do.* And Dad's gonna *die,* and
   I was feeling really *depressed.* And I was thinking to myself thoughts
   like, "Oh why can't I be normal?"

At this point in the story, William proposes *pretending* that they were
going to make the trip:

My husband said, "Let's just pretend."[1] He said, "Let's just make reservations. (.3 pause) We'll *pretend*. We'll— we'll make reservations."

Deciding to go ahead, Meg asks her co-workers to pray for her:

Meg: Please pray for me. And and don't *tell* anybody please because I— I may very well show up at work *tomorrow*.
Lisa: Um-hm
Meg: I— I— I'm not at all sure that I'm going to *do* this.
Lisa: Um-hm
Meg: But it's my *hope*.

Meg portrays herself as doubting that she would actually make the trip from the moment she left her house en route to the airport, to the moment she walked down the boarding ramp. But before she knew it, she and her family had fastened their seatbelts and were airborne. With tears in her eyes and awe in her voice, Meg recounts that several hours later, she arrived at the door of her childhood home for the first time in almost ten years. Meg was with her father when he died, and she paid tribute to him at his memorial service.

In contrast to Meg's panic stories, Meg's story of flying is a success story. Part of its success is rooted in critical features of the story events: (1) Meg herself proposes flying to Oregon; (2) Meg repeatedly and explicitly communicates her deep reservations; (3) Meg alters her environment to accommodate her reservations.

When we describe Meg's narrative as a success, we mean both that Meg has constructed a story in the genre of a success story, complete with a happy ending, and that she has been able to accomplish a goal that she herself has articulated:

Meg: Before you knew it we were in Portland. And by the time we got *there*, I knew it was less than one more hour on a short— very short
Lisa: Um-hm
Meg: You know

Lisa: Um-hm

Meg: Hop to Medford. And I knew that I had already *endured* the *worst*.

Meg, however, does not attribute her success to her own capabilities. As in the telling of panic narratives, Meg describes herself not as a rational and competent agent but, rather, as phobic and dependent on the actions of others. Meg needs prayers from her colleagues, medication from her doctor, and a game plan from her husband. Ultimately, she attributes the successful conclusion of these events to divine intervention:

> It was almost like a *fluke* or really an *act* of *God* in my eyes that I was able to do this in the midst of all that I'm going through with my *phobias*.

At this writing, Meg is experiencing a difficult reentry into her life in Southern California. Like Beryl Markham's Pegasus, "yielding his ethereal wings to wings of wood and steel," Meg is "less buoyant, less capable of bearing such cargoes of hope." She struggles over her own and others' expectations that she "should be able to do anything now." These expectations create added pressure and augment her feelings of abnormality and irrationality.

Salman Rushdie asks, "How does newness come into the world? How is it born? Of what fusions, translations, conjoinings, is it made?"[2] We believe that such fusions, translations, and conjoinings are waiting for Meg in her own words, in her own stories, in her own voice. Narrative insights into agoraphobia await integration into a life story that renders Meg ready and able to "fly" on freeways and surface streets, to theaters, markets, camping sites, and other destinations away from home and hearth.

Notes

1. The Agony of Agoraphobia

1. These interviews were conducted as part of the Epidemiological Catchment Area Survey, a comprehensive study of the prevalence of psychiatric disorders in the United States (Robins and Regier, 1991). See Eaton, Dryman, and Weissman (1991), chap. 7.

2. The nature and scope of agoraphobia across cultures invites further investigation by psychologists, linguists, and anthropologists.

3. Meg was diagnosed on the basis of diagnostic criteria in the *Diagnostic and Statistical Manual of Mental Disorders* (Washington, D.C.: American Psychiatric Association, 1987), or *DSM-III-R*. A newly revised manual, the *DSM-IV*, was published in 1994.

4. In studies involving samples of at least twenty-five subjects, the relative percentage of females has ranged from 63 percent (Snaith, 1968) to 90 percent (Solyom et al., 1974). In the two large surveys conducted in England, females make up 88 percent (Burns and Thorpe, 1977) and 95 percent (Marks and Herst, 1970) of the samples. The latter figure may have been inflated, however, as Foa, Steketee, and Young (1984) point out, because advertisements for the study were placed in media directed more at women than men.

5. Chambless and Mason (1986); Kleiner and Marshall (1987).

6. See Kendler et al. (1992a) and Weissman (1993) for reviews of family genetic studies of anxiety.

7. Torgersen (1983) compared the proband concordance rates for anxiety in monozygotic (identical) and dizygotic (fraternal) twins. See also Kendler et al. (1992a).

8. Comparing the psycho-physiological characteristics of anxious and non-anxious samples, Turner, Beidel, and Epstein (1991) have suggested that some

individuals' psycho-physiology may render them more vulnerable to anxiety and panic (see also Beidel, 1991). Although the biological underpinnings of these neurobiological processes remain unknown, most biological models of anxiety point to random "dysregulation" of biological processes, which results in "eruptions," commonly referred to as panic attacks.

9. A number of investigators have suggested that the onset of anxiety is precipitated by stressful or negative life events (Buglass et al., 1977; Doctor, 1982; Finlay-Jones and Brown, 1981; Franklin and Andrews, 1989; Kleiner and Marshall, 1987; Last, Barlow, and O'Brien, 1984; Mathews, Gelder, Johnston, 1981; Shafar, 1976; Sheehan, Sheehan, and Minichiello, 1981; Solyom et al., 1974).

10. Beck and Emery (1985), Clark (1989), Pollard and Frank (1990), and Rapee (1987) have elaborated the role of catastrophic misinterpretations; Belfer and Glass (1992), Fitzgerald and Phillips (1991), Foa, Steketee, and Young (1984), McNally and Foa (1987), and Roth and Tucker (1986) emphasize selective attention to internal physiological arousal deemed threatening; Hope et al. (1989) and Smith, Ingram, and Brehm (1983) highlight hypersensitivity to social-evaluative information; and Brodbeck and Michelson (1987) and Lavelle, Matalsky, and Coyne (1979) developed a model that emphasizes learned helplessness.

11. Rosenbaum and his colleagues (1988, 1991) developed this view based on their research on behavioral inhibition in children.

12. Silverman et al. (1988).

13. Barlow (1988, 1990).

14. Bacciagaluppi (1985, p. 369). See Bowlby (1973) on the relationships between parenting style and the development of secure and insecure parent-child attachments.

15. See Casat (1988) for a review of the literature on the relationship between childhood separation anxiety and adult agoraphobia.

16. De Ruiter and van IJzendoorn (1992) conducted a meta-analysis of studies that include retrospective accounts of overprotective, role-reversing caregiving style in parents of individuals with agoraphobia.

17. Briggs (1986); Cook-Gumperz (1986); C. Goodwin (1991, 1994); Goodwin and Goodwin (in press); S. B. Heath (1983); Gumperz (1982); Jacoby and Gonzales (1991); Kulick (1992); P. Miller (1982); Ochs (1988); Ochs, Jacoby, and Gonzales (1994); Schieffelin (1990).

18. Researchers suggesting that agoraphobia may be described in terms of interpersonal conflict, particularly within the marital relationship, include Barlow, Mavissakalian, and Hay (1981), Bowen and Kohout (1979), Chambless and Goldstein (1980), Fry (1962), A. J. Goldstein (1973), Goldstein and

Chambless (1978), Goodstein (1981), Hafner (1977, 1982), Holmes (1982), O'Brien, Barlow, and Last (1982), Roth (1959), Shafar (1976), Webster (1953), and Wolpe (1976).

19. Hafner (1979); Shafar (1976).

20. Controlled studies of the marital satisfaction of agoraphobic persons and their spouses have been conducted by Arrindell and Emmelkamp (1986) as well as by Buglass and his colleagues (1977). As reported in Arrindell and Emmelkamp (1986), these studies used the Maudsley Marital Questionnaire (Cobb et al., 1980; Crowe, 1978), the Marlowe-Crowne Social Desirability Scale (Crowne and Marlowe, 1964), and the following unpublished measures: the "General Marital Dissatisfaction Scale," the "Sexual Dissatisfaction Scale," the "Perceived Quality of Intimate Communication Scale," the "Need for Intimacy Scale," the "Emotional Dependency Scale," the "Exclusive-Partner-Centeredness Scale," the "Intentional Extra-Marital Involvement Scale," and the "Trait-Neuroticism Scale."

21. Arrindell and Emmelkamp (1986, p. 600), citing Symonds (1973).

22. Beth also completed a measure (Whalen et al., 1994a, 1994b) designed to assess normally developing children's perceptions of the prevalence and controllability of various health, environmental, and life-style risks, and their perceived vulnerability to such maladies in general and relative to same-aged peers.

23. For perspectives on cross-cultural language socialization, see Ochs (1988, 1993a), Ochs and Schieffelin (1984, in press), and Schieffelin and Ochs (1986).

24. Studies by Mufson, Weissman, and Warner (1992), Silverman et al. (1988), Sylvester, Hyde, and Reichler (1987), and Turner, Beidel, and Costello (1987) report elevated rates of anxiety among children of anxious parents; only Capps et al. (in press) and Silverman et al. ¿1988) evaluated and reported on children of agoraphobic parents in particular.

25. For studies of socialization through narrative, see Bruner (1990), Feldman (1989), M. H. Goodwin (1990), S. B. Heath (1982, 1983), Miller and Sperry (1988), Nelson (1989), Ochs et al. (1992), Ochs and Taylor (1992a, b), Schieffelin (1990), and Wolf and Heath (1992).

2. In Her Own Words

1. Silko (1977, p. 2).

2. Morrison (1994, p. 4).

3. Thorton (1987, p. 21).

4. Other writers, such as those whose works appear in the volume *We Are*

the Stories We Tell, edited by Martin (1990) echo this belief in the life-giving and preserving power of words and stories—the importance of giving voice to our personal and collective experiences.

5. Lifton (1993).

6. Even snapshots capture the point of view of the photographer through focus, distance, angle, lighting, and scope.

7. This quote was taken from "Life as Narrative" (Bruner 1987, p. 15). See also *Actual Minds, Possible Worlds* (1986) and *Acts of Meaning* (1990).

8. Where the teller is a protagonist, each narrative recasting may portray the teller in a different light, thereby transforming him or her into a different sort of person.

9. See Bruner (1986, 1990), Feldman (1989), Ochs et al. (1992) and White (1980) on narratives as theories. In addition, as Ochs and her colleagues (1992) note: "Debunking the image of the lone researcher tucked away in a personal laboratory, scholars have suggested that important explanations—in the form of theories—emerge out of everyday conversational interaction about collective observations among members of a research group and thus depend on a social interactional process" (Gilbert and Mulkay, 1984; Knorr-Cetina, 1981; Kuhn, 1962; Latour and Woolgar, 1986; Lynch, 1985). From this point of view, talk in social interaction is critical, in science as elsewhere, not only to the engendering of theories (theory construction) but also to the establishment of those theories as valid generalizations (theory critique).

10. Gay (1989, p. 68). Anna O. referred to the talking cure as "chimney sweeping." In reporting the case study of Anna O., Breuer and Freud note that Anna "knew that after she had given utterance to her hallucinations she would lose all her obstinancy and what she described as her 'energy.' "

11. These dynamics are simultaneously revealed in the transference relationship, in which the patient projects emotions and expectations onto the therapist.

12. This research is grounded in the idea that the context of therapy pulls for particular kinds of talk, and that therapies of different orientations function as distinct contexts. This perspective resonates with recent interdisciplinary discussions of psychotherapy, which argue that even to view emotional distress in mental health terms is itself determined within a framework of historically situated beliefs and practices. See Cederborg (1994), Ferrara (1994), Foucault (1979), Kleinman (1988), Lakoff (1990), Masson (1988), Mishler (1984, 1986), and Oremland (1991).

13. Labov and Fanshel (1977).

14. Schafer's (1976, 1980, 1992) work on action language is perhaps most largely responsible for the recent turn in psychoanalysis toward the language of

psychotherapeutic narratives. See also Gerhardt and Stinson (1994) and Spence (1982).

15. Havel (1983, p. 355).

16. In *Outline of a Theory of Practice* Bourdieu (1977) delineates how human behavior is guided by historical conventions, which he refers to as "habitus, understood as a system of lasting, transposable dispositions which, integrating past experiences, functions at every moment as a matrix of perceptions, appreciations, and actions . . . In short, habitus, the product of history, produces individual and collective practices, and hence history, in accordance with the schemes engendered by history" (p. 82). Bourdieu goes on to explain that "practices can be accounted for only by relating the objective *structure* defining the social conditions of the production of the habitus which engendered them to the conditions in which this habitus is operating." In the same spirit, Giddens's *Central Problems in Social Theory: Action, Structure, and Contradiction in Social Analysis* (1979, p. 69) speaks of the duality of structure, "which relates to the fundamentally *recursive character of social life, and expresses the mutual dependence of structure and agency*. By the duality of structure I mean that the structural properties of social systems are both the medium and the outcome of the practices that constitute those systems."

17. Freud fondly referred to himself as a kind of archeologist, believing that in the process of psychoanalysis he was uncovering pieces of the past (1932). See Polkinghorne (1988) and Spence (1982) for further discussion of Freud's blurring of the distinction between construction and reconstruction. Spence (1982, p. 176) writes, "Freud could never bring himself to give up the archeological model . . . The construction, initially hypothetical, gradually changes into a piece of reality in the clinical situation; in almost every instance his initial guess about an infantile event is assumed to be correct. There is no obvious difference between construction and reconstruction; the change in terminology does not alter Freud's persistent faith in the possibility of uncovering the past, a faith in the idea that psychoanalysis is an archeology of memories."

18. Freud (1932). Culler (1980), Polkinghorne (1988), and Spence (1982) discuss Freud's case of the Wolf Man in relation to the drive for narrative coherence in psychoanalysis and the dynamics between narrative fit and historical truth. See also Culler's *Structuralist Poetics* (1975), in which the author explores the distinction between a sequence of actions or events that are referred to in a narrative and the means by which these events are told.

19. Freud (1932, p. 223) writes, "It must therefore be left at this (I can see no other possibility): either the analysis based on the neurosis in his childhood is all a piece of nonsense from start to finish, or else everything took place just as I have described it."

20. Freud (1932, p. 260). See also Schafer (1983, 1992), wherein he develops a narrative approach to psychoanalysis based on the notion that the telling and retelling of stories in analysis involves not a search for the true past but rather a search for contemporary rightness.

21. See C. Goodwin's (1994) analysis of the practices that powerfully organized jurors' perceptions of the videotaped events.

22. Toobin (1995, pp. 30–31). The account continues with a description of the lead prosecutor, Marcia Clark: "What sets Clark apart—and puts her on at least equal footing with her adversaries in the Simpson camp is her sense of theatre . . . strengthened by the mysteries and thrillers she reads obsessively, Clark's dramatic instincts have allowed her to touch jurors in a way that captures both their hearts and their minds."

23. Johnson (1994, pp. 47–48).

24. Heidegger (1988[1975]). See also Jaspers (1925, pp. 1–2).

25. Schutz (1962).

26. See Fiske and Taylor (1984), Greenwald (1980), Nisbett and Ross (1980), Sackeim (1983), S. E. Taylor (1983), and Taylor and Brown (1988, 1994) on optimistic bias.

27. See Taylor and Brown (1988, 1994) on adaptive value of optimistic illusions. See Alloy and Ahrens (1987), Coyne and Gotlieb (1983), Ruehlman, West, and Pasahow (1985), and Watson and Clark (1984) for reviews of the literature comparing the world views of depressed and nondepressed persons.

28. Garfinkel (1967, p. 54).

29. Geertz (1983, p. 75).

3. Telling Panic

1. See Ochs (1979).

2. Interested readers may also refer to Capps and Ochs (1995), which contains fully annotated transcriptions of Meg's narratives.

3. Sharff (1982).

4. Stein and Glenn (1979).

5. The structure of personal narrative is delineated in Labov (1972), Labov and Waletsky (1967), Ochs et al. (1992), and Stein and Glenn (1979).

6. American Psychiatric Association (1987, p. 236).

7. *Niagara Story: Core Panic Episode Structure*

In the Niagara story, the climactic panic episode occurs when Meg and her family take an elevator to the base of Niagara Falls. Meg describes this climactic problematic event:

Meg: So I put on my little *rain* jacket that they give you. You can take this— this elevator that goes down this *shaft* through the rock and we [got on the elevator and went down and—

Lisa: [Um-hm

Meg: We got down and— (.5 pause) and— and— *inside* the rock is just like a— a *maze* of tunnels. And you— eventually you emerge to (.4 pause) a spot right behind where the actual (.4 pause) *water* is *falling*. And when I got down there I became *claustrophobic.*

Meg's account of becoming claustrophobic upon entering the waterfall casts this situation as a problem. Meg then articulates further psychological responses that continue to frame the event as a problem, including acute awareness that she is trapped:

Meg: And I— I *realized* there's no way out but through that *darn* elevator . . .

Meg goes on to narrate the third component of the dramatic core of panic narratives: a series of attempts to escape the problematic situation. Laced with psychological distress, such attempts take the form of communicative acts, first directed to her daughter Beth and then at her husband William:

Meg: And I *remembered* clutching onto my *daughter* and saying, "Beth I'm— *Mama's* really afraid." (.3 pause). And— and um (.4 pause) and um (.4 pause) I— er— I— I mean *instantly* regretted that I had (.4 pause) *told* her that I was afraid. But I— I *did.* I clutched on to her. And I remember asking her to *pray* with me because I was *so unnerved.* (.8 pause) And I— I said, "I wanna go *up* now." And (.4 pause) I told William, "I got to get out of here. I'm not— I'm not *feeling* good."

Ski Trip Story: Core Panic Episode Structure

In the Ski Trip story, Meg uses expressions of fear to cast traveling through remote areas en route to a ski vacation as a climactic problematic event:

Meg: Um well I remember looking for *signs* along the way. I— I would be scared in between turn-offs because I would think, "Here we are." You have to drive through some pretty remote

Lisa: Uh-huh

Meg: *areas,* through the desert and stuff to *get* there.

Meg goes on to voice additional psychological responses that emerge after they reach their destination. These expressed psychological states further cast the trip to Utah as a problem:

Meg: But I remember when we got to Utah, um the first night the anxiety *really* got to me.

As in the Niagara story, Meg then narrates anxiety-laden communicative attempts to alleviate the problem, this time through conversation with the pastor's wife:

Meg: And I remember um (.3 pause) calling back (.3 pause) to California and speaking with our pastor's wife . . . And I remember calling her and saying, "I just don't think I can *hack* this. I'm feeling terrible I'm really afraid." And I remember crying over the phone to her. She said some reassuring words and (.8 pause) somehow I— I— I can remember that the hotel where we were staying became like my safe base.

8. See Michael Hoey (1983, pp. 81–106) for a discussion of the multilayering of problems, responses, and solutions in written discourse.

4. A Grammar of Panic

1. Sapir (1931, p. 578).
2. Sapir (1924).
3. The principle of linguistic relativity has dominated the field of cultural anthropology. Cognitive psychologists, by contrast, have for many decades indicated ways in which human beings share common ways of categorizing the world despite radical differences in the grammatical structure of the languages they speak. Recently, however, the principle of linguistic relativity has been revived as language acquisition research in particular shows that "the world does not present 'events' to be encoded in language. Rather, experiences are filtered—(a) through choice of perspective, and (b) through the set of options provided by the particular language—into verbalized events" (Berman and Slobin, 1994, p. 9). See also Gumperz and Levinson (1991) and Hanks (1990).
4. In this sense, examining structures forms the basis of a post-structuralist analysis. Indeed, as Bourdieu pointed out in his discussion of gift giving, understanding the social construction of meaning requires systematic observation and analysis of particular practices.
5. American Psychological Association (1987).
6. See Ribeiro (1994, pp. 83–88) for a discussion of patients' use of "all of a sudden" to shift from the role of informant to that of narrator in the context of psychiatric interviews.
7. Although these expressions also indicate conditions of time ("all of a sudden") and space ("out of the blue"), in their narrative context they primarily convey that events took place for no reason.

8. Wooffitt (1991, 1992).

9. Anxiety Disorders Association of America (1993).

10. Quirk et al. (1985).

11. Bühler (1990[1934]).

12. Ibid., p. 150.

13. Heidegger (1962).

14. Ibid., p. 139.

15. C. Goodwin (1993) discusses other linguistic structures that index and anticipate circumstances that have not yet been specified, referring to them as "prospective indexicals."

16. Bergson (1911, p. 4).

17. Goffman (1959).

18. It is our hope that our analysis of these grammatical forms will be of use in characterizing and alleviating a range of disturbances that render a person helpless.

19. In a study of the effects of a therapeutic intervention for individuals with agoraphobia, Intoccia (1988) found that as treatment progressed, patients increasingly referred to themselves in agentive roles rather than as passive recipients of their circumstances.

20. Most of Meg's narratives are characterized by frustration and failed resolutions to predicaments; however, in a few narratives, Meg does portray herself as able to survive adverse circumstances.

21. Monod (1972).

22. Meg's makes herself invisible through ellipsis in much more than experiential roles. For example, Meg may omit herself as the expressed agent or actor in sentences involving action. In such sentences, Meg places the inanimate object affected by the action in the foreground rather than herself as agent/actor. In some cases, Meg appears to reject transitive sentences altogether in favor of intransitive sentences that describe an object in some state, without reference to her relationship to that object. In the following excerpt, Meg's daughter Beth portrays an event using a transitive sentence referring to herself and her mother as agents ("we"); while Meg at the same time portrays the 'same' event using an intransitive construction with the direct object ("car") of Beth's sentence as sentential subject:

Beth: And we go outside and [we can't get the car started
Meg: [and the *car* won't start.

23. See Bazerman (1988), Biber (1988), and Latour (1987).

24. See Duranti (1990, 1994) for a discussion of grammatical constructions that mitigate agency in discourse.

25. Quirk et al. (1985).

26. Ibid.

27. Brown and Levinson (1987).

5. Accommodation as a Source of Panic

1. This belief is articulated with respect to therapy with sufferers of agoraphobia by Guidano and Liotti (1983) and Liotti (1991).

2. Cott (1977). See also Belenky et al. (1986).

3. See Bellah et al. (1985) and Caplow (1982).

4. For studies linking self-sacrifice, depression, and women, see Jack (1991), Lerner (1987), Weissman and Klerman (1977, 1987), Weissman and Paykel (1974), and Zuroff and Mongrain (1987).

5. Jack (1991, p. 38).

6. Notice in this passage that Meg rephrases the proposal for collective action several times. She first aborts a comment that begins "we got—", where "got" may be a modal of extrinsic control, as in "we got to . . ." She then starts to recast this comment as a collective decision, but again halts its delivery. Ultimately, she formulates a proposal that takes the form of a "let's" imperative.

7. Brown and Levinson (1987); Sacks (1989).

8. Goodwin and Heritage (1990); Levinson (1983); Pomerantz (1975, 1978, 1984); Sacks (1987); Sacks, Schegloff and Jefferson (1974).

6. Nonaccommodation as an Outcome of Panic

1. The preponderance of "well" in Meg's reconstructions of her postpanic communications to William provides further evidence that Meg perceives these responses to be displeasing. "Well" is a characteristic preface to what conversation analysts call 'dispreferred responses,' such as rejections and disagreements and other disappointing replies (Levinson, 1983; Pomerantz, 1975, 1978, 1984; Sacks, Schegloff, and Jefferson, 1974). Meg uses "well" in representing her remarks to William (for example, "Well can't you get on the shoulder," "well I— I— I'm not *doing* very good," "Well— well you know I just— (.3 pause) I'm feeling *anxious*") and in quoting William's restatement of her remarks to a third party, Cousin Harriet (for example, "And he goes '*well* she uh' "; "Well she has claustro- *claustrophobia*"; "Well I think she's just a little claustrophobic"). Chapter 3 presents a fuller transcription of these remarks.

2. Freud (1936); Jones (1955[1944]) .

3. See, for example, Anderson and Stewart (1983), Newman (1994), and Schacht, Henry, and Strupp (1988).

4. Barlow, Mavissakalian, and Hay (1981); Goldstein and Chambless (1978); Hafner (1977, 1979, 1982); Kleiner and Marshall (1987); Liotti (1991); Shafar (1976); Wolpe (1976).

5. On individual-centered accounts of agoraphobia, see Beck and Emery (1985), Clark (1989), Marks et al. (1991), and Taylor and Rachman (1992).

6. Breuer and Freud (1957).

7. Szasz (1974).

8. See also Sass (1994).

9. Bateson (1972, p. 206).

10. Recent research on communication and schizophrenia has focused on the role of parents' communicative styles in predicting the onset and course of schizophrenia spectrum disorders. Studies show higher relapse rates among schizophrenic adolescents who return to a family environment marked by high levels of "expressed emotion" and "communicative deviance"—critical and over-intrusive comments (for example, Goldstein, 1987; Goldstein et al., 1989; Leff and Vaughn, 1985; Mishler and Waxler, 1968; Sass et al., 1984).

This line of study is being extended to individuals with affective disorders and their families, yielding similar results. Relapse rates are higher among persons suffering from depression and bipolar disorder who return to families with greater levels of expressed emotion than those returning to families with lower levels of expressed emotion (Miklowitz et al., 1988). Similarly, the onset of childhood depression and schizophrenia spectrum disorders is greatest among families with elevated rates of expressed emotion and communicative deviance (Cook et al., 1990). Finally, one study has examined communication in families where one parent suffered from a psychological disorder. Results suggest that anxiety in children is not related to communications in which parents contradict something the child has said, but rather to utterances in which the *child* disqualifies or contradicts his or her own messages (Wichstrom, Holte, and Wynne, 1993).

11. See Brown and Levinson (1987) for an extended theory of politeness and face-saving in social interaction.

7. Paradoxes of Panic

1. Ochs (1988).

2. The word *leaga*, "bad," in Samoan can be used also as an expression to mean "good," so that an utterance such as "e leaga le lelei" can mean literally "The good is bad," but "bad" is understood as a positive assessment.

3. Richards (1924).

4. Capps (1986); Capps, Bjork, and Siegel (1993).

5. Goffman (1964).

6. Strictly speaking, an apparent contradiction between two lexical meanings (for example, jumbo shrimp, cold heat) is an oxymoron; however oxymorons may be considered compressed paradoxes (see Brooks, 1947, pp. 3–21).

7. On double bind, see Bateson (1972). Hoffman (1981) discusses paradoxical techniques applied in Bowenian, strategic, structural, and systemic approaches to therapy. See also Minuchin and Fishman (1981) and Papp (1980).

8. Kant (1956[1788]).

8. Constructing the Irrational Woman

1. Arrindell and Emmelkamp (1986, p. 600).

2. See Duranti (1986), C. Goodwin (1986), M. H. Goodwin (1990), and Goodwin and Goodwin (1986).

3. Bahktin (1981, p. 283). See also Voloshinov (1973[1929]).

4. Griffiths (1994, p. 102).

5. The emphasis placed on collaborative narrative activity in this book is compatible with socio-cognitive paradigms, where cognition has been shown to be socially constructed (Cicourel, 1973; Cole and Cole, 1989; Lave and Wenger, 1991; Leont'ev, 1981; Luria, 1976; Rogoff, 1990; Vygotsky, 1978, 1986; Wertsch, 1985). It is also consistent with the conversation analytic approach to co-construction, which articulates an interactional architecture for the management of routine public behavior (Heritage, 1984; Sacks, Schegloff, and Jefferson, 1974; Schegloff, 1982, 1986; Schegloff and Sacks, 1973).

6. See Jacoby and Ochs (1995).

7. See C. Goodwin (1979), Goodwin and Goodwin (1992), and Goodwin and Heritage (1990).

8. Griffiths (1994, pp. 102–104).

9. See Ochs, Smith, and Taylor (1989), Ochs and Taylor (1992), and Ochs et al. (1992) on some of the positive outcomes of family interaction at dinnertime.

10. Meg initiates the telling of ten of seventeen stories recorded at dinnertime, and is principal protagonist in seven; all ten are directed at William as preferred responder. William initiates the telling of four stories, one of which involves him as a protagonist; he delivers two to Meg and the other two to the family at large. Beth initiates three storytelling sequences, two of which involve her as principal protagonist; directing them to her father. Sean does not initiate any stories, but serves as principal protagonist in three.

11. *Panopticon* was introduced by Bentham (1791) and later applied by Foucault (1979, 1980).

12. For more on Ochs's and Taylor's studies of dinnertime storytelling, see Ochs (1993b), Ochs, Smith, and Taylor (1989), Ochs and Taylor (1992, 1993), Ochs et al. (1992).

13. See also Aronsson and Rundstrom (1989) and Aronsson and Cederborg (1994) on child discourse and parental control in pediatric and psychiatric consultations, respectively; and Cederborg (1994) on participation frameworks/power differentials in the context of family therapy.

14. See Sacks, Schegloff, and Jefferson (1974), C. Goodwin (1981), and Pomerantz (1978, 1984) on pursuing a response through pausing and hesitation; and C. Goodwin (1981, 1986) and C. Heath (1984) on eye gaze.

15. See Pomerantz (1978) and Davidson (1984) on silence as a sign of disagreement/nonalignment.

16. See Pomerantz (1975, 1984) on escalating bids for responsiveness.

17. Mehan (1993, p. 267).

9. Socializing Emotion

1. As mentioned in Chapter 1, evidence that children of parents with anxiety disorders are at risk for anxiety is found in the results of epidemiological studies (Kendler et al., 1992b; Leckman et al., 1983; Rutter et al., 1976; Weissman et al., 1984); inquiries of first-degree relatives of adults with anxiety disorders (see Weissman 1993 for review); studies of the family histories of anxious children (Berg, Butler, and Pritchard, 1974; Last et al., 1987; Last, Phillips, and Statfeld, 1987; Livingston et al., 1985); and diagnostic evaluation of children of individuals with anxiety disorders (Breslau, Davis, and Prabucki, 1987; Mufson, Weissman, and Warner, 1992; Rosenbaum et al., 1988, 1991; Silverman et al., 1988; Sylvester, Hyde, and Reichler, 1987; Turner, Beidel, and Costello, 1987). See Bernstein and Borchardt (1991) for review of anxiety disorders of childhood and adolescence.

2. Silverman et al. (1988).

3. Crowe et al. (1980, 1983); Harris et al. (1983); Kendler et al. (1992b); and Torgersen (1983). See Weissman (1993) for review.

4. Torgersen (1983).

5. Comparing the psychophysiological characteristics of anxious and nonanxious samples, Turner, Beidel, and Epstein (1991; see also Beidel, 1991) have suggested that some individuals' psychophysiology may render them more vulnerable to anxiety and panic.

6. Rosenbaum and his colleagues (1988, 1991) develop this view based on their research on behavioral inhibition in children.

7. Silverman et al. (1988) propose the notion that children of agoraphobic parents internalize a fear-avoidance response.

8. See Barlow (1988, 1990).

9. See Capps (1993) and Capps et al., (in press).

10. Bacciagaluppi (1985) and Bowlby (1973) discuss the relationships between parenting style and the development of secure and insecure attachments between parents and children.

11. Casat (1988).

12. Fear Survey Schedule for Children (FSSC-R; Ollendick, 1983); Revised Children's Manifest Anxiety Scale (RCMAS; Reynolds and Richmond, 1978).

13. Though not as dramatically as Beth, many children of agoraphobic parents who participated in Lisa's dissertation research displayed notable degrees of indecisiveness across tasks (Capps, 1993). Because each child completed the questionnaires in pen it was possible to tally numbers of self-corrections. Between-group comparisons showed significantly greater number of corrections among children of agoraphobic parents than children of nonanxious parents.

14. Shotter (1978) describes how expected and accepted rules and approaches become institutionalized as "the way things are done." See also Berger and Luckmann (1967).

15. M. H. Goodwin (1990); S. B. Heath (1982, 1983); Kulik (1992); Ochs (1988); Ochs and Schieffelin (1984); Schieffelin (1990); Schieffelin and Ochs (1986); Wolf and Heath (1992).

16. This notion is consistent with a version of the Sapir-Whorf hypotheses (Mandelbaum, 1949), claiming that not only are language practices organized by world view, but they also create world views for language users carrying out these practices.

17. Apprenticeship has been used as a metaphor in language development (Adams and Bullock, 1986; Bruner, 1983; G. Miller, 1977; Moerk, 1985; Wells 1979) and has been applied in studies of youth and adults in skill training, academic learning, and career preparation of scientists and artists (Greenfield and Lave, 1982; John-Steiner, 1985).

18. Lave (1988) develops the notion of guided participation, suggesting that apprentices, by acting alongside people who do something well, learn to think, argue, act, and interact in increasingly knowledgeable ways.

19. See Goffman (1981) for extensive discussion of participation frameworks, particularly the status participants assume as a function of talk in progress. See also Lave and Wenger (1991).

20. John-Steiner (1985) writes, "It is only through close collaboration that the novice is likely to learn what the mentor may not even know: how he or she formulates a question or starts a new project."

21. Stone (1961, pp. 26–29).

22. See Rogoff (1990).

23. Wolf, in Rogoff (1990, p. 4).

24. For a classic reference on scaffolding, see Wood, Bruner, and Ross (1976).

25. Fraihberg, Adelson, and Shapiro's (1975) title, "Ghosts in the Nursery," captures this dynamic well.

26. Ovid (1916[7 C.E.], p. 181).

27. Strabo (1917[7 B.C.E.], p. 67).

28. See Pellowski's (1990) volume on storytelling.

29. Egblewogbe (1975, p. 47).

30. Toelken (1976, p. 98).

31. Pellowski (1990, p. 68).

32. See Pellowski (1990, pp. 44–95) on religious storytelling.

33. See C. Taylor (1994a, b), Miller et al. (1990), and Miller and Sperry (1988).

10. Socializing Anxiety

1. Capps (1993).

2. Collaborative accounts have been studied in child language studies and in conversation analysis. Child language researchers refer to such exchanges between caregivers and children as "propositions across utterances and speakers" (Keenan [Ochs] and Schieffelin, 1976; Ochs, Schieffelin, and Platt, 1979) and "vertical constructions" (Scollon, 1976). In conversation analysis, these collaborations are called "collaborative completions" (Lerner 1987).

11. Therapeutic Insights

1. Freud (1943). See also Polkinghorne (1988), Schafer (1980), and Spence (1982) on the development and use of case histories.

2. Freud (1943, p. 228).

3. See Anderson and Goolishian (1988, 1992), Epston, White, and Murray (1990), Gergen and Gergen (1988), McNamee and Gergen (1992), and White and Epston (1990).

4. For example, Schafer (1976, 1978, 1983, 1992) and Spence (1982).

5. Putnam (1989), Siegel (1993), Spiegel (1988), Terr (1991, 1994), and van der Kolk and van der Hart (1989) describe how the uncontrolled, intrusive nature of flashbacks prevents or impedes individuals from working through the

traumatic experience, as well as psychotherapeutic techniques used to integrate previously fragmented aspects.

6. Schafer (1992, p. 34). See also Polkinghorne (1988, pp. 150–155) on "self as narrative."

7. Anderson and Goolishian (1988); Cederborg (1994); McNamee and Gergen (1992); Schafer (1992); Spence (1982).

8. Spence (1982, p. 129).

9. Gergen and Kaye (1992).

10. Feldman et al. (1990, 1994).

11. Focusing on the role of the therapist as co-teller, the constructivist family therapists Harlene Anderson and Harold Goolishian (1988, 1990, 1992) prescribe therapeutic stances that facilitate the construction of narratives that promote growth and change. They suggest that by asking questions from a position of interested inquiry the therapist can create a climate in which clients feel that their point of view is understood, confirmed, and accepted. Anderson and Goolishian also refer to this stance as a "position of not knowing" (1992, p. 28.) From this perspective, the experience of receptivity, readiness to explore multiple viewpoints, and willingness to accept the relativity of meaning organize the restructuring of life narratives.

Similarly, the family therapist Terry Real (1990) proposes five stances that facilitate a social constructivist approach to therapy: an *eliciting stance*, communicating equal respect for competing constructs; a *probing stance* that allows him or her to reframe what individuals or family members have said; a *contextualizing stance* that shifts language from individuals toward patterns that tie individuals together; a *matching stance*, through which the therapist reflects and affirms the clients' perspective; and an *amplifying stance* that allows the therapist to evoke more information about a particular idea, affect, or theme that clients have introduced.

12. In describing the current state of constructivist therapies, for example, Gergen and Kaye (1992, p. 175) write, "We strongly endorse explorations into constructionist forms of practice . . . At the present time, however, we stand at a point of embarkation: a radical departure from traditional assumptions about knowledge, persons and the nature of the 'real' is at hand. Substantial deliberation and experimentation will be required before the results can be assayed."

13. White and Epston (1990).

14. Schafer (1976, 1978, 1983, 1992).

15. Schafer (1983, p. 226).

16. Relistening is the most basic of a set of procedures for exploring the organization of stories told in social interaction. Although repeated listening allows closer attention to how stories are built and the role of different inter-

locutors in co-authoring story versions, looking at transcripts of recorded storytelling is vastly more illuminating. Transcripts, together with the original recordings, highlight how emotions are verbalized through manner of delivery, grammar, and story structure. Further, as noted in Chapter 3, transcripts that represent utterances on different lines and show pauses, restarts, and overlaps articulate the linguistic and interactional architecture of stories more clearly than more compacted transcripts (see Ochs 1979).

17. Wolkstein and Kramer (1983), cited in Jack (1991).

18. Ochs and Taylor (1992a, b); Ochs et al. (1992).

19. Accommodators also may find it helpful to hear about strategies that people routinely employ to negotiate a proposal that maximizes the well-being of those involved. The antidote to excessive accommodation is no simple maxim such as "Just say no," but rather a set of politeness practices that preserve the face of the party who put forward the proposal while communicating reservations. The anthropologists Penelope Brown and Stephen Levinson suggest that the main function of politeness is precisely to soften the impact of face-threatening acts. Both the proposal and the rejection are face-threatening acts in that proposals impinge on someone's future activities and rejections indicate that interlocutors do not share wants and goals. In mitigating the affront of rejections, interlocutors routinely use politeness strategies such as (1) terms of endearment ("Honey, I can't"); (2) respect ("I can't, husband dear"); (3) partial agreement ("I would love to but I can't right now"); (4) flattery ("That's a great idea but I can't"); (5) sympathy ("I'm sorry but I can't"); (6) joking ("If only I had another body to bake twelve dozen cookies today, I would come"); (7) optimism ("I'm sure we'll be able to find a time while Cousin Harriet is here, but right now I can't"); (8) talking about common interests ("We love Cousin Harriet and she'll understand if we can't make it today"); and (9) giving reasons for being negative ("I have twelve dozen cookies to bake and presents to wrap").

20. Liotti (1991, pp. 217–218). Liotti adds, "Even those who do acknowledge that their personal difficulties may be related to their phobic anxieties, are unable consistently to deal with this anxiety as one may be expected to deal with a meaningful personal emotion. Most agoraphobics, in other words, attribute their painful feelings to an impending illness—either a somatic or a mental illness, but in any case an *illness*, that is, a process utterly alien to their experience and awareness of the Self." See also Guidano and Liotti (1983).

21. Furthermore, as we have shown in our analysis of the pit bull stories, well below the level of *discursive* reflection, Meg demonstrates what Giddens (1979) calls *practical consciousness* of her husband's flagging attention to her narrative account of an anxious experience. Her practical awareness and dissatisfaction

with the interaction is evident through her repeated attempts to reshape her narrative to involve her spouse as a more active participant. These observations suggest that different accounts of emotions, events, and relationships emerge when an agoraphobic person is responding to a questionnaire or structured interview than when an agoraphobic person is narrating a story about experiencing panic, where both explicit and implicit knowledge are communicated.

22. Aristotle (1982[4th cent. B.C.E.], p. 54).

23. The grammatical shifts we are suggesting are compatible with Schafer's proposed "language of action" (1976, 1978, 1983, 1992). Indeed, grammar is the foundation for the process he advocates.

24. Quirk et al. (1985).

25. See Beck, Epstein, and Harrison (1983) on cognition, attitudes, and personality dimensions in depression; and Beck et al. (1974) and Brown and Silberschatz (1989) on pessimism and hopelessness in particular.

Epilogue: Flying

1. Notice the "let's" imperative format of the proposal. But on this occasion it is Meg who has set the goal and means for attaining it. It is Meg who approaches her physician for medication, and it is Meg who enlists her family's support to make trial runs on the freeway, to the airport, and aboard the plane.

2. Rushdie (1988).

References

Adams, A. K., and Bullock, D. 1986. Apprenticeship in word use: Social convergence processes in learning categorically related nouns. In S. A. Kuczaj and M. D. Barrett, eds., *The development of word meaning: Progess in cognitive development research.* New York: Springer-Verlag.

Alloy, L. B., and Ahrens, A. H. 1987. Depression and pessimism for the future: Biased use of statistically relevant information in predictions for self versus others. *Journal of Personality and Social Psychology, 52,* 366–378.

American Psychiatric Association. 1987. *Diagnostic and statistical manual of mental disorders,* 3rd ed., rev. Washington, D.C.: American Psychiatric Association.

Anderson, H., and Goolishian, H. 1988. Human systems as linguistic systems: Evolving ideas about the implications for theory and practice. *Family Process, 27,* 371–393.

——— 1990. Beyond cybernetics: Comments on Atkinson and Heath's "Further thoughts on second-order family therapy." *Family Process, 29,* 157–163.

——— 1992. The client is the expert: A not-knowing approach to therapy. In S. McNamee and K. J. Gergen, eds., *Therapy as social construction.* London: Sage.

Anderson, C. M., and Stewart, S. 1983. *Mastering resistance: A practical guide to family therapy.* New York: Guilford Press.

Anxiety Disorders Association of America. 1993. *Panic and agoraphobia.* Rockville, Md.: Anxiety Disorders Association of America.

Aristotle. 1982[4th cent. B.C.E.]. *Poetics.* Trans. J. Hutton. New York: W. W. Norton.

Aronsson, K., and Cederborg, A. C. 1994. Voice and orchestration in family therapy talk: On co-narration in multi-party talk. *Text, 5(3).*

217

Aronsson, K., and Rundstrom, B. 1988. Child discourse and parental control in pediatric consultations. *Text, 8*, 159–189.

—— 1989. Cats, dogs, sweets in the clinical negotiation of reality: On politeness and coherence in pediatric discourse. *Language in Society, 18*, 483–504.

Arrindell, W. A., and Emmelkamp, P. M. G. 1986. Marital adjustment, intimacy, and needs in female agoraphobics and their partners: A controlled study. *British Journal of Psychiatry, 149*, 592–602.

Atkinson, J. M., and Drew, P. 1979. *Order in court: The organisation of verbal interaction in judicial settings.* London: Macmillan.

Atkinson, J. M., and Heritage, J. 1984. *Structures of social action.* Cambridge: Cambridge University Press.

Bacciagaluppi, M. 1985. Inversion of parent-child relationships: A contribution to attachment theory. *British Journal of Medical Psychology, 58*, 369–373.

Bakhtin, M. M. 1981. Discourse in the novel. In *The dialogic imagination*, trans. Caryl Emerson and Michael Holquist. Austin: University of Texas Press.

Barlow, D. H. 1988. *Anxiety and its disorders.* New York: Guilford Press.

—— 1990. Current models of panic disorder and a view from emotion theory. *American Psychiatric Press, Review of Psychiatry, 7*, 15–29.

Barlow, D. H., Mavissakalian, M., and Hay, L. R. 1981. Couples treatment of agoraphobia: Changes in marital satisfaction. *Behaviour Research and Therapy, 19*, 245–255.

Bateson, G. 1972. *Steps toward an ecology of mind.* New York: Ballentine.

Bazerman, C. 1988. *On rhetoric in science.* Madison: University of Wisconsin Press.

Beck, A. T., and Emery, G. 1985. *Anxiety disorders and phobias: A cognitive perspective.* New York: Basic Books.

Beck, A. T., Epstein, N., and Harrison, R. 1983. Cognitions, attitudes, and personality dimensions in depression. *British Journal of Cognitive Psychotherapy, 1*, 1–16.

Beck, A. T., Weissman, A. N., Lester, D., and Trexler, L. 1974. The measurement of pessimism: The Hopelessness Scale. *Journal of Consulting and Clinical Psychology, 42*, 861–865.

Beidel, D. C. 1991. Determining the reliability of psychophysiological assessment in childhood anxiety. *Journal of Anxiety Disorders, 5*, 139–150.

Belenky, M. F., Clinchy, B. M., Goldberger, N. R., and Tarule, J. M. 1986. *Women's ways of knowing: The development of self, voice, and mind.* New York: Basic Books.

Belfer, P. and Glass, C. 1992. Agoraphobic anxiety and fear of fear: Test of a cognitive-attentional model. *Journal of Anxiety Disorders, 6,* 133–146.

Bellah, R., Madsen, R., Sullivan, W. M., Swidler, A., and Tipton, S. M. 1985. *Habits of the heart: Individualism and commitment in American life.* Berkeley: University of California Press.

Bentham, J. 1791. *Panopticon.* London: T. Payne.

Berg, I., Butler, A., and Pritchard, J. 1974. Psychiatric illness in the mothers of school phobic adolescents. *British Journal of Psychiatry, 125,* 466–467.

Berger, P. L., and Luckmann, T. 1967. *The social construction of reality.* Garden City, N.J.: Doubleday.

Bergson, H. 1911. *Creative evolution.* Trans. A. Mitchell. Lanham, Md.: University Press of America.

Berman, R., and Slobin, D. A. 1994. *Relating events in narrative: A crosslinguistic developmental study.* Hillsdale, N.J.: Lawrence Erlbaum.

Bernstein, G. A., and Borchardt, C. M. 1991. Anxiety disorders of childhood and adolescence: A critical review. *Journal of American Academy of Child and Adolescent Psychiatry, 30(4),* 519–532.

Biber, D. 1988. *Variation across speech and writing.* Cambridge: Cambridge University Press.

Bourdieu, P. 1977. *Outline of a Theory of Practice.* Trans. Richard Nice. Cambridge: Cambridge University Press.

Bowen, R. C., and Kohout, J. 1979. The relationship between agoraphobia and primary affective disorders. *Canadian Journal of Psychiatry, 24,* 317–322.

Bowlby, J. 1973. *Attachment and loss.* Vol. 2: *Separation anxiety and anger,* pp. 292–312. New York: Basic Books.

Breslau, N., Davis, G. C., and Prabucki, K. 1987. Searching for evidence on the validity of generalized anxiety disorder: Psychopathology in children of anxious mothers. *Psychiatry Research, 20,* 285–297.

Breuer, J., and F., S. 1957. *Studies on hysteria.* Trans. J. Strachey and A. Freud. New York: Basic Books.

Briggs, C. L. 1986. *Learning how to ask: A sociolinguistic appraisal of the role of the interview in social science research.* Cambridge: Cambridge University Press.

Brodbeck, C., and Michelson, L. 1987. Problem-solving skills and attributional styles of agoraphobics. *Cognitive Therapy and Research, 11,* 593–610.

Brooks, C. 1947. *The well-wrought urn.* New York: Harcourt Brace Jovanovich.

Brown, P., and Levinson, S. C. 1987. *Politeness: Some universals in language usage.* Cambridge: Cambridge University Press.

Brown, J. D., and Silberschatz, G. 1989. Dependency, self-criticism, and depressive attributional style. *Journal of Abnormal Psychology, 98,* 187–188.

Bruner, J. S. 1983. *Child's talk: Learning to use language*. New York: Norton.

——— 1986. *Actual minds, possible worlds*. Cambridge, Mass.: Harvard University Press.

——— 1987. Life as narrative. *Social Research, 54*, 11–32.

——— 1990. *Acts of meaning*. Cambridge, Mass.: Harvard University Press.

Buglass, D., Clarke, J., Henderson, A. S., Kreitman, N., and Presley, A. S. 1977. A study of agoraphobic housewives. *Psychological Medicine, 7*, 73–86.

Buhler, K. 1990[1934]. *Sprachtheorie: Die darstellungsfunktion der sprache*. Jena: Gustav Fischer.

Burns, L. E., and Thorpe, G. L. 1977. Fears and clinical phobias: Epidemiological aspects and the National Survey of Agoraphobics. *Journal of International Medical Research, 5*, 1–7.

Caplow, T. 1982. *Middletown families: Fifty years of change and continuity*. Minneapolis: University of Minnesota Press.

Capps, L. 1986. From silence to serenity: An interpretation of the Vietnam Veterans' Memorial. Undergraduate honors thesis, Stanford University.

——— 1993. Psychological adjustment in children of agoraphobic parents. Ph.D. dissertation. University of California, Los Angeles.

Capps, L., Bjork, R., and Siegel, D. 1993. The meaning of memories. *UCLA Magazine, 4(4)*, 8–10.

Capps, L., and Ochs, E. 1995. Out of place: Narrative insights into agoraphobia. *Discourse Processes 19*.

Capps, L., Sigman, M., Sena, R., Henker, B., and Whalen, C. (in press). Psychological adjustment in children of agoraphobic parents. *Journal of Child Psychology and Psychiatry*.

Casat, C. D. 1988. Childhood anxiety disorders: A review of the possible relationship to adult panic disorder and agoraphobia. *Journal of Anxiety Disorders, 2*, 51–60.

Cederborg, A.-C. 1994. *Family therapy as collaborative work*. Dissertation. Linkoping University, Sweden.

Chambless, D. L. 1982. Characteristics of agoraphobia. In D. L. Chambless and A. J. Goldstein, eds., *Agoraphobia: Multiple perspectives on theory and treatment*. New York: Wiley.

Chambless, D. L., and Goldstein, A. J. 1980. The treatment of agoraphobia. In A. Goldstein and E. Foa, eds., *Handbook of behavioral interventions*. New York: Wiley.

Chambless, D. L., and Gracely, D. 1989. Fear of fear and the anxiety disorders. *Cognitive Therapy and Research, 13(1)*, 9–20.

Chambless, D. L., and Mason, J. 1986. Sex, sex role stereotyping, and agoraphobia. *Behavior Research and Therapy, 24*, 231–235.

Cicourel, A. V. 1973. *Cognitive sociology*. Harmondsworth: Penguin.

Clark, D. M. 1989. Anxiety states: Panic and generalized anxiety. In K. Hawton, P. M. Salkowvskis, J. Kirk, and D. M. Clark, eds., *Cognitive behavior therapy for psychiatric problems: A practical guide*. Oxford: Oxford University Press.

Cobb, J. P., McDonald, R., Marks, I. M., and Stern, R. 1980. Marital versus exposure therapy. *European Journal of Behavioral Analysis and Modification*, 4, 3–17.

Cole, M., and Cole, S. 1989. *The development of children*. New York: Scientific American Books.

Cook, W. L., Asarnow, J. R., Goldstein, M. J., Marshall, V. J., and Weber, E. 1990. Mother-child dynamics in early onset depression and childhood schizophrenia spectrum disorders. *Development and Psychopathology*, 2, 71–84.

Cook-Gumperz, J. 1986. *The social construction of literacy*. Cambridge: Cambridge University Press.

Cott, N. F. 1977. *The bonds of womanhood: Woman's sphere in New England, 1780–1835*. New Haven: Yale University Press.

Coyne, J. C., and Gotlieb, I. H. 1983. The role of cognition in depression: A critical appraisal. *Psychological Bulletin*, 94, 472–504.

Crowe, M. J. 1978. Conjoint marital therapy: A controlled outcome study. *Psychological Medicine*, 4, 623–636.

Crowe, R. R., Pauls, D. L., Slyman, D. and Noyes, R. 1980. A family study of anxiety neurosis: Morbidity in families of patients with and without mitral valve prolapse. *Archives of General Psychiatry*, 37, 77–79.

Crowe, R. R., Noyes, R., Pauls, D. L., and Slyman, D. 1983. A family study of panic disorder. *Archives of General Psychiatry*, 40, 1065–1069.

Crowne, D. P., and Marlowe, D. 1964. *The approval motive: Studies in evaluative dependence*. New York: Wiley.

Culler, J. 1975. *Structuralist poetics: Structuralism, linguistics, and the study of literature*. Ithaca, N.Y.: Cornell University Press.

—— 1980. Fabula and sjuzhet in the analysis of narrative: Some American discussions. *Poetics Today*, 1(3), 27–37.

Davidson, J. 1984. Subsequent versions of invitations, offers, requests, and proposals dealing with potential or actual rejection. In J. M. Atkinson and J. Heritage, eds., *Structures of social action*. Cambridge: Cambridge University Press.

De Ruiter, C., and van IJzendoorn, M. H. 1992. Agoraphobia and anxious-ambivalent attachment: An integrative review. *Journal of Anxiety Disorders*, 6, 365–381.

DiNardo, P. A., O'Brien, G. T., Barlow, D. H., Waddell, M. T., and Blanchard, E. B. 1983. Reliability of DSM-III anxiety disorder categories using a new structured interview. *Archives of General Psychiatry, 40,* 1070–1074.

Doctor, R. M. 1982. Major results of large-scale pretreatment survey of agoraphobics. In R. L. DuPont, ed., *Phobia: A comprehensive summary of modern treatments.* New York: Brunner/Mazel.

Duranti, A. 1986. The audience as co-author: Introduction. *Text, 6(3),* 239–347.

——— 1990. Politics and grammar: Agency in Samoan political discourse. *American Ethnologist, 17(4),* 646–666.

——— 1994. *From grammar to politics: Linguistic anthropology in a Western Samoan village.* Berkeley: University of California Press.

Eaton, W. W., Dryman, A., and Weissman, M. 1991. Panic and phobia. In L. N. Robins and D. A. Regier, eds., *Psychiatric disorders in America: The American Epidemiological Catchment Area Study.* New York: Free Press.

Egblewogbe, E. Y. 1975. *Games and songs as education media.* Accra: Ghana Publications Corp.

Epston, D., White, M., and Murray, K. 1992. A proposal for re-authoring therapy: Rose's revisioning of her life and a commentary. In S. McNamee and K. G. Gergen, eds., *Therapy as social construction.* London: Sage.

Feldman, C. F. 1989. Monologue as problem-solving narrative. In K. Nelson, ed., *Narratives from the crib.* Cambridge, Mass.: Harvard University Press.

Feldman, C. F., Bruner, J. S., Kalmar, D., and Renderer, B. 1994. Plot, plight, and dramatism: Interpretation at three ages. In W. F. O. and D. S. Palermo, eds., *The nature and ontogenesis of meaning.* Hillsdale, N.J.: Lawrence Erlbaum.

Feldman, C. F., Bruner, J., Renderer, B., and Spitzer, S. 1990. Narrative comprehension. In B. K. Britton and A. D. Pellegrini, eds., *Narrative Thought and Narrative Language.* Hillsdale, N.J.: Lawrence Erlbaum.

Ferrara, K. W. 1994. *Therapeutic ways with words.* New York: Oxford University Press.

Finlay-Jones, R., and Brown, G. W. 1981. Types of stressful life events and the onset of anxiety and depressive disorder. *Psychological Medicine, 11,* 801–815.

Fiske, S. T., and Taylor, S. E. 1984. *Social cognition.* Reading, Mass.: Addison-Wesley.

Fitzgerald, T. E., and Phillips, W. 1991. Attentional bias and agoraphobic avoidance: The role of cognitive style. *Journal of Anxiety Disorders, 5,* 333–341.

Foa, E., Steketee, G., and Young, M. 1984. Agoraphobia: Phenomenological aspects, associated characteristics, and theoretical considerations. *Clinical Psychology Review, 4,* 431–457.

Foucault, M. 1979. *Discipline and punishment: The birth of the prison.* New York: Random House.

———— 1980. *Power/knowledge: Selected interviews and other writings, 1972–1977.* Ed. Colin Gordon. New York: Pantheon.

Fraihberg, S., Adelson, E., and Shapiro, V. 1975. Ghosts in the nursery: A psychoanalytic approach to the problems of impaired infant-mother relationships. *Journal of the American Academy of Child Psychiatry, 14,* 387–421.

Franklin, J. A., and Andrews, G. 1989. Stress and the onset of agoraphobia. *Australian-Psychologist, 24,* 203–219.

Freud, S. 1932. *New introductory lectures on psychoanalysis.* Trans. J. Strachey. New York: Norton.

———— 1936. *Inhibitions, symptoms, and anxiety.* Trans. J. Strachey. London: Hogarth Press.

———— 1943. *A general introduction to psychoanalysis.* Garden City, N.Y.: Garden City Publishing.

Fry, W. F. 1962. The marital context of an anxiety syndrome. *Family Process, 4,* 245–252.

Garfinkel, H. 1967. *Studies in ethnomethodology.* Englewood Cliffs, N.J.: Prentice-Hall.

Gay, P. 1989. *The Freud reader.* New York: W. W. Norton.

Geertz, C. 1983. *Local knowledge: Further essays in interpretive anthropology.* New York: Basic Books.

Gergen, K. J., and Gergen, M. M. 1988. Narrative and the self as relationship. In L. Berkowitz, ed., *Advances in experimental social psychology.* New York: Academic Press.

Gergen, K. J., and Kaye, J. 1992. Beyond narrative in the negotiation of therapeutic meaning. In S. McNamee and K. J. Gergen, eds., *Therapy as social construction.* London: Sage.

Gerhardt, J., and Stinson, C. 1994. The nature of therapeutic discourse: Accounts of the self. *Journal of Narrative and Life History, 4(3),* 151–191.

Giddens, A. 1979. *Central problems in social theory: Action, structure, and contradiction in social analysis.* Berkeley: University of California Press.

Gilbert, G. N., and Mulkay, M. 1984. *Opening Pandora's box: A sociological analysis of scientists' discourse.* Cambridge: Cambridge University Press.

Gittelman, R., and Klein, D. 1984. Relationship between separation anxiety and panic and agoraphobic disorders. *Psychopathology, 17,* 56–65.

Goffman, E. 1959. *The presentation of self in everyday life*. Garden City, N.J.: Doubleday.

—— 1964. The neglected situation. In John J. Gumperz and Dell Hymes, eds., *The ethnography of communication*. *American Anthropologist, 66, 6, pt. II*, 133–136.

—— 1981. Footing. In E. Goffman, ed., *Forms of talk*. Philadelphia: University of Pennsylvania Press.

Goldstein, A. J. 1973. Learning theory insufficiency in understanding agoraphobia: A plea for empiricism. In J. C. Brengelmann and W. Tunner, eds., *Behaviour Therapy–Verhaltenstherapie*. Munich: Urban and Schwarzenberg.

Goldstein, A. J., and Chambless, D. L. 1978. A reanalysis of agoraphobia. *Behavior Therapy, 9*, 47–59.

Goldstein, M. J. 1987. The UCLA high risk project. *Schizophrenia Bulletin, 13*, 505–514.

Goldstein, M. J., Miklowitz, D. J., Strachan, A. M., et al. 1989. Patterns of expressed emotion and patient coping styles that characterize the families of recent onset schizophrenics. *British Journal of Psychiatry, 155*, 107–111.

Goodstein, R. K. 1981. Agoraphobia: Fear and the family. *Journal of Psychiatric Treatment and Evaluation, 3*, 423–427.

Goodwin, C. 1979. The interactive construction of a sentence in natural conversation. In G. Psathas, ed., *Everyday language: Studies in ethnomethodology*. New York: Irvington Publishers.

—— 1981. *Conversational organization: Interaction between speakers and hearers*. New York: Academic Press.

—— 1986. Audience diversity, participation, and interpretation. *Text, 6(3)*, 283–316.

—— 1991. Situated literacy in the workplace. Paper presented at the Department of Applied Linguistics, UCLA.

—— 1993. Transparent vision. Manuscript.

—— 1994. Professional vision. *American Anthropologist, 96(3)*, 606–633.

Goodwin, C., and Goodwin, M. H. 1992. Assessments and the construction of context. In A. Duranti and C. Goodwin, eds., *Rethinking context*. Cambridge: Cambridge University Press.

Goodwin, C., and Heritage, J. 1990. Conversation analysis. *Annual Reviews of Anthropology, 19*, 283–307.

Goodwin, M. H. 1990. *He-said-she-said: Talk as social organization among Black children*. Bloomington, Ind.: Indiana University Press.

Goodwin, M. H., and Goodwin, C. 1986. Gesture and coparticipation in the activity of searching for a word. *Semiotica, 62(1/2)*, 51–75.

Greenfield, P., and Lave, J. 1982. Cognitive aspects of informal education. In D. Wagner and H. Stevenson, eds., *Cultural perspectives on child development*. San Francisco: Freeman.

Greenwald, A. G. 1980. The totalitarian ego: Fabrication and revision of personal history. *American Psychologist, 35*, 63–618.

Griffiths, P. 1994. Berio becoming Berio. *New Yorker*, May 30, pp. 102–104.

Guidano, V. F., and Liotti, G. 1983. *Cognitive processes and emotional disorders*. New York: Guilford.

Gumperz, J. J. 1982. *Language and social identity*. Cambridge: Cambridge University Press.

Gumperz, J. J., and Levinson, S. 1991. Rethinking linguistic relativity. *Current Anthropology, 32*, 613–623.

Hafner, R. J. 1977. The husbands of agoraphobic women: Assortive mating or pathogenic interaction? *British Journal of Psychiatry, 130*, 233–239.

—— 1979. Agoraphobic women married to abnormally jealous men. *British Journal of Medical Psychology, 52*, 99–104.

—— 1982. The marital context of the agoraphobic syndrome. In D. L. Chambless and A. J. Goldstein, eds., *Agoraphobia: Multiple perspectives on theory and treatment*. New York: Wiley.

Hallam, R. S. 1985. *Anxiety: Psychological perspectives on panic and agoraphobia*. London: Academic Press.

Hanks, W. F. 1990. *Referential practice: Language and lived space among the Maya*. Chicago: University of Chicago Press.

Harris, E. L., Noyes, R., Crowe, R. R., and Chaudhry, M. D. 1983. Family study of agoraphobia. *Archives of General Psychiatry, 40*, 1061–1064.

Havel, V. 1983. *Letters to Olga*. New York: Henry Holt.

—— 1987. The power of the powerless. In *Living in truth*. London: Faber and Faber.

Heath, C. 1984. Talk and recipiency: Sequential organization in speech and body movement. In M. Atkinson and J. Heritage, eds., *Structures of social action*. Cambridge: Cambridge University Press.

Heath, S. B. 1982. What no bedtime story means: Narrative skills at home and school. *Language in Society, 11*, 49–76.

—— 1983. *Ways with words: Language, life, and work in communities and classrooms*. Cambridge: Cambridge University Press.

Heidegger, M. 1962. *Being and time*. Trans. J. Macquarrie and E. Robinson. New York: Harper and Row.

—— 1988[1975]. *The basic problems of phenomenology*. Revised edition. Translation, introduction, and lexicon by Albert Hofstadter. Bloomington: Indiana University Press.

Heritage, J. 1984. *Garfinkel and ethnomethodology*. Cambridge: Polity Press.

Hoffman, L. 1981. *Foundations of family therapy*. New York: Basic Books.

Hoey, M. 1983. *On the surface of discourse*. London: George Allen and Unwin.

Holmes, J. 1982. Phobia and counterphobia: Family aspects of agoraphobia. *Journal of Family Therapy, 4*, 133–152.

Hope, D., Rapee, R., Heimberg, R., and Dombeck, M. 1989. Representation of the self in social phobia: Vulnerability to social threat. *Cognitive Research and Therapy, 14*, 177–190.

Intoccia, M. 1988. Agoraphobia: The syndrome and internal life changes which occur throughout treatment. Ph.D. dissertation, New School for Social Research, New York, N.Y.

Jack, D. C. 1991. *Silencing the self*. Cambridge, Mass.: Harvard University Press.

Jacoby, S., and Gonzales, P. 1991. The constitution of expert-novice in scientific discourse. *Issues in Applied Linguistics, 2(2)*, 149–181.

Jacoby, S., and Ochs, E. 1995. Co-construction: An introduction. *Research on Language and Social Interaction, 28(3)*.

Jaspers, K. 1925. *Psychologie der weltanshaaugen*, 3rd ed. Berlin: Springer.

Johnson, J. 1994. Witness for the prosecution. *New Yorker*, May 16, p. 42–51.

John-Steiner, V. 1985. *Notebooks of the mind: Explorations of thinking*. Albuquerque: University of New Mexico Press.

Jones, E. 1955[1944]. *The life and work of Sigmund Freud*. New York: Basic Books.

Kant, I. 1956[1788]. *Critique of practical reason*. New York: Macmillan.

Keenan (Ochs), E., and Schieffelin, B. B. 1976. Topic as a discourse notion: A study of topic in the conversations of children and adults. In C. N. Li, ed., *Subject and topic*. New York: Academic Press.

Kendler, K. S., Neale, M. C., Kessler, R. C., Heath, A. C., and Eaves, L. J. 1992a. Generalized anxiety disorder in women: A population-based twin study. *Archives of General Psychiatry, 49*, 267–272.

Kendler, K. S., Neale, M. C., Kessler, R. C., Heath, A. C., and Lindon, J. E. 1992b. The genetic epidemiology of phobias in women. *Archives of General Psychiatry, 49*, 273–281.

Kleiner, L., and Marshall, W. L. 1987. The role of interpersonal problems in the development of agoraphobia with panic attacks. *Journal of Anxiety Disorders, 1*, 313–323.

Kleinman, A. 1988. *The illness narratives: Suffering, healing, and the human condition*. New York: Basic Books.

Knorr-Cetina, K. 1981. *The manufacture of knowledge: An essay on the constructivist and contextual nature of science*. New York: Pergamon.

Kuhn, T. 1962. *The structure of scientific revolutions*. Chicago: University of Chicago Press.

Kulick, D. 1992. *Language shift and cultural reproduction: Socialization, self, and syncretism in a Papua New Guinean village.* Cambridge: Cambridge University Press.

Labov, W. 1972. *Language in the inner city: Studies in the Black English vernacular.* Philadelphia: University of Pennsylvania Press.

Labov, W., and Fanshel, D. 1977. *Therapeutic discourse: Psychotherapy as conversation.* New York: Academic Press.

Labov, W., and Waletzky, J. 1967. Narrative analysis: Oral versions of personal experience. In J. Helm, *Essays on verbal and visual arts.* Seattle: University of Washington Press for the American Ethnological Society.

Labov, W., and Waletzky, J. 1968. Narrative analysis. In W. Labov et al., eds., *A study of the non-standard English of Negro and Puerto Rican speakers in New York City.* New York: Columbia University.

Lakoff, R. 1990. The talking cure. In *Talking power: The politics of language in our lives.* New York: Basic Books.

Last, C. G., Barlow, D. H., and O'Brien, G. T. 1984. Precipitants of agoraphobia: Role of stressful life events. *Psychological Reports, 54,* 567–570.

Last, C. G., Hersen, M., Kazdin, A. E., Francis, G. and Grubb, H. J. 1987. Psychiatric illness in the mothers of anxious children. *American Journal of Psychiatry, 144,* 1580–1583.

Last, C. G., Philips, J. E., and Statfeld, A. 1987. Childhood anxiety disorders in mothers and their children. *Child Psychiatry and Human Development, 18,* 103–112.

Latour, B. 1987. *Science in action: How to follow scientists and engineers through society.* Cambridge, Mass.: Harvard University Press.

Latour, B., and Woolgar, S. 1986. *Laboratory life: The social construction of scientific facts.* Princeton: Princeton University Press.

Lave, J. 1988. *Cognition in practice.* Cambridge: Cambridge University Press.

Lave, J., and Wenger, E. 1991. *Situated learning: Legitimate peripheral participation.* Cambridge: Cambridge University Press.

Lavelle, T. L., Metalsky, G. I., and Coyne, J. C. 1979. Learned helplessness, test anxiety, and the acknowledgment of contingencies. *Journal of Abnormal Psychology, 88,* 381–387.

Leckman, J. F., Weissman, M. M., Merikangas, K. R., Pauls, D. L., and Prusoff, B. A. 1983. Panic disorder and major depression: Increased risk of depression, alcoholism, panic, and phobic disorders in families of depressed probands with panic disorder. *Archives of General Psychiatry, 40,* 1055–1060.

Leff, J., and Vaughn, C. 1985. *Expressed emotion in families.* New York: Guilford Press.

Leont'ev, A. N. 1981. The Problem of Activity in Psychology. In J. V. Wertsch, eds., *The concept of activity in Soviet psychology*. Armonk, N.Y.: M. E. Sharpe.

Lerner, G. H. 1987. Collaborative turn sequences: Sentence construction and social action. Ph.D. dissertation, University of California at Irvine.

Levinson, S. C. 1983. *Pragmatics*. Cambridge: Cambridge University Press.

Lifton, R. J. 1993. *The Protean self: Human resilience in an age of fragmentation*. New York: Harper and Row.

Liotti, A. 1991. Insecure attachment and agoraphobia. In P. Marris, J. Stevenson-Hinde, and C. Parkes, eds., *Attachment across the life cycle*. New York: Routledge.

Livingston, R., Nugent, H., Rader, L., et al. 1985. Family histories of depressed and severely anxious children. *American Journal of Psychiatry, 142*, 1497–1499.

Luria, A. R. 1976. *Cognitive development: Its cultural and social foundations*. Cambridge, Mass.: Harvard University Press.

Lynch, M. 1985. *Art and artefact in laboratory science*. London: Routledge and Kegan Paul.

Mandelbaum, D. G., ed. 1949. *Selected writings of Edward Sapir in language, culture, and personality*. Berkeley: University of California Press.

Markham, B. 1983. *West with the night*. San Francisco, Calif.: North Point Press.

Marks, M. P., Basoglu, M., Alkubaisy, T., Sengun, S., and Marks, I. M. 1991. Are anxiety symptoms and catastrophic cognitions directly related? *Journal of Anxiety Disorders, 5*, 247–254.

Marks, I. M., and Herst, E. R. 1970. A survey of 1,200 agoraphobics in Britain. *Social Psychiatry 5*, 16–24.

Martin, W. 1990. *We are the stories we tell*. New York: Random House.

Masson, J. M. 1988. *Against therapy*. New York: Atheneum.

Matthews, A. M., Gelder, M. G., and Johnston, D. W. 1981. *Agoraphobia: Nature and treatment*. New York: Guildford Press.

McNally, R. J., and Foa, E. 1987. Cognition and agoraphobia: Bias in the interpretation of threat. *Cognitive Therapy and Research, 11*, 567–581.

McNamee, S., and Gergen, K., 1992. *Therapy as social construction*. London: Sage.

Mehan, H. 1993. Beneath the skin and between the ears: A case study in the politics of representation. In S. Chaiklin and J. Lave, eds., *Understanding practice: Perspectives on activity and context*. Cambridge: Cambridge University Press.

Miklowitz, D. J., Goldstein, M. J., Nuecherterlein, K. H., Synder, K. S., Mintz,

J. 1988. Family factors and the course of bipolar affective disorder. *Archives of General Psychiatry*, 45, 225–231.

Miller, G. 1977. *Spontaneous apprentices*. New York: Seabury Press.

Miller, P. 1982. *Amy, Wendy, and Beth: Learning language in South Baltimore*. Austin: University of Texas Press.

Miller, P., Potts, R., Fung, H., Hoogstra, L., and Mintz, J. 1990. Narrative practices and the social construction of self in childhood. *American Ethnologist*, 17, 292–311.

Miller, P., and Sperry, L. 1988. Early talk about the past: The origins of conversational stories of personal experience. *Journal of Child Language*, 15, 293–315.

Minuchin, S., and Fishman, Charles, H. 1981. *Family Therapy Techniques*. Cambridge, Mass.: Harvard University Press.

Mishler, E. G. 1984. *The discourse of medicine: Dialectics of medical interviews*. Norwood: Ablex.

————— 1986. *Research Interviewing: Context and Narrative*. Cambridge, Mass.: Harvard University Press.

Mishler, E. G., and Waxler, N. 1968. *Interaction in families: An experimental study of family processes and schizophrenia*. New York: John Wiley and Sons.

Moerk, E. L. 1985. A differential interactive analysis of language teaching and learning. *Discourse Processes*, 8, 113–142.

Monod, J. 1972. *Chance and necessity*. Trans. A. Wainhouse. London: Collins.

Moran, C., and Andrews, G. 1985. The familial occurrence of agoraphobia. *British Journal of Psychiatry*, 146, 262–267.

Morrison, T. 1994. The Nobel lecture in literature. New York: Alfred A. Knopf.

Mufson, L. 1992. Depression and anxiety in parents and children: A direct interview study. *Journal of Anxiety Disorders*, 6, 1–13.

Mufson, L., Weissman, M., and Warner, V. 1992. Depression and anxiety in parents and children: A direct interview study. *Journal of Anxiety Disorders*, 6, 1–13.

Naylor, G. 1990. Gloria Naylor. In M. Pearlman and K. U. Henderson, eds., *A voice of one's own: Conversations with America's writing women*. Boston: Houghton Mifflin.

Nelson, K. 1989. *Narratives from the crib*. Cambridge, Mass.: Harvard University Press.

Newman, C. F. 1994. Cognitive therapy of anxiety disorders. In B. B. Wolman and G. Strickler, eds., *Anxiety and related disorders: A handbook*. New York: John Wiley and Sons.

Nisbett, R. E., and Ross, L. 1980. *Human inference: Strategies and shortcomings of social judgment.* Englewood Cliffs, N.J.: Prentice-Hall.

Oates, J. C. 1990. Joyce Carol Oates. In M. Pearlman and K. U. Henderson, eds., *A voice of one's own: Conversations with America's writing women.* Boston: Houghton Mifflin.

O'Brien, G. T., Barlow, D. H., and Last, C. G. 1982. Changing marriage patterns of agoraphobics as a result of treatment. In R. L. DuPont, ed., *Phobia: A comprehensive summary of modern treatments.* New York: Brunner/Mazel.

Ochs, E. 1979. Transcription as theory. In E. Ochs and B. B. Schieffelin, eds., *Developmental pragmatics.* New York: Academic Press.

—— 1988. *Culture and language development: Language acquisition and language socialization in a Samoan village.* Cambridge: Cambridge University Press.

—— 1993a. Constructing social identity: A language socialization perspective. *Research on Language and Social Interaction, 26(3),* 287–306.

—— 1993b. Stories that step into the future. In D. Biber and E. Finegan, eds., *Perspectives on register: Situating register variation within sociolinguistics.* Oxford: Oxford University Press.

Ochs, E., Jacoby, S., and Gonzales, P. 1994. Interpretive journeys: How physicists talk and travel through graphic space. *Configurations 2(1),* 151–172.

Ochs, E., and Schieffelin, B. B. 1984. Language acquisition and socialization: Three developmental stories. In R. A. Shweder and R. A. LeVine, eds., *Culture theory: Essays on mind, self, and emotion.* Cambridge: Cambridge University Press.

Ochs, E., and Schieffelin, B. B. 1995. The influence of language socialialization on grammatical development. In P. F. and B. MacWhinney, eds., *Handbook on child language development.* Oxford: Basil Blackwell.

Ochs, E., Schieffelin, B. B., and Platt, M. 1979. Propositions across utterances and speakers. In E. Ochs and B. B. Schieffelin, eds., *Developmental pragmatics.* New York: Academic Press.

Ochs, E., Smith, R., and Taylor, C. 1989. Dinner narratives as detective stories. *Cultural Dynamics, 2,* 238–257.

Ochs, E., and Taylor, C. 1992a. Family narrative as political activity. *Discourse and Society, 3(3),* 301–340.

Ochs, E., and Taylor, C. 1992b. Mothers' role in the everyday reconstruction of "Father Knows Best." In K. Hall, ed., *Locating power: Proceedings of the 1992 Berkeley Women and Language Conference.* Berkeley: University of California at Berkeley.

Ochs, E., Taylor, C., Rudolph, D., and Smith, R. 1992. Story-telling as a theory-building activity. *Discourse Processes, 15(1)*, 37–72.

Ollendick, T. H. 1983. Reliability and validity of the revised Fear Survey Schedule for Children (FSSC-R). *Behavior Research and Therapy, 21*, 685–692.

Olsen, T. 1978. *Silences*. New York: Delacorte Press.

Oremland, J. 1991. *Interpretation and interaction: Psychoanalysis or psychotherapy?* Hillsdale, N.J.: Analytic Press.

Ovid (1916[7 C.E.]). *Metamorphoses*. Trans. F. J. Miller. New York: Loeb Classical Library.

Papp, P. 1980. The Greek chorus and other techniques of paradoxical therapy. *Family Process, 19(1)*, 21–37.

Pellowski, A. 1990. *The world of storytelling*. Bronx, N.Y.: H. W. Wilson.

Polkinghorne, D. E. 1988. *Narrative knowing and the human sciences*. Albany, N.Y.: State University of New York Press.

Pollard, C. A., and Frank, M. A. 1990. Catastrophic cognitions and physical sensations of panic attacks associated with agoraphobia. *Phobia Practice and Research Journal, 3*, 3–18.

Pomerantz, A. 1975. Second assessments: A study of some features of agreements/disagreements. Ph.D. dissertation. University of California at Irvine.

——— 1978. Compliment responses: Notes on the co-operation of multiple constraints. In J. Schenkein, ed., *Studies in the organization of conversational interaction*. New York: Academic Press.

——— 1984. Agreeing and disagreeing with assessments: Some features of preferred/dispreferred turn shapes. In J. M. Atkinson and J. Heritage, eds., *Structures of social action: Studies in conversation analysis*. Cambridge: Cambridge University Press.

Putnam, F. W. 1989. *Diagnosis and treatment of Multiple Personality Disorder*. New York: Guilford Press.

Quirk, R., Greenbaum, S., Leech, G., and Svartvik, J. 1985. *A comprehensive grammar of the English language*. New York: Longman.

Rapee, R. 1987. The psychological treatment of panic attacks: Theoretical conceptualization and review of evidence. *Clinical Psychology Review, 7*, 427–438.

Real, T. 1990. The therapeutic use of self in constructionist/systemic therapy. *Family Process, 29*, 255–272.

Reynolds, C. R. and Richmond, B. O. 1978. What I think and feel. *Journal of Abnormal Psychology, 6*, 271–280.

Ribeiro, B. T. 1994. *Coherence in psychotic discourse*. Oxford: Oxford University Press.

Richards, I. A. 1924. *Principles of literary criticism*. London: Routledge and Kegan Paul.

Robins, L., and Regier, L., eds. 1991. *Psychiatric disorders in America: The American Epidemiological Catchment Area Study*. New York: Free Press.

Rogoff, B. 1990. *Apprenticeship in thinking*. New York: Oxford University Press.

Rosenbaum, J. F., Biederman, J., Gersten, M., et al. 1988. Behavioral inhibition in children of parents with panic disorder and agoraphobia. *Archives of General Psychiatry, 45*, 463–470.

Rosenbaum, J. F., Biederman, J., Hirshfeld, D. R., Bolduc, E. A., Faraone, S. V., Kagan, J., Snidman, N., and Reznick, S. J. 1991. Further evidence of an association between behavioral inhibition and anxiety disorders: Results from a family study of children from a non-clinical sample. *Journal of Psychiatric Research, 25*, 49–65.

Roth, M. 1959. The phobic anxiety-depersonalization syndrome. *Proceedings of the Royal Society of Medicine, 52*, 587–595.

Roth, M., and Tucker, D. 1986. Neural systems of emotional control on information processing. In R. E. Ingram, ed., *Information processing approaches to clinical psychology*. New York: Academic Press.

Ruehlman, L. S., West, S. G., and Pasahow, R. J. 1985. Depression and evaluative schemata. *Journal of Personality, 53*, 46–92.

Rushdie, S. 1988. *The Satanic verses*. New York: Viking Press.

Rutter, M., Tizard, J., Yule, W., Graham, P., and Whitmore, K. 1976. Research report: The Isle of Wight studies, 1964–1974. *Psychological Medicine, 6*, 313–332.

Sackheim, H. A. 1983. Self-deception, self-esteem, and depression: The adaptive value of lying to oneself. In J. Masling, ed., *Empirical studies of psychoanalytic theories*. Hillsdale, N.J.: Analytic Press.

Sacks, H. 1987. On the preferences for agreement and contiguity in sequences in conversation. In G. Button and J. R. E. Lee, eds., *Talk and social organisation*. Clevedon, England: Multilingual Matters.

———— 1989. Lectures, 1964–1965. Edited by Gail Jefferson, introduction/memoir by Emanuel A. Schegloff. *Human Studies, 12(3–4)*, 1–408.

Sacks, H., Schegloff, E. A., and Jefferson, G. 1974. A simplest systematics for the organization of turn-taking for conversation. *Language, 50*, 696–735.

Sapir, E. 1924. Culture, genuine and spurious. *Journal of Sociology, 29*, 401–29.

———— 1931. Conceptual categories in primitive languages. *Science, 74*, 578.

Sass, L. A. 1994. *Paradoxes of delusion: Wittgenstein, Schreber, and the schizophrenic mind*. Ithaca, N.Y.: Cornell University Press.

Sass, L. A., Gunderson, J. G., Singer, M. T., and Wynne, L. C. 1984. Parental communication deviance and forms of thinking in male schizophrenic off-spring. *Journal of Nervous and Mental Disease, 172,* 513–520.

Schacht, T. E., Henry, W. P., and Strupp, H. H. 1988. Psychotherapy. In C. G. Last and M. Hersen, eds., *Handbook of anxiety disorders.* New York: Pergamon Press.

Schafer, R. 1976. *A new language for psychoanalysis.* New Haven: Yale University Press.

—— 1978. *Language and insight: The Sigmund Freud memorial lectures, University College London, 1975–1976.* New Haven: Yale University Press.

—— 1980. Narration in the psychoanalytic dialogue. In W. J. T. Mitchell, ed., *On narrative.* Chicago: University of Chicago Press.

—— 1983. *The analytic attitude.* New York: Basic Books.

—— 1992. *Retelling a life: Narration and dialogue in psychoanalysis.* New York: Basic Books.

Schegloff, E. A. 1982. Discourse as an interactional achievement: Some uses of 'uh huh' and other things that come between sentences. In D. Tannen, ed., *Georgetown University Roundtable on Languages and Linguistics.* Washington, D.C.: Georgetown University Press.

—— 1986. The routine as achievement. *Human Studies, 9,* 111–151.

Schegloff, E. A., and Sacks, H. 1973. Opening up closings. *Semiotica, 8,* 289–327.

Schieffelin, B. B. 1990. *The give and take of everyday life: Language socialization of Kaluli children.* Cambridge: Cambridge University Press.

Schieffelin, B. B., and Ochs, E. 1986. *Language socialization across cultures.* Cambridge: Cambridge University Press.

Schutz, A. 1962. *Collected papers.* Vol.1: *The problem of social reality.* The Hague: Martinus Nijhoff.

Scollon, R. 1976. *Conversations with a one-year-old: A case study of the developmental foundation of syntax.* Honolulu: University Press of Hawaii.

Shafar, S. 1976. Aspects of phobic illness: A study of 90 personal cases. *British Journal of Medical Psychology, 79,* 221–236.

—— 1982. *The elements of cinema: Toward a theory of cinesthetic impact.* New York: Columbia University Press.

Sheehan, D. V., Sheehan, K. E., and Minichiello, W. E. 1981. Age of onset of phobic disorders: A reevaluation. *Comprehensive Psychiatry, 22,* 544–553.

Shotter, J. 1978. The cultural context of communication. In A. Lock, ed., *Action, gesture, and symbol.* London: Academic Press.

Siegel, D. J. 1993. Childhood memory: An introduction. Paper presented at the meeting of the American Academy of Child and Adolescent Psychiatry, October, San Antonio, Tex.

Silko, L. M. 1977. *Ceremony*. New York: Penguin Books.

Silverman, W. K., Cerny, J. A., Nelles, W. B., and Burke, A. E. 1988. Behavior problems in children of parents with anxiety disorders. *Journal of the American Academy of Child and Adolescent Psychiatry*, 27, 779–784.

Smith, T. W., Ingram, R. E., and Brehm, S. S. 1983. Social anxiety, anxious self-preoccupation, and recall of self-relevant information. *Journal of Personality and Social Psychology*, 44, 1276–1283.

Snaith, R. 1968. A clinical investigation of phobias. *British Journal of Psychiatry* 114, 673–697.

Solyom, L., Beck, P., Solyom, C., and Hugel, R. 1974. Some etiological factors in phobic neurosis. *Canadian Psychiatric Association Journal*, 19, 69–78.

Spence, D. P. 1982. *Narrative truth and historical truth: Meaning and interpretation in psychoanalysis*. New York: W. W. Norton.

Spiegel, D. 1988. Dissociation and hypnosis in post-traumatic stress disorders. *Journal of Traumatic Stress*, 1, 17–33.

Stein, N., and Glenn, C. G. 1979. An analysis of story comprehension in elementary school children. In R. O. Freedle, ed., *New directions in discourse processing*. Norwood, N.J.: Ablex.

Stein, N., and Policastro, M. 1984. The concept of a story: A comparison between children's and teacher's viewpoints. In H. Mandl, N. Stein, and T. Trabasso, eds., *Learning and comprehension of text*. Hillsdale, N.J.: Erlbaum.

Stone, I. 1961. *The agony and the ecstacy*. New York: Doubleday.

Strabo. 1917[7 B.C.E.]. *Geography, Book I, Part 2*. Trans. H. L. Jones. New York: Loeb Classical Library.

Sylvester, C., Hyde, T. S., and Reichler, R. J. 1987. The diagnostic interview for children and personality inventory for children in studies of children at risk for anxiety disorders or depression. *Journal of the American Academy of Child and Adolescent Psychiatry*, 26, 668–675.

Symonds, A. 1973. Phobias after marriage: Women's declaration of independence. In J. B. Miller, ed., *Psychoanalysis and women*. Harmondsworth: Penguin.

Szasz, T. 1974. *The myth of mental illness*. New York: Harper and Row.

Taylor, C. 1994a. Child as apprentice-narrator: Socializing voice, face, and self-esteem amid the narrative politics of dinner. Ph.D. dissertation. University of Southern California, Los Angeles.

——— 1994b. "You think it was a fight?": Co-constructing affect, cognition, face, and family in dinnertime interaction. Paper presented at the meeting of the American Association for Applied Linguistics, Baltimore, May.

Taylor, S. E. 1983. Adjustment to threatening events: A theory of cognitive adaptation. *American Psychologist, 38*, 1161–1173.

Taylor, S. E., and Brown, J. D. 1988. Illusion and well-being: A social psychological perspective on mental health. *Psychological Bulletin, 103*, 193–210.

——— 1994. Positive illusions and well-being revisited: Separating fact from fiction. *Psychological Bulletin, 116(1)*, 21–27.

Taylor, S., and Rachman, S. J. 1992. Fear and avoidance of aversive affective states: Dimensions and causal relations. *Journal of Anxiety Disorders, 6*, 15–25.

Tearnan, B. H., and Telch, M. J. 1988. Etiology of agoraphobia: An investigation of perceived childhood and parental factors. *Phobia Practice and Research Journal, 1*, 13–24.

Terr, L. 1991. Childhood traumas: An outline and overview. *American Journal of Psychiatry, 148*, 10–20.

——— 1994. *Unchained memories*. New York: Basic Books.

Thorton, L. 1987. *Imagining Argentina*. New York: Basic Books.

Toelken, B. 1976. The pretty languages of yellowman. In D. Ben-Amos, ed., *Folklore genres*. Austin: University of Texas Press.

Toobin, J. 1995. Annals of law: Marcia Clark. *New Yorker*, February 7, pp. 30–37.

Torgersen, S. 1983. Genetic factors in anxiety disorders. *Archives of General Psychiatry, 40*, 1085–1089.

Turner, S. M., Beidel, D. C., and Costello, A. 1987. Psychopathology in the offspring of anxiety disorders patients. *Journal of Consulting and Clinical Psychology, 55*, 229–235.

Turner, S. M., Beidel, D. C., and Epstein, L. H. 1991. Vulnerability and risk for anxiety disorders. *Journal of Anxiety Disorders, 5*, 151–166.

Van der Kolk, B. A., and Van der Hart, O. 1989. Pierre Janet and the breakdown of adaptation in psychological trauma. *American Journal of Psychiatry, 146*, 1530–1540.

Vidler, A. 1992. *The architectural uncanny: Essays in the modern unhomely*. Cambridge, Mass.: MIT Press.

Voloshinov, V. N. 1973[1929]. *Marxism and the philosophy of language*. Trans. Ladislav Matejka and I. R. Titunik. New York: Seminar Press.

Vygotsky, L. S. 1978. *Mind in society: The development of higher psychological processes*. Cambridge, Mass.: Harvard University Press.

——— 1986. *Thought and language*. Trans. Alex Kozulin. Cambridge, Mass.: MIT Press.

Watson, D., and Clark, L. A. 1984. Negative affectivity: The disposition to experience aversive emotional states. *Psychological Bulletin, 96*, 465–490.

Webster, A. S. 1953. The development of phobias in women. *Psychological Monographs: General and Applied, 67,* 1–18.

Weissman, M. M. 1993. Family genetic studies of panic disorder. *Journal of Psychiatric Research, 27(1),* 69–78.

Weissman, M. M., and Klerman, G. L. 1977. Sex differences and the epidemiology of depression. *Archives of General Psychiatry, 34,* 98–111.

——— 1987. Gender and depression. In R. Formanek and A. Gurian, eds., *Women and depression: A lifespan perspective.* New York: Springer.

Weissman, M. M., and Paykel, E. S. 1974. *The depressed woman: A study of social relationships.* Chicago: University of Chicago Press.

Weissman, M. M., Leckman, J. F., Merikangas, K. R., Gammon, G. D., and Prusoff, B. A. 1984. Depression and anxiety disorders in parents and children. *Archives of General Psychiatry, 41,* 845–852.

Wells, G. 1979. Apprenticeship in meaning. In K. Nelson, ed., *Children's language.* New York: Halsted Press.

Wertsch, J. 1985. *Culture, communication, and cognition: Vygotskian perspectives.* Cambridge: Cambridge University Press.

Whalen, C. K., Henker, B., O'Neil, R., Hollingshead, J., Holman, A., and Moore, B. 1994a. Preadolescents' perceptions of AIDS before and after Earvin Magic Johnson's announcement. *Journal of Pediatric Psychology, 19,* 3–17.

——— 1994b. Optimism in children's judgments of health and environmental risks. *Health Psychology, 13(4),* 319–325.

White, H. 1980. The value of narrativity in the representation of reality. In W. J. T. Mitchell, ed., *On narrative.* Chicago: University of Chicago Press.

White, M., and Epston, D. 1990. *Narrative means to therapeutic ends.* New York: Norton.

Wichstrom, L., Holte, A., and Wynne, L. C. 1993. Disqualifying communication and anxiety in offspring at risk for psychopathology. *Acta Psychiatrica Scandinavia, 88,* 74–79.

Wolf, S. A., and Heath, S. B. 1992. *The braid of literature.* Cambridge, Mass.: Harvard University Press.

Wolkstein, D., and Kramer, S. N. 1983. *Inanna, queen of heaven and earth: Her stories and hymns from Sumer.* New York: Harper and Row.

Wolpe, J. 1976. *Theme and variations: A behavior therapy casebook.* New York: Pergamon Press.

Wood, D., Bruner, J., and Ross, G. 1976. The role of tutoring in problem solving. *Journal of Child Psychology and Psychiatry, 17,* 89–100.

Wooffitt, R. 1991. I was just doing X . . . when Y': Some inferential properties of a device in accounts of paranormal experiences. *Text, 11(2),* 267–288.

Woolf, V. 1970[1929/1942]. Professions for women. In *The death of the moth and other essays.* New York: Harcourt Brace Jovanovich.

Zuroff, D. C., and Mongrain, M. 1987. Dependency and self-criticism: Vulnerability factors for depressive affective states. *Journal of Abnormal Psychology, 96,* 14–22.

Acknowledgments

Our collaboration began in the winter of 1990, when we both participated in a seminar on narrative directed by Jerome Bruner and Carol Feldman, who were visiting scholars at UCLA. The seminar brought together psychologists, psychiatrists, and linguists to contemplate the complexities of narrative thought. This common experience formed the basis of our joint enterprise relating narratives to lives in the making, particularly lives clouded by mental suffering.

Our enterprise blends methods from anthropology, sociology, linguistics, and psychology. The anthropological turn of the project brought Lisa into Meg's home and family life. The Logan family's continuing openness and generosity allowed us to capture the intricacies of informal, day-to-day interaction, giving our work the authenticity that is vital to understanding how anxiety penetrates lives. The sociological and linguistic sides of this project draw from research on conversational discourse and from ongoing discussions with our colleagues Alessandro Duranti, Per-Anders Forstorp, Patrick Gonzales, Charles Goodwin, Sally Jacoby, Emmanuel Schegloff, Bambi Schieffelin, John Schumann, and Susan Strauss. We greatly benefited from their close readings of early drafts of this work, as well as from Nathan Brostrom's responses to successive revisions. Our project also builds on psychological research, particularly a study of children of agoraphobic parents that Lisa carried out with Marian Sigman, Rhonda Sena, and Barbara Henker. We are grateful to them for rich insights into the perpetuation of anxiety in families. We are also indebted to members of our cognitive neuroscience study group and to participants in a seminar on language, culture, and interaction. These meetings never fail to spark stimulating questions and debate. We thank Jerome Bruner and Carol Feldman, who remain a constant source of energy and innovation. Through conversation and commentary on the text itself we have learned how to articulate new syntheses between disciplines.

The gestation of this book concided with that of Lisa's baby, David. His arrival, five weeks before the manuscript's completion, provided joyful inspiration. We thank those who tended to David while we worked: Nathan Brostrom, Sharon Brostrom, Lois and Walter Capps, and Sandro and Marco Duranti. We are most grateful to our families for their unwavering support of our works-in-progress. Finally, we thank two anonymous reviewers for their comments and suggestions, Angela Von der Lippe, Lynne Raughley, and Elizabeth Gretz of Harvard University Press, and Betsy Rymes, who helped us tighten our prose, clarify our presentation, and bring this book to completion.

Index

abnormalizing devices, 58

accommodation: communicative consequences of, 92–95, 112; communicative dilemmas and, 17, 84, 111–112; panic and, 83–84, 89–91, 95–96; psychological disorders and, 83; women and, 82–84, 184

adverbs, 56–58, 80, 159–162, 184, 191, 206nn6,7

agency: agent, 67, 70–71, 108, 187, 207nn19,20; diminished agentive roles, 69–77, 207n19; experiencer, 67, 69, 187, 207n22; mitigating, 207n24; nonagentive roles, 67–69, 108, 170–71, 207n22

agoraphobia: avoidance and, 47, 99, 135; cognitive theories of, 5–6, 135, 200n10, 212n7; as a communicative disorder, 16–17, 44–45, 82, 87, 91, 95–96, 100, 102–104, 184; definition of, 3, 46–47, 66, 99, 160; demographic characteristics of, 1; epidemiological studies of, 1; genetic studies of, 4–5, 134–135, 199nn6,7; guilt and, 36; interpersonal conflict and, 6–7, 87, 100, 104, 200–201n18; labeling and, 92, 98, 101–102, 113, 116, 132, 191; prevalence of, 1; psychodynamic models of (*see also* separation anxiety), 6, 100, 135–136; psychophysiological studies of, 5, 135, 199–200n8; sex roles and, 2; sick role and (*see also* secondary

gain), 6, 100; socialization and, 7; spouses of, 6–7; stress as precipitant, 200n9; as warrant for displeasing communication, 92, 100–102, 165, 171; as women's syndrome 2, 159

"agoraphobic personality," 2

alignment, 131

anxiety: children at risk for, 10, 149; epidemiological studies of, 1, 211n1; genetic studies of, 4–5, 134–135, 199nn6,7, 211nn1–4; pyschophysiological studies of, 5, 135, 199–200n8, 211n5; socialization of, 5–6, 11, 19, 27, 37–38, 134–136, 148–149, 153–172

apprenticeship, 145–152, 179, 212n17

Aristotle, 186

Arindell, W. A., 7

assessments, 123–124, 157; downgraded, 126–127

attachment security, 200n14, 212n10

audience, 15, 110. *See also* co-authorship

authority, narrator's, 119–133, 166, 181. *See also* storytelling roles

autobiography, 33

avoidance, 3, 6, 34–36, 47, 99, 135

Bahktin, Mikhail, 116

Bateson, Gregory, 103, 106

behavioral inhibition, 200n11

Berio, Luciano, 117–118

Breuer, Josef, 17, 103